THE
Ethics
OF
Teaching
AND
Scientific Research

Other books published in cooperation with the University Centers for Rational Alternatives:

THE IDEA OF A MODERN UNIVERSITY (1974)

THE PHILOSOPHY OF THE CURRICULUM (1975)

THE UNIVERSITY AND THE STATE: THE PROPER ROLE OF GOVERNMENT IN HIGHER EDUCATION

(forthcoming)

THE
Ethics
OF
Teaching
AND
Scientific Research

edited by

Sidney Hook
Paul Kurtz
Miro Todorovich

ℙ *Prometheus Books*
Buffalo, N.Y. 14215

LB
2331.4
. E86

Published by Prometheus Books
1203 Kensington Avenue, Buffalo, New York 14215

Copyright © 1977 by Prometheus Books
All rights reserved

Library of Congress Catalog Card Number 76-56902
ISBN 0-87975-068-5

Printed in the United States of America

THE
Ethics
OF
Teaching
AND
Scientific Research

Contents

Contents

Introduction

Sidney Hook

The two themes to which this volume is dedicated—the ethics of teaching and the ethics of research—are closely related. Nonetheless the connecting issues reflect rather different pressures and interests. In the main the problems that have provoked a renewed interest in the ethics of teaching stem from the politicalization of institutions of higher education, or rather from the politicalization of student bodies and faculty members in some of our most prestigious centers of learning. The common law, so to speak, of academic life—the freedom to teach and learn—has been challenged during the last decade or so, not so much by the state or by political demagogues or by groups outside the academy, as by fanatical elements within the academy itself. Certain doctrines in biology, psychology, sociology, political science and international affairs which have been interpreted, rightly or wrongly, as having anti-social consequences, have been declared taboo! Their proponents are denounced as having forfeited their rights of protection under the canons of academic freedom regardless of the care or conscientiousness with which they have reached their conclusions. This has brought some campuses to violent disruption of classes and meetings.

The rash of these excesses has temporarily abated but questions about the rights and responsibilities of teachers and students in institutions of higher education are more topical than ever. The right to dissent, to protest, to demonstrate is not in question. The mode in which it is done, is. How far can teachers and students go in expressing dissent? If all things are not to be permitted, at what point should they be checked? How and by whom? Is academic objectivity a will of the wisp? If so, does everything go? Is there a difference between teaching and indoctrination? Can or should indoctrination be avoided? What are the rights and responsibilities of academic freedom? These are some of the themes explored under the rubric of the ethics of teaching.

Problems concerning the ethics of research are, in the main, of a different order. Here, too, irrelevant political considerations have often blocked research in various fields and the publication of results. But on the whole, the ethical problems in this area arise from a genuine conflict of values in which possible benefits to men and society must be balanced against costs, risks and violations of privacy. Even if the community were all of one political mind, which is not likely ever to be the case, we would still have to decide whether to run the risks of research on recombinant DNA for the possible benefits of alleviating or abolishing the scourge of cancer and other evils. Wise men have always realized that although knowledge has both intrinsic and instrumental value, it is better not to know some things about personal affairs. In some human situations we do not ask questions because we prefer not to know the answer. Other values may have overriding priority because of the unhappy consequences of some knowledge. Except in special circumstances, only a foolish man would want to know the precise moment of his death. For in effect he would die many times before that moment. From the moment of his awareness his experience would become a cone focusing on the fatal event.

When it comes to social affairs it is hard to think of any kind of knowledge that it would be better not to have, although one may justifiably be unwilling to sanction the costs of the inquiry or the cruel experimental procedures required to get the knowledge. In many situations in which there seems to be a conflict between the value of knowledge and other values in the moral economy, the conflict is not between possessing the knowledge and, say, human safety, but between the things that must be done to get the knowledge. Leaving aside the costs, moral and material, and the dangerous consequences of acquiring knowledge of some phenomenon, which may warrant our foregoing its pursuit, there is always a *prima facie* justification for possessing knowledge of the truth in any problematic situation in which there is genuine doubt as to what is truly the case. The justification is that the knowledge, aside from the intrinsic value, if any, of possessing it, may enable us to remedy or mitigate evils. But since there are cases in which it is likely that the knowledge in question, despite all feasible safeguards, will be used to generate evils of even greater magnitude, we may declare a moratorium on its quest or forbid its dissemination on reasonable moral grounds.

Without some general ethical principles no reasonable decision can be taken in a situation when we are in doubt whether to undertake research that may have dangerous fallout. And it goes without saying that knowledge of what these possible benefits and dangers are is a *sine qua non*. That is why we cannot draw up in advance, and independently of the study of specific situations, what is or should be permissible research.

It is always helpful in cases of dispute and controversy over what should legitimately be investigated, to try to clarify the real issues in dispute. The contents of this volume represent an attempt at such clarification. In substance it presents the proceedings of the Third National Conference of University Centers for Rational Alternatives at Rockefeller University, New York City, on April 24th and 25th 1975. No attempt was made to reach a consensus on the resolution of any issues. Each contributor, including the editor, speaks for himself alone and not for any organization with which he is affiliated. Untitled contributions were given titles by the editor. Technical difficulties made it impossible to reproduce the spirited discussion from the floor that followed each major session.

University Centers for Rational Alternatives takes pride in the fact that its deliberations and conferences from the time of its founding have called the turn in focusing the intellectual attention of American scholars and educators on the perennial and yet ever topical issues of the nature of the university, the philosophy of the curriculum, and the ethics of teaching and research. At the present juncture all of these issues are affected by the ever growing role of government in educational affairs. In consequence, it is proposed at the next National Conference of UCRA to make the question of what the proper role of government should be in higher education the focus of the deliberations.

Grateful acknowledgments are made to the Smith Richardson Foundation for aid in making the Third Conference possible.

Objectivity
and Indoctrination

Teaching About
Politics as a Vocation

Martin Diamond
Northern Illinois University

Our subject is the "ethics of teaching" relative to the problem of "objectivity and indoctrination in the classroom." This means, of course, *political* objectivity and *political* indoctrination; that is, objectivity and indoctrination are ways of teaching about political questions. And political knowledge must be understood broadly as comprehension of the fundamental moral and social ordering of the political community. We are talking not only about political science teaching and social science teaching in general, but also about the whole range of teaching in all the human disciplines so far as they touch on the fundamental political questions about human existence.

Regarding the way educators teach about such political questions, objectivity and indoctrination seem to represent the polar extremes. Objectivity represents the purely scientific approach to teaching, a deliberate abstraction from political or value considerations. The objective teacher systematically seeks to refrain from shaping the fundamental political views of students. Indoctrination represents the deliberately political approach to education, the placing of political or value considerations at the center of teaching. The indoctrinating teacher systematically seeks to influence the moral and political outlook of students and to direct them toward what he believes is the right moral order of society. Two such polar extremes compellingly invite one to seize upon the middle point between them. The intention of this paper is to offer a kind of mean that satisfies the compound ethical requirements of the teaching of political subjects. The tension between scientific objectivity and political indoctrination can be likened to the problem of rendering things both to Ceasar and God. It is intended here, however, not to propose a division of things as between science and the polity, but rather to search for an optimizing mean that unites the scientific and political aspects of the teaching vocation.

Common sense tells one that there is a tension, if not an ultimate contradiction, between the aims and needs of teaching about political matters, and the aims and needs of the polity. Education and the political seem to belong somehow to separate and perhaps even rival realms. That is, teaching has a scientific duty to seek and convey the truth about the political—the truth wherever and whatever it is; whereas the political achieves or preserves what a particular polity holds true no matter what others elsewhere may say or believe. On the other hand, teaching about the political is also somehow quintessentially political; teaching what is true about the political is perhaps the profoundest influence on what people do politically—and hence on the polity. For example, to teach as true what John Locke said about the origin and end of political society, will tend to produce different citizens and statesmen than are produced by teaching as true what Karl Marx said.

This common sense awareness—that teaching about political matters is caught in a tension between the conflicting demands of science and the polity—sets the poles of our inquiry into the problematic relationship between the teacher and the polity. The task is to see how the teaching of political subjects both is and is not political in character. One must understand what makes education and the polity separate and even rival realms, and what simultaneously draws them together toward unity. If one understands this dual tendency, one may find ways to conciliate the conflicting interests of education and the polity.

The political is ultimately bound up with *doing,* with the uncertainty and tumult and changefulness of things being made and done. The scientific is ultimately bound up with *knowing,* with a movement toward the certainty, silence, and permanence of things being seen and grasped. Science, as the root of the word indicates, means simply knowing and, as such, culminates in a will-less seeing and understanding. Yet the political is a will to action and never culminates but is a ceaseless shaping of events. This difference is manifested in the dissimilar kinds of human beings that politicians and professors become. Professors, when true to their calling, usually are not politically gifted people; and politicians, however wise and learned, ordinarily are not academic in character. So great is the tension between the political and the scientific that Max Weber, for example, thought of them as wholly separate vocations or callings. He made this point dramatically in two famous speeches he gave one year under the deliberately paired and polarized titles, "Politics as a Vocation" and "Science as a Vocation." This total dissevering of the political and the scientific is, of course, an expression of Weber's dissevering of value and fact. The political belongs, for Weber, to the world in which the will passionately acts out values, while the scientific belongs to a world in which fact is dispassionately studied and known for its own sake. Weber's fact-value distinguishing positivism led him thus to treat the political and the scientific as constituting unbridgeably separate worlds.

The title of this paper—a play on the titles Weber used—points to the need to understand the political and the scientific in both their separateness and unity, as that duality or tension confronts the political science teacher or any teacher dealing with fundamental political questions. The teaching vocation holds both the political and the scientific together in such a way that the duality or tension—both the separateness and the unity—is at the center of the action. Political science teachers are not simply citizens or statesmen; but neither are they simply scientists engaged in a silent, solitary study of politics. It is in their teaching that the duality or tension of the political and scientific comes into play.

Weber understood that an academician, unlike a solitary scientist, "must qualify not only as a scholar but also as a teacher."[1] Indeed, he even calls this the "dual aspect" of the "academic process."[2] But, by dual aspect, Weber does not in the least refer to the political dimension of teaching. He means only that the academic scientist, in addition to his scientific qualifications, must also accidentally possess the pedagogic art as a "personal gift."[3] Weber understands pedagogy narrowly, as having no authoritative status of its own but as simply ancillary to the scientific vocation. Teaching seems little more than a happy flair for presenting "scientific problems in such a manner that an untutored but receptive mind can understand them . . . (most important) come to think about them independently."[4] Thus, Weber gives only passing attention to the question of teaching; moreover, he does so only under the rubric of scientific vocation and, so, obscures what links teaching to the political. One must understand, instead, that teaching about politics is a peculiar, hybrid vocation in which the aims of the scientific and the political are at once drawn both together and apart.

That teachers are not simply scientists, but hybrids who also deal with the political, sounds almost blasphemous and certainly unpersuasive to those who derive from Weber. This is in part because the term "political" is used here differently from the way Weber uses it. The persuasiveness of Weber's separation of science and politics, and his subsuming of teaching under the scientific vocation, resulted from his definition—his too narrow definition—of politics. Weber understood the political as follows: "politics for us means striving to share power or striving to influence the distribution of power, either among states or among groups within a state."[5] If the political is thus understood, then the teaching of political science should be utterly remote from the political. There should never be any "striving" in the classroom "to influence the distribution of power . . . within the state." If the political is narrowly confined to the question of power, then teaching political science is most emphatically not a political act.

To argue that the teaching of political science is itself political is to proceed from a different understanding of what the political is. One must understand politics as comprehending, at least equally with power, the purposes of power. And this means purposes not as mere givens, not as mere subjective preferences determined by irrational underlying forces, but purposes as authentic ideas. These ideas include people's arguments and reasonings, their opinions—about what sort of country they want—the ideas of justice and human excellence they proclaim and live by or betray. What forms and influences such opinions, and what they influence in turn, is political in its essential quality. Such opinions, whether in the form of normative prescription or empirical description, are formidable causes of political behavior—indeed, the fulcrums by which the levers of power work. And such opinions are precisely what teachers teach about, thereby inescapably influencing the fundamental political outlook of their students and affecting the shape of the political order.

Perhaps every political scientist, no matter how narrowly like Weber he limits his formal definition of politics to the question of power, proceeds in the classroom on the basis of the broader understanding of politics suggested here. For example, in an American government course, surely every political scientist would treat as a political dimension of the presidency what Theodore Roosevelt called "the bully pulpit." Indeed, most political scientists think a president fails in his political duties if he does not do well in his pulpit. Presidents speaking *ex cathedra* powerfully affect public opinion on underlying moral and philosophic principles, by the force of which "opinion ultimately governs the world." Professors speak from a different chair, and the difference in the chair must constrain severely the manner and substance of their speaking. But theirs too is a bully pulpit. Teaching about political matters inevitably speaks directly and closely to the purposes of power, to the normative issues of justice and human excellence, to factual questions of the nature and limits of politics. Political science teachers have an inescapable impact on opinion; and their subject matter, unlike geometry or logic, draws one inexorably into the political realm—both as it brings one to the interested attention of the political world and as one influences others in political directions. Formally limiting the definition of politics to manipulations of power will not exorcize the reality: If one is teaching about politics, he or she is thereby in the business of influencing politics.

Perhaps at this point it is illuminating and prudent to quote a great political philosopher whose good standing with modern political and social thinkers is matched only by that of Machiavelli—namely, Thomas Hobbes. He says that, in defending their political interests, men switch from custom to reason and back again, depending on which at the moment supports and flatters them. That is why the claim of scientific reasoning, he tells us, in matters like "the causes, and original constitution of right, equity, and justice . . . . is perpetually disputed, both by the Pen and the Sword: Whereas the doctrines of Lines, and Figures, is not so; because men care not, in that subject what be truth, as a thing that crosses no mans ambition, profit, or lust."[6] In the effort to teach about politics, the truth inevitably "crosses . . . mans ambition, profit, or lust." Although it shares with teaching about "Lines and Figures" a scientific concern with truth, teaching political matters is a compound of the scientific and political vocations.

It remains now to explore that compound or dual nature by examining how the political and scientific are drawn together in teaching, how they yet remain separate, and how one may live with this duality.

II

An obvious fact immediately differentiates the simply scientific enterprise from teaching: Teaching requires students and money; it cannot be done unaided and alone. And therewith politics must intrude upon the teaching of political science. In contrast, the scientific study of political matters can be conducted without the knowing consent of others—silently, alone, even covertly, and as cheaply as it takes the scientist to keep body and soul together. The solitary scientist can live like a spy in the land, free behind his mask to behave solely in accordance with the ends and needs of his science. But when he becomes also a political science teacher, he must come out into the open and accept the consequences. A teacher must do whatever is necessary to secure students and money, and he must do justice to these students and that money in ways appropriate to the general nature and ends of teaching and to its scientific ends in particular.

Someone always has to supply the books, real estate, food, wages, and necessary equipment—a lot of necessary equipment. Mark Hopkins' log would hardly suffice for contemporary appetites and needs. But even more important, someone always has to supply the young men and women who are to be educated. Those who pay the money and provide the young always derive from or speak for the ruling political elements, whether it be parents, citizens, philanthropists, church, or state. Their money and their young are rightly precious to them and, ultimately, will be supplied only on terms, political terms. These terms vary with the needs of each polity and with the peculiar political and social demands that each places on education in general and the teaching of political science in particular. The constant—namely, the scientific study and teaching of universal truths about the political—has always to interact with the variable, the particular polity within which it must function. The nature and history of the varying interaction between a teacher's scientific aims and his constraining political environment, form an intellectual subject of paramount importance. Accommodation to the political is a precondition of teaching about politics, and such teaching is itself a fundamental phenomenon demanding scientific study.

Moreover, there is an obvious and compelling prudential reason for such a study. To put it harshly as possible, if teaching about politics is to be possible—and there are hideous times when it is not—some tribute must be paid to the dominant forces of each society. If there is no accommodation to political necessity, there will be no students, no money, no teaching of political science. Sheer need compels teachers to come to terms with the political element that is ineluctably part of their profession. Prudence dictates, when one must come to terms with something, not just to lament the necessity but to figure out in advance the best possible terms.

On both judicious and scientific grounds, then, the question is whether the best possible terms have been worked out in the given political circumstances. Whether the best possible has been achieved is the thing most worth knowing scientifically. Only by looking at the best possible can one see and deal with departures from it, just as disease is seen and treated as a departure from health.

The honorable teaching of politics is that which manages optimally, in its peculiar political circumstances (the variable), to preserve its scientific integrity (the constant) while teaching the young—that is, teaching that manages to secure for itself the best terms. Judgments about what are such terms would have to be treated as scientifically defensible in principle and not just as resting on cognitively indefensible value preferences.

One may draw out the implications of this argument by considering it in terms of *political socialization,* a concept that has lately been prominent in political science. "Political socialization" is the process whereby people learn and accept the political roles and values their community assigns to them, and is typically deemed indispensable to the existence of any society. How does teaching—the teaching of all who deal with political questions in the broad sense—affect this indispensable process? Does the instruction undermine what political socialization does? Should it? Will society indefinitely permit something indispensable to its existence to be undermined by those whom they pay and to whom they give their young? Should it? These questions would have occurred to Socrates; he would have seen the hemlock in them. But they have been ignored despite the fact that they must be asked, on both prudent and scientific grounds.

We have ignored or blunted our awareness of such questions because we live in a liberal democracy that defers to higher education, clumsily perhaps, but with a mild and lavish hand that is unprecedented. This country has been not only financially generous beyond all earlier expectations but also startlingly permissive in the intellectual latitude it has allowed to universities. However, we must not be deceived into imprudent complacency or into scientific unawareness by the fact, for example, that Archie Bunker never brutally inquires into just what the "Meathead" is learning at that college he goes to. If only he knew. Inevitably some day he will. Then the political constraints on teaching about political matters will become dangerously clear. Now, while the going is good, is the time to avert that outcome by taking a scientific, cautious account of the political constraints intrinsic to teaching.

It is not only a matter of necessity or expediency that obliges the teacher to come to some sort of terms with the polity. Justice likewise dictates such terms. If professors are to take students and money, what are they to give in return? Justice requires that they return some sort of good to the students and society, or perhaps an assortment of goods according to the variety of students and the various aspects of society. In any event, teachers must at least be sure that they do as little harm as possible. They may have a hard time convincing others that what they do is truly good, but they must at least be able to convince themselves.

Little thought seems to have been given in recent years to this problem of a just return, to the good that teachers claim results for students and society from education. It is not enough, for example, to have instruments that test the factual knowledge or the general reasoning skills students acquire in their courses. Responsible teachers would search out deeper consequences of their teaching and then justify these consequences or seek to avoid those that cannot be justified. For example, have the students' attachments to their old pieties and loyalties been weakened as a result of their education? Have the students been improved by such a weakening? If so, precisely how? The customary justification is a sort of gadfly notion that only by being emancipated from received opinions can students become critically independent. No doubt. But is it only an old dogma that such critical independence is good, or can a philosophic argument be made to support this claim? Consider this from the perspective of contemporary value-free political and social science. If ultimate political and moral values are equal from the standpoint of scientific or cognitive reasoning, as is now widely believed, just how can it be claimed that critical independence is superior to uncritical dependence in the realm of ultimate values? If values are ultimately beyond the jurisdiction of cognitive reasoning, why is it better that a student hold such cognitively indefensible values in a critical and independent way? Indeed, in that realm of ultimate noncognitive givens, what could the words "critical" and "uncritical," "independent" and "dependent," possibly mean? It is vulgar to assert superiority merely as an article of faith; it requires a philosophic argument to sustain the idea of critical independence as the end and justification of education. That argument or justification originated in the Socratic tradition, which modern political and social thinkers have largely rejected. Having rejected the foundation, some teachers continue to assert the end; having rejected the argument, they still brandish the slogan and claim its privileges. Yet if they are to justify their impact on students—their weakening of students' old pieties and loyalties by the claim of critical independence—then it behooves them to restore scientific entitlement to that justification. They are morally obliged to show precisely how this weakening results in a new outcome that is good for the student and, thus, is the just return.

Even if teachers can show precisely what good they accomplish, can they claim to succeed with all, most, or many students? Can teachers claim that all or most students achieve some superior new condition that alone justifies the gadfly teaching function? Or do teachers in fact leave most students with their old beliefs disordered but without anything like the qualities of mind in their place that warrant the disordering? The range of capacity and character in the various strata of students has always been and, so long as human capacities vary, will always be a major theoretical and practical problem for education. Are these strata not extraordinarily varied now because of our peculiar political situation, that is, a movement toward mass democratic higher education? Must teachers take more rhetorical pains than ever to achieve the best results among all these strata? And if so, how?

This is only to begin to raise the necessary moral questions regarding the consequences of teaching. In contrast, the silent, solitary scientist has no such problem with consequences because, in his capacity, he only sees and grasps; acting upon others is not at the heart of his enterprise. But in their capacity, teachers do act upon others; affecting students is at the heart of teaching. Teachers cannot take refuge in the position that may, or very well may not, shelter their colleagues in the physical sciences. Teachers cannot say that they only discover and teach the facts and that their students and society may do with these facts what they wish. The physical scientist and the teacher of the physical sciences may in fact agonize over and try to affect the uses to which their discoveries and teaching are put; those who teach about political matters are surely not the only ones with ethical problems. However, there remains this immense difference: the scientists' ethical difficulties are extrinsic and posterior to their science and teaching; the political science teachers' difficulties are intrinsic to and coeval with their teaching. The scientist's problems result from the uses to which society puts his findings and teaching; the political science teacher's ethical troubles result from the uses to which his findings and teaching put the society. Nothing in what the physical scientist teaches about atoms and enzymes, for example, necessarily causes conviction in his students' minds as to what should be done with atoms and enzymes. But what political science teachers tell their students about politics does. The physical scientist teaches about matters external to the students; political science teachers teach students about themselves. What the latter teach—whether descriptively about the nature, possibilities, and limits of the political or about the standards to be drawn—inescapably affects the most important political element, the fundamental opinions of students about how they and their society should live. No brandishing of an alleged distinction between facts and values, no positivist scruple, will prevent one's actions from having consequences nor lessen one's responsibility for them.

Now this good that teachers supply must conform to the constraint of propriety and must be appropriate to their vocation. It must be a good compatible with and given in their capacity as teachers of political things, as sharers in an educational enterprise. That is how one solicits the money and the students, by promising the good that teachers can give. If they try to be therapists, statesmen, or revolutionaries to our students, the teachers are taking money under false pretenses. That is a fraud, and not less culpably so for professors than for other people. Some may be first-rate therapists or statesmen or revolutionaries. That is fine. Let them be, in their private capacities, or let them fulfill their destinies elsewhere in the appropriate places. But the concern here is the vocation of teaching, and nothing in the estate of teaching supplies a moral or legal warrant for anything else than first-rate teaching. Teachers have got to give only that good to students and to society that they can claim to be peculiarly qualified and warranted to give, that is appropriate to teaching about politics.

III

Necessity, justice, and propriety have emerged as standards or inhibitions for teachers in their relationship with the polity. Stressing the political constraints on teaching, it would seem to push one towards a mere subservience to the state. This emphasis is deliberate. Both the "Weberians" and those who reject Weber from the Left fail to appreciate the inevitable and legitimate claims that derive from teachers' relationships with the polity. This is, of course, to stress only one side of the teacher-polity relationship, the side tending toward unity of the two. It is imperative to examine equally the other side, the extent to which the aims of the polity and of higher education belong to separate and possibly opposed realms. Thus, indispensable as it is that one come to terms to secure money and students, it is equally essential that these terms satisfy the other side of education—the side having to do with scientific autonomy, with the search for and teaching about political truth without deference to any particular form of government.

One must look for a middle ground, a mean—not simply a compromise, an arithmetic mean that reconciles by merely splitting the difference but a middle state between the purely political and the purely scientific. This mean is an "extreme of a kind" and thereby enables the teaching vocation to achieve its fullest self, optimally satisfying both sides of its hybrid nature. Usually this sort of mean is found by taking one's bearings from the prevailing opinions regarding the matter under consideration. In recent years, there have been two predominant, sharply opposed opinions regarding the subject of teaching politics—the Weberian view and that which opposes it from the Left. By testing each position against the standards proposed (necessity, justice, and propriety), the inadequacy of Weber's ideas and of those who refute him will perhaps become evident; and, thereby, the mean that one is seeking may begin to emerge.

The critics on the Left have challenged and shaken what might have become too thick a "cake of custom." For example, they have usefully criticized the value presuppositions of positivistic political and social science. They have rightly sympathized with some students' yearnings for political science classes that shed light on society's moral and political concerns. These critics have insisted that the study of political questions is inseparable from problems regarding justice, the good life, and the best political order. Had they stopped there—or, more precisely, had they really dug in there and truly reopened these questions—they might have vastly improved contemporary political science teaching.

None of these leftist critics of the behavioral establishment and of the "fact-value distinction" has really taken seriously the rich, ennobling perplexities of justice and of the good life, or of the value question in general. In most instances, they have simply dogmatically embraced one fundamental version of justice and the good life—namely, democracy understood only as equality, democracy made more and more democratic by equility being made more and more equal. They do not ask at least that political thought reopen the value question; rather, they in effect close it once and for all. These critics have not questioned their own ultimate values. They treat these values as settled, and demand that political scientists devote themselves to carrying out democratization and egalitarianism. The critics then have stormily demanded that educators politicize themselves to achieve these goals in the way the critics have embraced them. The rhetoric of the critics calls for criticism and hence for creative political thought and teaching. But the criticism is nearly always from the Left, and the creativity is usually in that direction. Leftist critics have complained, for example, that American political science has been closed, but they have opened it only to the Left, which is really the exchange of one closure for another. Instead, educators must truly renew the value question and prudently and appropriately follow it in their pursuit of science and in their teaching, as far as they can go.

Further, the issues raised by these critics of positivistic political science do not rest simply at the level of intellectual criticisms and questionings. There is also the problem of "politicization." Recent leftist critics have vehemently insisted that teaching about politics is a political act, and they have sought to make campuses and the teaching profession the centers of direct political action. But the critics utterly ignore society's constraints on educators. Use of a classroom to press political causes will not be tolerated indefinitely by those who supply students and resources to the schools. The proposed new kind of "politicization" of classrooms by professors would and should result in old-fashioned, harmful intervention by society. An aroused public, goaded into repressiveness by an incontinent faculty, would never allow the freedom that the academy now enjoys. Even if the community remained uncharacteristically torpid, the proposed politicization would lead to ludicrous and intolerable results within the educational institution. It would turn into a political community with majorities and minorities, tyrannies and factions—or into rival political communities with conservative colleges, liberal colleges, all kinds of political colleges. In moderation, such divisions are inevitable, tolerable, and even healthy in small doses as a special brand of pluralism. But the degree of politicization recently sought, and its elevation to high principle, would produce intolerable results.

It is interesting that many who call for militant politicization themselves implicitly acknowledge the intolerable impropriety of counter-regime politicization, that is, as a regular principle for education. They usually argue that they live in a moment of unique urgency: Things are now so abominably and critically bad that every resource, including especially the academy, must be thrown into the struggle. However, this is just a variation of the old argument that, in a revolutionary crisis, anything goes; everyone may have to be perverted from his proper character and temporarily made to serve the revolution. Such revolutionaries do not intend to allow teaching to continue the same kind of political act in their new society; postrevolutionary regimes take great pains to ensure that no revolutionaries will teach in the universities. These regimes know that permanent "politicization" is an untenable principle for education. One does not have to wait until a revolution to see what happens in universities, like some in western

Europe as well as in America, when they are captured by such "politicizers."

The viewpoint of the critics of Weber may be summed up in terms of the standards that have been proposed. As to the need to come to terms with the polity, these critics not only refuse terms but, on the contrary, insist that critical teaching and political action are a teacher's duties. Taking money and students from society, the critics claim the right—both by teaching and by direct political action on campus—to rally the students and, thus, society in whatever radically new directions they conceive. They are relatively safe because a sober majority of their colleagues shield them. And, because most western countries have been amazingly mild and permissive, the leftist critics seem to ignore the counter-revolution that their revolution—if on a large enough scale—would inevitably and disastrously bring. As to what a teacher justly owes his students and society, far from ignoring the obligation, the critics make great claims. They claim to heighten the moral sensitivity of their students, summoning them to idealism and helping them conceive a truly just political order. This is what a provocative approach to teaching about politics gives to all who are capable of receiving it. It is splendid if the good that these critics promise means they are teaching their students the poignant ambiguities of morality. Or that, if by idealism, they mean to help their students become more virtuous—that is, more courageous, moderate, contemplative, and so forth; and if they labor to open their students to the rival claims of various political orders. Instead, the critics seem merely to encourage militant moral certainty; idealism largely means indulging in the easy pleasure of railing at society and postponing its moral transformation. For them, a just political order is not a standard to be lived by but a goal passionately here and now to be grasped by the will and pursued at any cost. As to the question of propriety—what a teacher may fitly do in contrast to what a therapist, statesman, or revolutionary may do—the leftist critics seem to have given no consideration at all.

Regarding Weber's position, one may reverse the procedure and begin by similarly summing it up before examining certain features in detail. On the subject of propriety, Weber and his successors have said much that is true and valuable regarding the chastening constraints that the scientific student of politics must accept when teaching. They have said much less about the problem of conforming to necessity—that is, the problem of coming to terms. But there seems to be an implicit Weberian strategy that must be examined. The greatest difficulty arises regarding justice and the good that Weberians claim to give their students.

How does Weber come to terms with the polity? There are two strategies in Weberian teaching: clarifying values and showing how in the "real world" these values may be maximized or optimized. For example, Weber says that teachers should compare the various forms of democracy and then compare these with nondemocratic forms so that "the student may find the point from which, in terms of *his ultimate values,* he can take a stand."[7] Weberians seem to believe that this neutrality will purchase freedom for their scholarly and educational enterprise, for—if one promises equal service to all—will not everyone be nice and not interfere? Unfortunately, this works only in a liberal democracy. Only easygoing liberal democrats will allow Weberians to compare all kinds of regimes and let the student ultimately take his pick. Regimes other than liberal democracies—and not just modern totalitarian tyrannies but historically typical nontyrannical regimes like the Puritan, Spartan, and medieval regimes—would not allow any such freedom. Weberian terms and political principles would be unacceptable to them and could not be taught. Is it not a fatal parochialism to limit the teaching of politics to one epoch and to one country?

Liberal political teaching is only possible in progressive democracies, if it has no serious effect; that is, so long as the majority of students emerge from such instruction relatively unimpaired from the viewpoint of the liberal polity. If one takes seriously Weber's prescription that the teacher present to the student the various kinds of government, then many students might actually opt against liberal democracy. But if this really happened on a massive scale, the democratic government would soon have to clamp down on the subversive instruction or else it would soon be replaced by some illiberal system chosen by the nondemocratic students. Once again Weberian teaching would be impossible. A Weberian philosopher then can come to terms with the polity, but only a liberal polity in which he does not upset the applecart. This may do for a while and is sufficient for a parochial political and social science, but not for one that claims a universal scientific standing.

Weberian teaching necessarily serves all comers; that is, it presents its scientific findings in the same way to all students, leaving intact their various ultimate values. Such education serves especially the ruling element in the polity, which is what typically prevails among the comers. This is why the leftist critics have justifiably complained that Weberianism is a species of Establishment science. By abjuring scientific jurisdiction over ultimate values, the Weberian teacher leaves these values unchallenged; that is he leaves the prevailing ones—the status quo—unchallenged. By assigning ultimate values to the realm of will and not of reason, Weber in effect removes these values from the possible challenge and condemnation of reason in order to shield the established powers from a weapon historically invaluable to antiestablishment forces. Since ultimate values belong to the realm of will, only a superior will or the prevailing power can decide what the values are. This is the element of truth in the recent Leftists' critiques.

However, there is more to the whole story. Whereas the Weberian mode does not submit the ruling ultimate values to cognitive challenge, it does not in fact leave these or any values quite untouched. It undermines them and all political values by its radical distinction between fact and value and by its denial of cognitive status to the realm of value. All normative opinions and values typically claim to derive from reality. Political and social scientists may postulate an unabridgeable distinction, but all real-world actors believe and claim to derive their oughts from ises. They believe and claim to see in reality, how humans ought to live. Communities hold in common normative opinions and values. Weberianism does not say that these opinions and values are false; it only says that science proves that no one can *know by reason* whether they are false or true.[8] Cautious as this is, it is corrosive of political life, which exists with the conviction that its beliefs are grounded in reason.

If the vast majority of mankind believes its ultimate values have a cognitive foundation—and if polities are constituted by such a belief—then the Weberian mode, far from serving all comers, is ultimately, nihilistically destructive of all political values held in the real world. For example, American political life rests on (or at least once rested on) the conviction that certain truths are self-evident. The Weberian answers that no moral or political values, such as those in the Declaration of Independence, can be objective or inherently self-evident. Most Weberians may prefer to believe in the Declaration's truths, but science compels them to say that these are only truths to people with ultimate values. And they must, therefore, be treated by science with inverted commas firmly in place, merely as givens, varying from individual to individual, people to people, and age to age, but all incapable alike of cognitive foundation.[9] To use a phrase from Lincoln, "see what a mere wreck—mangled ruin—it makes of our once glorious Declaration," to read it on this positivist basis: "We hold these 'ultimate values' to be ours, incapable of self-evident or any other rational evidentiary foundation, but ours nonetheless; that among these 'ultimate values' are, etc." At first one might think that this would produce a tolerant liberalism—you respect my ultimate values and I will respect yours. But in the end such an approach nihilistically deprives all values of a grounding in reason. In such a bleak world, tolerance does not in fact prevail. Rather, brutish values grounded chiefly in some dangerous doctrine of the will, have the ultimate advantage over all those values that seek to rest on reason.

This completes the discussion of the Weberian strategy for coming to terms. Now we must consider how Weberianism meets the test of the just return. To students it says, "Bring us your muddled values and we will help you clarify them. We will teach you to treasure consistency and thinking things through; we will help you think your values through and make them consistent one with another." As to the deepest values, one's ultimate values that are the foundation of all else, students are told not to try to think them through; it can't be done. Precisely when teachers should lead their ablest students to the deepest thoughts, Weberianism would seem to assure them that they need not make the effort. It assures them that they need not disturb their deepest prejudices, only their inconsistent ones. This ensures scientifically that the world is one of blind will, that a student's value system is a kind of weapon that he must point while blindfolded, with micrometric accuracy.

What of the second good promised by Weberian instruction, namely helping the student to maximize or optimize his clarified values in the real world by means of scientific factual knowledge? The performance of this good would depend on whether the important real-world political facts would be accurately disclosed by a political and social science that scrupulously abstracted from value considerations. If the important political facts are seen as such only on the basis of a particular value-orientation, then they would truly be facts only on the basis of the true value-orientation. If this could be shown, then the Weberian study of politics—since it abjures the possibility of a true value-orientation—would thereby be incapable of disclosing factual reality. This is not merely to say that values determine what the scientist chooses to study; that is an old problem. Something more is suggested here: that in all important cases, the facts themselves are always such only in virtue of value considerations. If the latter are arbitrary, so are the former; if there can be no cognitive knowledge of values, then there can be no cognitive knowledge of facts.

There may seem something perverse in all this to those who are Weberian scholars. The difficulty may lie in the word *value*. Only two centuries ago did the word come to be used in contradistinction to *fact*. This modern usage has a rhetorical effect requiring that one think of facts as radically separated from values. First one sees the facts, and then separately one values or likes or does not like them. The question is not whether one likes or values the facts, but rather a question of the nature of important political facts. For example, one does not ask a doctor: Is that cancer? Do you like it? In medicine, the whole value problem is intrinsic to the factual diagnosis of cancer. One asks a doctor: Is that healthy or diseased tissue, no matter whether you like, value, or dislike it? A doctor cannot *see* except on the basis of a true understanding of the distinction of health and disease, no matter which he happens to prefer. What students of political science are concerned about is much more like the relationship between health and disease than between valuing or liking. Once the questions of health and disease are restored to a factual, cognitive basis, there will be plenty of time to worry about people who dislike health and prefer disease.

Some of the difficulty can be traced, perhaps, to the way the English language translates as *virtue* the ancient Greek *arete*. For us, virtue came to mean morality that became moral preference, which became liking or valuing. But *arete* meant something more like health or excellence. Thus, Plato and Aristotle spoke about the health or excellence of the body as *arete* and also, using the same word and the same idea, of the political excellences and the excellences of heart and mind. They did not understand how the body could have its health or excellences—discoverable by appropriate scientific inquiry—and the heart and mind not have theirs, discoverable similarly but with much more difficulty and uncertainty.

It seems inescapable to speak of a fact-*value* distinction—fact separately first and values or the question of whether you like the facts, separately later. But can one likewise speak of a fact-*health/excellence* distinction—facts separately first and the question of health or excellence separately later? One cannot say that medical facts come first and judgments about health or disease come later. Physical health and disease are manifestly factual; there can be no scientific grasp of the medical *is* without there being also scientific knowledge of the medical *ought*—namely, health. Political facts and political health are likewise not radically disjoined; indeed, important facts are such only in the light of a true grasp of what is healthy or excellent political tissue. This is the crucial issue. The question of whether one should regard political health as the political ought, whether one should like healthy rather than diseased tissue, would not prove very troubling.

Perhaps the only worthy study of political things—whether in political science, social sciences, or in the arts and letters—is one that undogmatically without any pretence to having the answers, rediscovers the perennial questions about political health and excellence. Such a study takes its best-reasoned shot at these questions, always aware how easy it is to err and, therefore, always awaiting the discovery of its own errors to improve its questioning and answering. Students must be taught that there is no cognitive basis for ultimate questions and answers about political health and excellence, to arm them with a scientific defense against all the pain of political inquiry. Thereby, students become vulnerable to those modern armed messiahs who offer a cheap substitute for that pain.

IV

Teaching in the Weberian manner may be the defect that is relative to the mean one is seeking; the contemporary Left's teaching principle is its excess. Weberianism falls short of the mean by clinging to science's pole; the Left rushes past the mean headlong toward the pole of politics. There is a kind of political science teaching that forms a mean between the two extremes. However, it is always easier to show what are the defects and excesses to be avoided than to state positively what the mean is. That does not lessen its reality or one's access to it; although it may not be painted in bold colors, it is still there and visible in the central area not shaded in on either side.

As to necessity and the problem of coming to terms, if the polity is truly abominable, then open higher education in political matters is simply impossible. Teachers and students will be able to proceed only covertly, if at all. After all, the good man can no more be a good political science professor than a good citizen in a truly bad regime; there is not sufficient health or decency in such a regime to supply the prerequisite common ground for teacher, student, and society. In any decent regime, and not just in a liberal democracy, a study of politics oriented to the question of political health and excellence will come to honorable teaching terms.

To come to respectable terms capable of satisfying both the scientific and political needs of teaching, is to give to the decent polity and its opinions a central and respected place in political education. One should begin by considering what the decent polity regards as its own excellences. For example, an obvious way to do this in America is to look at the Declaration of Independence and the United States Constitution. One must also teach the student to see as deeply as possible what are the claims of his government, what it regards as the proper human ends and the modes of their political attainment, and what is distinctive in all this as compared with political behavior elsewhere. It would mean that one would study—by the light of those ends and putative modes of attainment—American political institutions, processes, events, and behaviors in all their manifestations.

To make this the starting point and the rhetorical mode whereby the student commences the study of politics, is the way to secure the best possible terms for political instruction. The polity is thereby assured from the outset that, whatever may be inherently dangerous to it in the academic teaching of the young about politics, the danger has been minimized by a prudent mode of instruction. Such instruction will win for itself the greatest possible latitude to pursue its autonomous scientific ends. This is the sine qua non of authentic education. Moreover, to come to such terms is not only a prudent concession to necessity but also a dialectically sound way to begin an educational ascent. The dialectical procedure is to take delight in showing what is wrong in a proposed opinion.

The Socratic procedure, as in the opening discussion with Cephalus in the *Republic*, is to begin pleasantly with what is sensible and healthy in the proposed opinion. Since Socrates is at that moment securing students for himself, and if not money at least a place in which their education may occur, his pleasant and prudent treatment of

Cephalus' opinion is paradigmatic of the way philosophic teaching should address itself to authority. Moreover, the dialectical ascent requires not just Socrates' showing what is deficient in Cephalus' opinion but also his showing what is sound in it. The sound element in opinion is the footing on which the ascent to knowledge rests. By such means, a student is led affirmatively toward the full explication of what he believes politically. To explicate fully means to develop precisely the meanings, nuances, grounds, and implications of opinions. But when affirmative explication of opinions is completed, their problematic aspects will also have been disclosed. One will have begun with the familiar and then step by step rendered it problematic. By this means the deeper, universal questions that transcend any particular polity and are part of an autonomous scientific study of political life, will have been raised. Full explication of opinions culminates in philosophic understanding. Thus, what begins as a prudent condescension to necessity satisfies also the independent scientific needs of teaching. To examine what is politically healthy and unhealthy in one's own government opens the path to the mean that will balance as far as possible the dual tendencies of the hybrid vocation of teaching—both the tension and the unity of its relation to the polity.

The same mean meets also the test of propriety, that is, our obligation to function only in a manner conformable to teaching. Minimally, this requires that the teacher renounce political coercion and persuasion. However, some will think that restoring the value question to the purview of scientific reasoning will plunge the teacher into the political thicket; and that, licensed by the mean proposed here, the teacher will use political persuasion to draw students toward his values. This kind of thinking misses the vital distinction regarding persuasion. When appropriate to the inquiry, the teacher will indeed offer students the reasoning that leads them to their own value conclusions. The teacher will share with the students his own reasoned quest for these conclusions. This does not constitute political persuasion. Some students, of course, become attached to their teachers and imitate them and their views. All teachers experience this at least once, and no mode of teaching can wholly prevent it. But this persuasion fallout does not belie the distinction between educational persuasion and political persuasion. Unlike the politician who does seek to persuade and wants agreement and votes whether or not voters understand issues, the teacher—when true to his vocation—wants agreement only when students understand. The teacher does not want to win votes from students for his values; he wants them to agree or disagree with him only after they have used reason to reach conclusions. The validity of this distinction can be seen in the contempt one feels for colleagues who betray their vocation by desiring to win a partisan following or mere popularity by means of political or other inappropriate persuasion. Restoration of the value question to cognitive learning does not, therefore, draw the teacher improperly into political persuasion; he remains committed to reasoned persuasion proper to scientific pursuit.

What could be more faithful and proper to teaching than the effort to instruct each student according to his capacity to learn, rejecting political means of coercion and persuasion and raising every consideration—as Weber says, "that tells against one's own position" —holding nothing back and drawing from each student something excellent relative to the study of politics? By freeing oneself from the self-denying ordinance of the fact-value distinction and turning instead to the question of what is healthy and diseased in political life, one can find a proper posture—neither unconstrained scientist nor committed politician but that of a teacher mediating between the two.

As to the justice and good teachers must supply, they should support and philosophically consider the American liberal democracy, for this approach has the great advantage of avoiding the harm they may do inadvertently. Unfortunately, some of the millions going to colleges and universities, are incapable of achieving higher education. The study of politics is strong stuff; it can injure those unable to handle its demands. Every teacher has probably had the experience (although not all realize it) of unintentionally injuring some of his students. Some teachers cheerfully shatter religious beliefs, others debunk sexual mores, and others mock the values of the marketplace. Still others incautiously or too loudly teach philosophic truths that cannot be understood readily by the young. The danger is not only that individual students can be left disoriented, less decent, less capable of common sense; the danger is on a large enough scale now that liberal democracy may be deprived of the kinds of citizens it needs. This danger is averted if the sympathetic consideration of the American form of government is properly stressed in teaching about politics. Each student is then more likely to take away from his education what he is capable of receiving. Those students who can go all the way will receive sound guidance; those who inevitably drop out will have their opinions and characters improved by what they were able to understand. Nothing should be held back from anyone. It is all there, democratically available, in books and discussion. No information is let in to the exclusion of other material; no admission decisions have to be made. The presentation is structured so that the desirable facts simply select themselves.

Teachers must strive for something more than a just return for the money and students they receive. Teachers must seek for themselves the good and delight of their jobs. A quotation from Leo Strauss illustrates this. His teaching experience shows what I have said here to a greater extent than I can acknowledge. The quote is from a class lecture given at the University of Chicago shortly after the death of Winston Churchill.

We have no higher duty, and no more pressing duty, than to remind ourselves and our students, of political greatness, human greatness, of the
peaks of human excellence. For we are supposed to train ourselves and
others in seeing things as they are, and this means above all in seeing their
greatness and their misery, their excellence and their vileness, their nobili-
ty and their baseness, and therefore never to mistake mediocrity, however
brilliant, for true greatness. In our age this duty demands of us in the first
place that we liberate ourselves from the supposition that value statements cannot be factual statements.

Let us liberate ourselves from that supposition. Let us reopen the
question, the perennial question of political health and human excellence. We will then avoid the defect of making science sterile and,
probably, unphilosophically smuggling our values in, thereby deceiving
others or ourselves. We will also avoid the excess of taking our values
as settled, needing only our passionate political commitment to them.
If only we liberate ourselves, we may find the mean and then return to
the proper task of raising the perennial questions, offering the evidence
against our answers as well as the evidence that inclines us to them,
and sharing prudently but wholly with our students the love of asking
and seeking.

NOTES

1. *From Max Weber: Essays in Sociology*, eds. H. H. Gerth and C. Wright Mills (New York:
Oxford University Press, 1946), p. 133.
2. Ibid., p. 130.
3. Ibid., p. 134.
4. Ibid.
5. Ibid., p. 78. American political scientists typically define politics in a manner similar
to Weber's. Cf. Robert A. Dahl: "A political system is any persistent pattern of human relationships that involves, to a significant extent, power, rule, or authority," in *Modern Political Analysis*, 2nd ed. (Englewood Cliffs, N.J.: Prentice Hall, 1970), p. 6. Since there are many
kinds of power, rule, or authority, Dahl's definition perhaps begs the question: What *kind* of
power, rule, or authority, is *political*?
6. *Leviathan*, I, 11.
7. *Max Weber*, p. 145. Emphasis added.
8. See Arnold Brecht, *Political Theory* (Princeton, N.J.: Princeton University Press, 1967),
pp. 9-10, 124-26.
9. Cf. Leo Strauss, *Natural Right and History* (Chicago: University of Chicago Press, 1953),
pp. 1-2.

Facts, Values,
and Responsible Choice

Charles Frankel
Columbia University

The subject of the ethics and responsibilities of members of the academic community lies, in my opinion, at the heart of the entire subject of academic freedom. Ethics and responsibilities are at the core of reconstructing in our time, under changed circumstances, a sensible and defensible rationale for the preservation of academic freedom.

Traditional doctrines of academic freedom emerged in societies in which the regnant philosophies and practices carefully walled off certain kinds of inquiry. Physics and chemistry, though they implicitly challenged traditional religious beliefs, were nevertheless taught in Germany and the United States. But these courses were taught in classrooms in which the religious implications of the new sciences were muted or ignored. Indeed, classic philosophical positions like Descartes' helped to justify this separation of physics and chemistry from fundamental questions such as the nature of man and human destiny. Similarly, although history was taught, it was taught with careful concern for the past. And most historians left the implications for the present tacit rather than explicit. Around a hundred years ago, however, something new emerged. This was the effort to be scientific—or at least dispassionate and descriptive—in treating social and political affairs. There was a time when people were fired from American universities for suggesting that the gold standard was questionable. However, during the last hundred years a whole new branch of inquiry was domesticated in universities. An area of fundamental controversy in the society at large was incorporated into the university—namely, politics and the subjects that surround it, up to and including the role of religion and science and the learned professions in the construction of society's destiny. Consequently, a new theory of academic freedom had to be developed. In that context, Max Weber, John Dewey, and others developed what has been until recently the prevailing rationale for academic freedom.

The question of objectivity and indoctrination with respect to teaching political and social subjects raises, as it did early in this century, the fundamental challenge as to the meaning and justification for academic freedom. For it is in teaching these subjects that one takes vital and controversial matters of society at large and brings them into the university while at the same time claiming that one is not being political.

In many ways, I disagree with Professor Diamond's position. I would begin, however, by stressing the areas of agreement between us. First, like Diamond, I believe that our actions as teachers and scholars have consequences, particularly political consequences. Therefore, it is incumbent on us to approach our actions in the classroom as morally responsible agents. Second, while it is not clear what it is that radical students demand, I do agree that a humanistic and philosophical approach is desirable in teaching social and political sciences. And this is true whether or not one carries the title of professor of philosophy. I believe the teacher's basic responsibility is to invite, cajole, provoke, irritate, or seduce his students into confronting their values and trying to determine where their consciences and senses of human decency lie and what their ideals really are. On this issue, I applaud Diamond's views and his excellent critique of the "politicization" of American and other universities. Finally, I would stress my agreement with a statement that Diamond makes towards the close of his essay: " . . . one does not ask a doctor: Is that cancer? Do you like it?. . . One asks (him): Is that healthy or diseased tissue, no matter whether you like, value, or dislike it?" I agree. And Diamond's formulation indicates that there is a distinction between recognizing facts and liking them. I agree so much with him on this point that my only problem is whether he agrees with himself.

My observations will fall into three parts: first, my comments on Diamond's views; second, what the Weberian distinction between fact and value involves in my opinion; and third, comments on the question of objectivity and indoctrination.

It seems to me that Diamond sometimes states the facts falsely and, in most cases, in such an exaggerated and highly abstract form that he erases the actual problems that exist and the necessary distinctions that have to be made. He has the habit of turning intellectual distinctions into "realms" (his word, not mine). He suggests that whenever you make a distinction, say, between the intellectual and the political, you are establishing two jurisdictions rather like China and Russia. The problem then is to find some sort of mean or compromise between these two sovereign elements. On the contrary, I believe that one needs to seek not a mean between two polar opposites but a set of distinctions that allow one to take account of the actual facts, and to come out with a reasonable and consistent program of action with regard to the issues.

Professor Diamond begins by saying that "education and the political seem to belong somehow to separate . . . realms." But philosophers have, with few exceptions, said the opposite. All important philosophers of education — Plato, Rousseau, John Locke, John Dewey — have dealt with education as fundamentally a political affair. Does that mean they had no common sense? On the contrary, ask any common-sense person whether education is political. He will probably tell you that he is supporting it with his taxes and that it surely is political.

Note the definitions that Diamond employs. He says that teaching has to do with the truth, while the political has to do with achieving and preserving what is dear to us no matter what others may say or believe. But much teaching has to do with values other than truth. One, for example, is to set a decent example of self-respect as a teacher in a classroom, to be a moral model. Other functions of education include the deepening of esthetic sensitivities, the transmission of civic rituals. Moreover, much teaching is in fact political and doctrinal. As for politics, how about Diamond's definition? Is politics the activity of achieving or preserving what is dear to us, no matter what others may say or believe? Only sometimes, but not in the minds of democratically minded people with whom I have worked. Politics for them is not the attempt to win, "no matter what others elsewhere may say or believe." It is persuasion, compromise, bargaining — all expressive of a principle of respect for others. Diamond defines education in terms of a preselected ideal, and defines politics opprobriously in terms of a "realistic" model. No wonder the contrast is so glaring, the gap to be crossed so wide.

A second proposition fundamental to Diamond's argument is that the political is wholly bound up with doing, and the scientific with knowing. As a description of facts this, too, is false. Some of the most obvious things about American politics, for example, are the reports, panels, investigations, and documents that are produced to support positions and refute others. Inquiry and argument are observable parts of the political process. Similarly, part of the educational process comprises elements of political behavior such as jockeying for position, logrolling, and beating the competition to the printer. Moreover, there is a doubtful epistemology in Diamond's account. "Certainty" and "silence" seem to me the last words to use, though they are the ones he uses to describe the objectives of scientific inquiry. What conclusions usually produce are not certainty, but probability; not silence but debate; not the "permanence of things seen or grasped." What can this mean? Does it mean statements not subject to further rectification, or the objects or relations described by these statements? Does it mean no active experimental observation? As for the political, it was Plato who said that the object of politics is to seek permanence, secure possession of the good. What I think Diamond has done is to exaggerate a distinction between the cognitive and other activities. Cognition is a process that goes on within a communal forum, and it has an internal politic. In compensation, politics has cognitive aspects.

Perhaps what is most important is what I think is a misreading of Max Weber's basic point. Weber, in writing his two essays on science and politics, had both intellectual and practical political objectives in mind. Those essays were written to support Weber's effort to find places in the German universities for Social Democrats. He was trying to show that even, if you were a Social Democrat, you were not disqualified from teaching in universities. Weber would not have understood what it meant to talk about "dissevering" science from politics; he was a deeply committed political man. He did not believe that in becoming a professor he was required to give up the political causes he thought were just and right. His effort, like Diamond's, was to show how a man could serve both masters honorably; and how a full, decent life demanded this harmonious marriage of intellect and politics. Weber suggested proper moralities for science and for politics and showed that these two moralities, far from being opposed, can be harmonized in the lives of morally responsible individuals.

One of the most troublesome and central propositions in Diamond's argument stems from his talk of "realms," "severances," and the like. He says that if teaching is to be possible, some tribute to the dominant forces of society is required. This sounds more ominous than it really needs to be. The empirical question has to be raised, and Diamond nowhere raises it: What is the character of the dominant forces in society? In our society, the dominant forces are overwhelmingly allied to a constitutional ethic and a philosophy of free debate. What, then, is this "tribute" that teachers must give to the dominant forces? The tribute, it seems, is to preserve the forum of free debate and to conduct oneself honorably within it. It certainly is not tribute in the sense of not saying things that would irritate the powers that be. And to pay tribute to free debate is simply to pay respect to one's professional obligations as a scholar.

This is not just an abstract argument for argument's sake with Professor Diamond. His view seems to lead to a radical misinterpretation of the actual facts of our present situation. He says something like,

"We had better be good boys, at least moderately good boys, or Archie Bunker will eventually get us." Archie Bunker has actually been leaving scholars and teachers pretty much alone. The greatest threats to scholarly integrity and scientific honesty in recent years have come not from the public at large—either Archie Bunkers or Archie Bunker's enemies—but from within the intellectual community itself. If honesty, integrity, and freedom are threatened in society (and I think they are), they are threatened by the lack of conviction and sometimes the demagoguery of people inside the intellectual community. I do not see the picture as composed of the threatening polity on one side and honest scholars on the other. The problem is scholarly probity and integrity and the disagreements among academicians about what they are and should be.

As I understand Diamond, he sees that the fundamental problem of Weberians is that they leave it to the individual student to choose his position in the light of his ultimate values. The Weberians make no comment about ultimate values. When Weber used the words "ultimate values," he meant the kind of empirical, practical situation most professors face in colleges and universities. If a student in Germany in Weber's time, for example, was a Catholic and living in the Weimar Republic, one would describe the Weimar Republic, criticize it, and compare it to other regimes. But, in the end, one would not try in a course in political philosophy to tell that student not to be a Catholic. Now Diamond draws what he takes to be a most damaging implication from this position. He argues that this kind of attitude, in which one presents various points of view and leaves it to the student to make his own choice in terms of his values, is something that would work only in a liberal democracy. It would not work in Puritan England, Sparta, or Stalinist Russia. Of course, I agree. But what's damaging about this? One of the excellences of liberal democracy lies precisely in this fact. It is a reason why, as professional truth-seekers, scholars have a strong reason to value liberal democracy.

Diamond believes that something like political science is taught in all societies. Of course, but some societies insist that physics be theology and that animal breeding be a proof of political dogmas. To say that a certain kind of cultural and political setting is indispensable for accomplishing certain scientific goals is not to say that the conclusions reached are politically and culturally limited in validity. This is a genetic fallacy.

Let me turn, then, to the basic question of facts and values. What is the issue? Is it really true that Weber removes all value questions from the field of rational debate? Admittedly, some of his formulations are less than satisfactory and resemble the more extreme, unguarded statements of early logical positivism. Nevertheless, Weber's position in his essays on politics and science is quite clear, and I do not think it can be accurately described as Diamond attempts to do. Weber's fundamental distinction is between the "ethics of responsibility" and the "ethics of ultimate ends." It is the latter that, he believes, lies beyond scientific jurisdiction, because the people who are guided by such an ethic refuse to submit it on principle to scientific scrutiny. In contrast, within an ethics of responsibility, one is so committed to his or her ends that one is prepared always to examine them in relation to their consequences, conditions, and byproducts.

In any context of thought and action there are, of course, some values that are not treated as problematic. To take the example of medicine, it has not been argued by most doctors through the ages whether they should or should not save life. It was a given that their task was to save human life and reduce pain. But when new medical technologies and science emerged, these goals became in part problematic. Saving life and reducing pain have come into conflict with the values of individual autonomy. New inquiry is needed into the proper balance to be achieved. What Weber was proposing with his distinction between "is" and "ought" was, among other things, general scientific inquiry into the legitimacy of one's notions of what ought to be.

Professor Diamond sees a kind of deal between professors and the polity, a kind of necessary effort of placation on the part of scholars. I would look at the matter differently. It seems to me that the political and the scientific are conjoint activities. We walk into our classrooms, let us hope, as full human beings. And we walk in having accepted a professional ethic: that ethic requires that certain rules of inquiry and teaching be employed in the classroom. Why are these professional rules justified? For their intellectual and political functions. These functions have been determined to be indispensable to a decent, enlightened civilization. One goes into the classroom, one analyzes various points of view, and one tries with the help of one's students to present as many points of view as fairly and justly as possible. In doing that one is also a political actor, spreading the ethic of tolerance—an ethic that affects the distribution of values in society. Diamond says that people don't hold their values in this tentative way. That is a fact. But if one distinguishes between facts and values, one would wish to assert that generally the educated people in society should learn to consider their values as hypotheses, as programs of action to be tested by their consequences. It seems odd and demoralizing to suggest that, to maintain an ethic of free inquiry, it is desirable that scholars accept an implicit demand of the surrounding society and limit that free inquiry when it enters dangerous waters. Though Professor Diamond would describe himself, I imagine, as absolutistic and me as a relativist, I think he is much more relativistic than I am about this matter.

The Problem
of Indoctrination

Francis Canavan, S. J.
Fordham University

In a real sense, I am professionally committed to indoctrination. Yet I do not personally regard indoctrination in the classroom as a practical problem, because I am so convinced that the effort to indoctrinate is largely futile.

I can perhaps explain why I so regard it by quoting a line I read in a book review years ago — so many years ago that I have forgotten in what journal I read it and what book was under review. But the line that stuck in my memory was this: "You can persuade a class of sophomores that Ernest Hemingway is the greatest writer who ever lived; but the sophomores will grow up, and they will despise you." Of course one can play upon the immaturity and insecurity of students, but only at the risk that they will eventually grow up and see through what has been done to them. Any teacher worth his salt, however convinced he may be of the truth of his own views, must want results more lasting than that.

To the extent, then, that he aims at assent at all, a good teacher must aim at *reasoned* assent. That is, he must strive, at most, for agreement based on a genuine understanding of the fundamental questions involved in the subject under study, of the possible answers to those questions, and of the reasons for what he thinks are the right answers. Then he must leave the matter up to the judgment of the students. And he will do this, not primarily out of respect for the students' rights, but out of recognition of the nature of their minds.

For it is impossible to teach anyone to think the truth without teaching him to think and to think critically. If one is content to have students accept what one regards as true because of one's personal authority or the persuasive power of one's rhetoric, one builds on sand, not on rock, and the building may soon collapse. The only lasting convictions are those founded on the exercise of personal judgment.

The reader will notice that I say personal judgment, not private judgment. I am not speaking of the right to intellectual freedom but of something antecedent to and more basic than it: the reality of intellectual freedom. People, even young ones, are in fact free and they will make up their own minds, whether they have a right to do so or not. I find nothing wrong in principle with trying to get students to see something if one thinks it is there to be seen. But I do not know how to *make* anyone see anything. and so I see no point in trying.

What is wrong with the political activist in the classroom, then, is not that he has convictions. It is rather that, in Professor Diamond's words, he has "militant moral certainty" about the just social order as "a goal passionately here and now to be embraced by the will and pursued at any cost." Objectivity need not depend on a rejection of all moral certainty—I happen to believe that it is objectively unjust to punish a man for a crime which one knows he did not commit, for example—but it does depend on an ability to transcend mere will and passion.

For this reason, I think that Professor Diamond's substitution of "health" and "excellence" for "value" is sound. Value may be a purely subjective preference. But, arguably at least, health and excellence are objects of intellectual cognition because they are not added to that which is understood, but are implicit in the very act of understanding it. One cannot understand the human body, let alone cure its ills, if one insists on maintaining a "value-free" attitude that regards health as a subjective preference of the patient or the doctor, but not as the right order of the body. As Michael Polanyi has put it, "All physiology is teleological, . . .Physiology is a system of rules of rightness, and as such can account only for health."[1] Similarly, although more subtly, one cannot understand the human psyche without understanding that excellence which constitutes its right order, and one cannot understand the body politic with understanding its right order.

These propositions, it seems to me, rest in turn on the Scholastic adage, *bonum et ens convertuntur,* good and being are convertible terms. The "good," that is to say, is not a preference projected on the real but is an aspect of the real. To state this is, of course, to make an assertion which many will deny and which certainly is not proved by the mere act of asserting it. But the assertion does point out that political philosophy, like moral philosophy generally, depends on the answer to a metaphysical question.

Plato was surely right when he said that the supreme idea in political thought is the Idea of the Good. All politics is a kind of action, and action always aims at some end which men hold (however subjectively) to be good. Politics cannot be understood without understanding the good at which it aims. The ultimate question in political philosophy, therefore, is the metaphysical status of the Idea of the Good.

If its status is that of non-being — if, in other words, the Idea of the Good has no foundation in objective reality but is rooted only in men's subjective desires — then political questions are ultimately unanswerable on intellectual grounds. If that is true, then we must accept it as true. But whether it is true is a valid metaphysical issue and a most important one. We cannot escape the issue by pronouncing a priori that discussion of it is barred by the scientific method.

There is indeed a moral certainty all too easily arrived at by shallow people who are more interested in action than in thought and who implicitly assert the superiority of practice to theory. But Professor Diamond's paper is, among other things, a plea for the possibility of philosophy in general and of political philosophy in particular. It is therefore an assertion of the superiority of theory to practice. In this I think Professor Diamond is right, because I see no other intellectual check on political moralism and proselytism than to maintain that political theory is both possible and superior to practice.

I therefore doubt the wisdom of making the case against indoctrination in the classroom rest on a rejection of the possibility of a valid political philosophy. To be sure, anyone interested in seeking truth — particularly, I should think, in the area of politics — will cultivate an attitude of mind which may appear to be skepticism because it makes one hesitant about jumping to conclusions on complex matters. But that habit of mind is better described as critical judgment than as skepticism.

A true skepticism denies in advance that answers to the basic questions of ethics and politics are intellectually available. In so doing, it tries to safeguard against indoctrination by denying the possibility of true doctrine. But it thereby denies that practice can be guided by theory, or action by reason. And so it removes the intellectual barriers to that very subjectivism and mindless activism that it fears. We should protect objectivity more effectively, I suggest, if we admitted the possibility that valid answers to the basic questions are available. Political philosophy would then once again become what the classics took it to be: an inquiry into the principles of right political order conducted in accordance with critical theoretical standards.

Let me now turn to a complicating factor, namely, the relationship between the teacher and the community. Although at first hearing it sounds shocking, I believe that Professor Diamond is right when he says that the community supplies the teacher with money and students on political terms. Academic freedom is, of course, a right belonging to the teacher as an individual. But it is a right that can be established and defined only by the community—for the reason that, if a community does not recognize and protect academic freedom, it does not exist in that community.

Now, the community will make its decision on academic freedom in the light of its understanding of its own interest. After all, even John Stuart Mill in *On Liberty* was trying to persuade the community of the utility of liberty. The teacher, therefore, has to persuade the community that, in Edmund Burke's phrase, he owes it, not obedience but judgment, and that it is good for the community that he should furnish it with mature, dispassionate and critical judgment.

On the institutional scale, this means that the university and the community come to terms with each other in a mutual agreement that the university serves the community by performing its proper function, and that its function is defined broadly as the pursuit of knowledge and understanding. As Professor Diamond says, society will not indefinitely tolerate the politicization of the academy, because politicization is a conversion of the academy from its intellectual function to political activism. When that happens, society may cease to see any reason why it should protect the academy and guarantee its privileges. Not only is that a risk which academics in prudence should not take. It is a perversion of the academy which in conscience they should not permit because it deprives society of the service which the academy ought to render and which is the basis of the academy's claim upon society.

There is a further dimension of the relationship of the university to the community which I should like to mention. Professor Diamond, in his paper, had in mind the political community which, as political, is one. But the community today is religiously, philosophically and culturally plural. It is a community, not only of individuals, but of communities. It is this reality, I take it, that we designate when we speak of a pluralist society. The question arises, then, whether in a pluralist society we could not have different kinds of university serving different communities.

To explain what I mean, I will present here a sketch of an intellectual project in which I, as a Catholic, would be interested in engaging. It is not meant to be a description of what actually goes on in any Catholic university in America today. It is only my view of how one might conceive of the function of a Catholic university. *Mutatis mutandis,* it could be applied to a university conducted by any group of people holding a common religious belief or even simply a common *Weltanschauung* of a philosophical nature. But I shall speak of a Catholic project because it is the one that would attract me.

Let us begin with a problem that confronts every thinking Catholic or, indeed, any intelligent believer in what professes to be a revealed religion. A believer has the lifelong task of harmonizing his revealed faith with the findings of human reason that are available in his time. He could shake off the problem, of course, by abandoning his faith, just as one can get rid of a headache by taking a gun and blowing his brains out. But my assumption is that we are dealing with a man who wants to keep his faith, who regards it as a boon rather than a burden, and who finds that it helps, not hinders, him in understanding the world in which he lives. Such a person will nonetheless have the never-finished task of bringing the teachings of faith and the conclusions of reason into some kind of coherent and harmonious relationship.

But, if establishing a coherent world view, based on both faith and reason, is a project for the individual Catholic, then the project can be institutionalized. What one can and must do for himself, he may do in cooperation with others. A Catholic university, then, can be conceived of as an institution designed to enable Catholics collectively to attack the intellectual problems that any one of them has to face individually.

Note that such an institution assumes the truth of the Catholic religion. It does not have to enter into the question whether its religion is true before it can begin its work. The institution exists for persons who have already answered that question, on grounds which they find satisfactory. Those who do not find them satisfactory will presumably attend or work in other institutions. But these persons have answered the question and intend to move on to the further questions arising out of what is believed by faith, what is known or speculated about by reason, and the relationship between them.

It does not follow that a Catholic university is an institution dedicated primarily to studying and teaching revealed religion, or that its purpose is indoctrination. To perform adequately the task that I have very sketchily described, it must study and teach all the subjects that make up the ordinary curriculum of universities in its time and place. It is through the study of these subjects that the members of the university will confront that rationally known reality which they wish to harmonize with faith and to understand in the light of faith, and in whose light faith itself must be interpreted. A relation, after all, always has at least two terms; if one wishes to reflect upon the relationship between physics and theology, for instance, it is as necessary to know physics as it is to know theology.

A Catholic university cannot do its work properly unless it studies and teaches these subjects objectively—though I must say again that "objective" is not a synonym for "neutral," "agnostic," or "value-free." It means only that the first intellectual duty of any man, believer or non-believer, is to understand the real as it is, to the best of his ability, without distorting it to fit the needs of his general point of view.

On the other hand, it is one thing for a physicist to insist that physics must be studied on its own terms and by its own methods. It is quite another thing to say that any effort to integrate physics into a broader and more comprehensive view of the world is ruled out in advance as an attack on the autonomy of physics. The latter position is nothing but the narrow-mindedness of a specialist who has no interest in anything beyond his own discipline and therefore refuses to think beyond its frontiers.

One could, of course, admit that science must somehow be integrated with philosophy, but deny that it can or should have anything to do with religious faith. One could hold—as many do—that revealed religion is an absurdity, that a Catholic university is a contradiction in terms, and that therefore the work of a Catholic university as described here is impossible to perform. But I wonder on what grounds one would deny others the right to try to perform it. It can hardly be on the ground of "objectivity" unless one defines objectivity as meaning agreement with oneself.

The objection to a Catholic university, however, can be pressed further. This kind of university, it is said, is not only a contradiction in terms but is incompatible with the fundamental principle of a free and pluralist society.

Pluralism, in this view, connotes a wide diversity of beliefs held by individuals, all of whom are equal. But to found a university on a particular belief is to give that belief a privileged position in the university. It is therefore to deny the equality of all individuals and their beliefs, and so is an attack on pluralism. The only kind of university that ought to exist in a pluralist society is one organized as a free marketplace of ideas. The university, as a university, must stand for nothing but the free expression of ideas, all of which are equal in its sight.

Now, the proper name for this theory is not pluralism. A pluralist society is one which accepts the plurality not only of individuals but of groups. It recognizes the right of each group to hold its beliefs, to regard them as true and therefore superior to other and conflicting beliefs, and to institutionalize its efforts to deal with the intellectual problems connected with its beliefs. A Catholic university, far from being an attack on pluralism, is an expression of it.

The real premise of the charge that a Catholic university is incompatible with a free society is not pluralism but a radical individualism according to which the rights of the group and its institutions must always yield to the individual's claim to freedom. But this is to beg the question: when freedoms conflict, which should prevail? It is true that the group's freedom to organize its own institutions for its own purposes necessarily limits the freedom of individuals who do not share those purposes but who, for one reason or another, want to be part of the institutions. But if we absolutize the freedom of the individual and give him a veto power over what an institution may do, we deny the freedom of the group. A genuine plurality of universities serving the needs of different groups then becomes impossible, and there is only one legitimate kind of university, that is, one founded on the principles of liberal individualism. But this is a view that seems to be, in its own way, fully as sectarian as the views it rejects.

It is clear that I, for my part, reject liberal individualism and its premises in political theory, epistemology and metaphysics. But it is also clear to me that there is little prospect in today's world of general agreement on matters of faith. There is just as little prospect of agreement on the conclusions of reason about matters of fundamental importance to men: if religion is not about to convert the world, neither is philosophy. To return to where I began, the most that one might hope for in modern universities is agreement on the critical standards of judgment that define objectivity and prohibit mere indoctrination.

Even that, however, is more than we are likely to get. In the social sciences at least, epistemological debate is endless. What we can know, and how we can know that we know it, is a controverted question, to put it mildly. Yet the mere fact of the controversy offers us some common ground. For it assumes, among all parties to the dispute, an antecedent agreement that there ought to be critical standards and that they can in principle be established by argument. It is this antecedent agreement, minimal though it is, that makes some degree of shared respect for objectivity possible and enables us to distinguish those who respect it from those who do not. It is not much to go on, but it may be enough to keep the barbarians outside the gates of the academy.

NOTES

1. Michael Polanyi, *Personal Knowledge*. New York & Evanston: Harper & Row, 1964, p. 360.

Teaching and the Shaping of Souls

Robert A. Goldwin
*Special Consultant on Education to
the President of the United States*

I start with an anecdote, which, I think, may be helpful in telling you the background of my views and may also throw some light on our topic. When I was dean of St. John's College, it used to be a practice for people to sit around a certain table in the coffee shop and try to think of academic jokes. For instance, I once made up a motto that any college could adopt: "Where the truth lies."

One day we were trying to think of unlikely lecture titles. Someone thought of "Hegel's Use of Metaphor"; another was "The Humor of Immanuel Kant"; and I invented one: "Euclid's Rhetoric." I thought it was an excellent joke because it was so unlikely; for whether you read Euclid in the original or in translation, or whether you simply studied geometry years ago you know that he made no rhetorical effort. That is, proposition after proposition after proposition starts out with the statement of a problem, with a list of what was given, with a series of arguments—first step, second step, third step, and so on—and a conclusion that now this has been proven, q.e.d., and on to the next theorem.

The more I thought about it, however, the more I felt that I had made not a good joke, but a good discovery. I began to think of it this way. Suppose you were Euclid in Athens, or wherever he was, and suppose you wanted to give form to a nation, a people, a city where geometry would be taken very seriously. It would be necessary to develop a certain taste, a certain inclination, a certain inner discipline that would begin to pervade the whole society. It would be receptive to

37

this unusual inquiry so that serious men—not just children but fully grown, serious men—would devote themselves to the enterprise of trying to understand more about lines and triangles and squares and circles and solid figures and numbers and ratios. Euclid's first step would be to start shaping souls open to geometry.

Now, I take that to be a clue to what the enterprise of teaching is and, I think, in a certain sense we have been talking about it in the right direction but in an inadequate and insufficiently comprehensive way. Professor Diamond makes a distinction. What scientists teach is radically different, he says, from the teaching of political or social subjects, because a scientist's subject (and he takes the example of enzymes although he might have said a geometer and used the example of lines and figures) are external to us. Whereas, he says, "we (political scientists and others in related fields) teach them about themselves." Now, I have the feeling that this is misleading in words and in thinking.

The best teaching of science understands that science and mathematics are liberal arts or humanistic studies. When I say that science and mathematics are humanistic studies, I mean that part of the enterprise is to understand ourselves better as human beings, by understanding the kinds of things we can do with our mind.

I was not and am not a mathematician. From my study of Euclid—I now remember very little of the theorems—there was the tremendously enlightening sensation that "I am one hell of a guy" to be able to understand some of those propositions. I didn't mean it was significant personally. What was significant was that it showed me something about what it means to be a human being with a functioning mind, and how far the power of the human mind can be carried.

Professor Diamond seems to think that studies of things like geometry are external to us and do not arouse the same kinds of difficulties that the study of politics engenders. He refers to a great authority, Hobbes, "a great political philosopher whose good standing with modern political scientists is matched only by that of Machiavelli," and "he [Hobbes] says that, in defending their political interests, men switch from 'custom' to 'reason' and back again, depending on which at the moment supports and flatters them. That is why the claim of scientific reasoning and matters like 'the causes and original constitution of right, equity, and justice are perpetually disputed both by the pen and the sword: whereas the doctrine of lines and figures [meaning geometry] is not so; because men care not in that subject what be truth, as a thing that crosses no man's ambition, profit or lust.'"

One of the advantages of an undergraduate education in the Great Books, such as one gets at St. John's College, is that certain little tidbits stick in your mind. I remember that Hobbes engaged in a tremendous controversy over geometry. The great Thomas Hobbes thought that he had figured out how to square the circle. He wrote a paper called, "Six

Lessons to the Professors of the Mathematics, One of Geometry, the Other of Astronomy, and the Chair Set up by the Noble and Learned Henry Savile in the University of Oxford." In those papers he apparently claims not only to square the circle but also to duplicate the cube, two problems that have since been proven impossible to accomplish. A well-known and, apparently, excellent contemporary mathematician, named John Wallis wrote a response with the mild title "A Due Correction for Mr. Hobbes in School Discipline for Not Saying His Lessons Right." Now, behind that mild title is the fact that, according to the *Dictionary of Scientific Biography*, Wallis attacked Hobbes for errors in Greek, for his West Country manner of speech, for being a rustic, for disloyalty to the Crown, and so on. Hobbes, of course, replied; the *Dictionary of Scientific Biography* says that Hobbes' replies were better mannered. But listen to the title of Hobbes' reply to Wallis: "Stigmae or Marks of the Absurd Geometry, Rural Language, Scottish Church Politics, and Barbarisms of John Wallis."

Now that, I think, is an interesting example of what can happen in a controversy over "lines and figures," which Hobbes assured us does not become as heated as political controversy, because "men care not in that subject what be truth, as a thing that crosses no man's ambition, profit, or lust."

In short, I think, danger lies about us everywhere. Even in the study of geometry, if teaching has not formed characters receptive to the subject, passion can overwhelm reason. Professor Diamond spoke of ethos and ethnos, that is, the effort of teaching must take place in some society, somewhere, and that every society has a character, and every honest teacher must want that society to be one that is suitable, accommodating, hospitable for the teaching he thinks is appropriate. As a minimum, he has to hope that he will be allowed to teach unnoticed if he cannot make the society what he wants it to be. Professor Diamond raises the question: What molds values, what are the ideas of excellence? That is the essential question in any society, he says, and he then undertakes to teach prudence to the very people, he says, who lack the political art.

Now, I know about this matter of being a professor and being in politics. I have done both, not always very well, from time to time, for many years now. There is a kind of disjunction between the two worlds of study and action. One of the evidences is this: when I first became active in a political campaign in Chicago more than ten years ago, the politicians called me "Perfessor," and that was, I am sure, a persistent and deliberate reminder to me that I was an outsider. They had all sorts of strange notions of what I was an outsider about. For instance, the first time I sat in on a meeting in which political patronage was discussed, one of them said to me afterwards, "Well, Perfessor, I guess that's something you don't learn about in your textbooks." I was a little embarrassed because if he could have read what political science literature says about the importance to politicians of patronage and graft and other such activities, he would have been embarrassed. The politicians themselves are much less sure that those things are right than hardboiled political scientists who write textbooks and knowing articles about American politics. The sense that their grounds were different from mine was, I think, evident, and I have always kept it in mind and think it is a reality. The worlds of study and politics are related but different. The professor in politics remains an outsider, or ceases to be a professor. This effort to teach prudence—that is, the political art—to a professor who lacks it, according to Diamond, is essential if he is to be a good teacher. I think that's the difficult—maybe impossible—but certainly difficult task that Diamond poses to himself.

At St. John's College a member of the faculty said that he was unfairly being asked to leave. He had the impression it was because he was too much of a scholar, and he asked derisively whether having a Ph.D. disqualifies one from being a member of the faculty at St. John's College. The answer was "No, it does not disqualify you, but you are expected to rise above it."

Professor Diamond's point is that every teacher's teaching takes place in some society that does have views, and therefore every professor must have some notion of prudence. But, I think it is also important to rise above it. A teacher who is nothing but a politician is not a teacher. A teacher who lacks any political sense may also turn out not to be a teacher. But to the extent that he is aware of the setting and acts in accordance with it, he is being prudent; and to the extent that he can—and that would depend very much on his understanding, his ability, his grasp of his subject matter, and his understanding that he has an obligation to shape students—he must rise above considerations of prudence.

I return, therefore, to the point about Euclid. Professor Frankel said that most philosophers—and he mentioned a number of them, including Plato—would surely say that education is fundamentally political. Locke may have said that or meant it. Plato, I am sure, did not mean that, unless by *fundamentally* we mean only *initially*. Education must be more than the political, and one must rise above the political to be a good teacher. When Professor Diamond says, "Let us reopen the question of human excellence," it's clear that the problem is broader than politics. I won't say it is broader than he *thinks it is*. It's broader than he *seems to say it is*.

When you reopen the question of human excellence, then the most fundamental beliefs of any society begin to be questioned and you are back with your old trouble. That's what I mean by rising above the considerations of prudence. If you don't reopen the question of human excellence, then you are not an honest teacher, and if you do, you cannot be called prudent essentially, although you may use prudence to get yourself to the point. Once that question is honestly re-opened, seriously pursued, no one knows what the outcome may be, and you face the problem that Socrates faced, ultimately. That, I think, is a responsibility of a good teacher and that, I hope, is what we have been talking about.

The Ethics of Teaching
Political Science: Another Perspective

Abraham H. Miller
University of Cincinnati

It is appropriate that a political scientist should initiate our discussion on the ethics of teaching and research. Political scientists have experienced much conflict and critical self-examination in recent years over the values and ethics of teaching and research. Whether anything can be learned from our internal and often internecine conflict is, of course, another matter entirely. Perhaps reflection on and assessment of our experiences will simply illustrate the futility of using one's intellectual resources in the quest for solutions to unresolvable problems. For, in the final analysis, values are some of the most immutable of man's creations. Values tend to be far more reflective of basic psychological needs and predispositions than of conclusions based on rational assessment. They are part of the infrastructure of one's presentation of self and, as such, remain generally unresponsive to reasonable, dispassionate argument. This is not to say that raising poignant and important value questions serves no useful function.

Recent confrontations with basic value questions that affect teachers' and researchers' conduct have caused reexamination of professional behavior and even the objectivity of some of the most cherished theories. Some intellectual catharsis has resulted from this experience. Certain people who were intimidated by the weight of conventional, professional wisdom have felt less constrained to speak out, and graduate students have been exposed to issues that a few short years ago were nonexistent. Yet, none of the value problems have been resolved. Those who insist on the view of political science as a dispassionate, objective, scientific discipline whose research can — in terms of scientific method — attain the standards of the natural sciences are more convinced than ever of the correctness and necessity of their position. Those who see the study of politics as intimately linked to questions of political and social values remain convinced of their position. And some individuals feel that the only proper function of the political sciences is to carve out a "humane" set of social and political ethics and transmit them to one's students. The justification for this pursuit, which I believe violates the basic responsibility of the teacher, is that this is what is being done anyhow — only in a more devious, subtle, and mendacious form under the guise of science.

This is the state of affairs in our profession. Wherever questions of values are involved, solutions are not easily achieved. Consequently, Professor Diamond aspires beyond his reach in attempting to resolve what he perceives as another value dilemma uniquely affecting the teacher of political science. The solution he does offer is an exercise in the facile replacement of substance with rhetoric. But, before addressing Diamond's attempt at finding a solution, it is important to step back somewhat and consider the accuracy of his diagnosis of the problem.

Many who do teach political science, do not perceive a tension between the aims and goals of education and those of the polity. This is because they see both their pedagogical pursuits and the foundation of the polity as being based on freedom of inquiry. Even if they were to ignore the special preserve of academic freedom, the ethos on which the polity is based derives from freedom of expression and inquiry. Diamond says that a tension exists between seeking the truth "wherever and whatever it is," which he describes as the function of teaching; and achieving or preserving "what a particular polity holds true no matter what others elsewhere may say or believe," which he sees as polity's function. Does this tension not also exist in other and equally important spheres of society, such as the press and the citizenry at large?

The ethos of the fraternity of journalists is no less moral than that of teachers — to report the truth wherever and whatever it is. The social and political ramifications of being a journalistic truth-seeker and following the dictates of one's professional conscience are perhaps even more in conflict with the polity and have far greater immediate political implications than virtually anything a teacher says in the classroom. The Nixon-Agnew administration's vicious attacks on the press, its attempt to intimidate the news media — as well as its direct assaults on the licensing privileges of television broadcasting facilities operated by the *Washington Post* — signify dramatic pressures administered by the White House, which did not believe the press was paying proper homage to the body politic.

The same tension, if conceived the way Professor Diamond has portrayed it, exists for the citizenry at large. How does one render homage to the polity and maintain independence of thought, opinion, and action? One must recognize that homage is paid to the polity through free debate, free thought, free inquiry, and loyal opposition. When one steps beyond this, then one does not pay homage to the polity at all. One may become a sycophant for particular administrations and an apologist for given policies and programs, but ephemeral administrations and ideologies do not represent the public. This *l'état, c'est moi* approach—where those who occupy short-lived administrative positions or enunciate and implement transient policies claim they are the embodiment of the society—has nothing to do with the true nature of the polity.

One of the basic flaws in Diamond's argument is the supposition that the powers that be are a personification of the polity, the dominant ethos of society. Former President Nixon delighted in such logic; he had some pragmatic reasons for playing the role of Louis XIV. But, as a political scientist, Diamond should know better. His ethical argument that teachers must accommodate themselves to the desires of the power elite is still in no way justified. I do not think the school of thought that political scientists call democratic pluralism can be entirely ignored. Power does vary from issue to issue and from situation to situation. Appeasing one group only leads to making enemies of other groups. Politics is an arena of pluralistic coalitions competing with each other for scarce resources, uniting with various groups on different issues.

I do not perceive the basic tension to which Diamond alludes. If this tension exists for teachers of political science, it also exists for other pursuits within the sociopolitical order. The teaching of politics does engage political questions, but is this really much different from the professions of teaching most, if not all, other subjects? Certainly it is more difficult to ignore political issues that arise in the course of teaching political science than it is in teaching some disciplines where such matters are tangential to the main subject matter. Ignoring political questions is not really an option for those who consider themselves students of politics. How then are these political issues to be addressed? Should one address these questions with reasoned dispassion or pay dues to society by becoming its apologist and inculcator? Despite periodic attempts to deny these roles, they are the only ones that Diamond would have political science teachers play to keep peace with the polity. As he notes, "... when he becomes ... a political science teacher, he must come out into the open and accept the consequences. A teacher must do whatever is necessary to secure students and money, and he must do justice to these students and that money in ways appropriate to the general nature and ends of teaching and to its scientific ends in particular."

Few teachers would have any quarrel with doing what is just and appropriate. Unfortunately, it is difficult to get any agreement on what is just and appropriate classroom behavior. Certainly, the vision of the New Left depicts the just and appropriate in ways that most reasonable scholars would find intolerable. But most would also find it equally intolerable to do whatever is necessary to secure students and money. At some points and in some situations, as Diamond rightly notes, teaching is not possible. And one of those times must be when the teacher's basic values are subverted by the expediency of securing students and money. In fact, the current financial malady affecting academe has made securing students and money a primary consideration, often at the expense of educational standards and integrity. For some, that may render teaching impossible; and the continuation of such a situation will result ultimately in more students and money and less talent to deal with them. The better minds will then seek alternatives that are not so compromising of their integrity.

Diamond points out that teachers must come to terms with the polity and still satisfy their commitment to scientific autonomy. That is only possible in a society where there is prior recognition of and ultimate commitment to science for the sake of man's unrelenting curiosity and desire for truth. Diamond is quick to note that large segments of society do not share that goal. Yet, as a political scientist, he should understand that the public's dominant character does not rest on the day-to-day fluctuations in its sentiments. If it did, the Bill of Rights would be meaningless, the Constitution would be a scrap of paper, lynching would still exist, racial tensions would flare into open warfare, and the rule of law would be impossible.

Public sentiments do have an impact on the quality and largess of resources expended on educational institutions. However, what are the options? Does one compromise the unrelenting pursuit of truth for fear that the public may not wish to hear one's revelation? Diamond would probably say that he would not advocate such a position. But he does—at least he comes terribly close when he says, "If there is no accommodation to political necessity, there will be no students, no money, no teaching of political science. Sheer need compels teachers to come to terms with the political element that is ineluctably part of their profession." This is nothing less than the worst form of manipulation of the individual person's mind by the ephemeral whims of mass politics and culture. If one is to be haunted by perpetual fear of the probable ramifications that will ensue if the Archie Bunkers of the world learn what is going on in the classroom, then the quality of intellectual life will never transcend the quality of mass opinion.

This is not a realistic fear, for mass opinion is not going to be directly translated into institutional policies except in the most extreme circumstances—witness the late 1960s. Even then democracy's basic safeguards acted in no small measure as countervailing forces. Moreover, in the late 1960s the public outrage against American universities was largely justified. The public intervened long after these institutions had renounced their normative commitments. The masses were not the first to violate the universities. Significant groups in the academic community first transgressed their own norms respecting dispassionate, objective inquiry and sought to politicize the campuses for their own purposes.

Before one turns the university over to the Archie Bunkers (and by default at that), one might begin by doing a better job of educating the public and students about the nature, meaning, and purpose of higher education. One might also try to resocialize some of his or her own colleagues who have contributed more to the assault against academe than has any other element in society.

As noted earlier, it is not simply Diamond's delineation of the problem with which I find difficulty, but the thrust of his attempt at a solution as well. Assuming that the tension between the public's demands and the political science teacher's goals does exist as he describes it, how well does his prescription fare?

Professor Diamond notes that one must come to terms with the polity:

> To come to respectable terms . . . is to give the decent polity and its opinions a central and respected place in political education. One should begin by considering what the decent polity regards as its own excellences. For example, an obvious way to do this in America is to look at the Declaration of Independence and United States Constitution. One must also teach the student to see as deeply as possible what are the claims of his government, what it regards as the proper human ends and the modes of their political attainment. . . .

The solution provided in this approach would result in as many answers as there are political scientists to ask the questions. Diamond may seriously believe that this is a solution, but it is so only if one assumes there is a type of value homogeneity. But such homogeneity is unrealistic. It is doubtful, for example, that most Marxists (and many non-Marxist youths as well) would accept the premise that Americans constitute a decent polity. Moreover, even if by force of logic one could persuade the Marxists that there is such a polity, it would be equally difficult to obtain any consensus on whether or not Americans have met their own standards of excellence. That exercise requires formidable value judgments. Also, the opinions on such matters would vary exponentially among the students confronted with the problem and the professors who pose it. Teaching would probably deteriorate into an indoctrination session under a professor's direction. This would hardly resolve the tension between political science teachers and the public, but it might go a long way toward exacerbating it.

As a political scientist interested in the political uses of terror, I thought naively that most civilized, decent human beings could agree without much difficulty to condemn political terrorism. Yet, a recent United Nations conference could not even reach any agreement about what terrorism is, let alone issue a proclamation condemning it. This conference was conducted in a transnational setting that was, of course, different from that of an American classroom. But it well illustrates how much ideology acts as a force field blocking normative perceptions that do not agree with previous value predispositions.

This inability to achieve any consensus when dealing with normative issues is not surprising. For this reason, among others, political science as a discipline has dramatically and increasingly moved away from purely standard approaches to political questions. Political scientists have found in the Weberian approach and in the ensuing fact-value distinction, the only intellectual pursuits that can claim scientific dispassion and objectivity.

As a scientist then, the scholar of politics does not suffer any greater tension than does any other member of the scientific community. The political scientist's primary obligation both as teacher and researcher is to science—to the unbiased search for truth, wherever it may lead—and to society's interests only when they are in accord with the norms of science. Obviously, such a relationship can exist only in a society that places a special value on the freedom of inquiry. History has noted repeatedly the tragedy that results when scientific quest is subsumed in homage to political accommodation. Most recently, the Soviet Union's use of psychiatry as a weapon against political dissidents is a poignant example of the betrayal of science to accommodate the state. In their moving, personal account, A Case of Madness, Zhores and Roy Medvedev graphically depict the human and social tragedies that occur when science prostitutes its values to conform to the ruling regime.

How long can a regime remain decent once its intellectual community adopts a policy of political expediency? Whatever tension exists between what scientists do and what the polity requires of them, that tension is insignificant when compared to the strain of trying to function as a scientist while paying homage to society. The only tribute a scientist and a teacher should pay to society is the pursuit of truth. Anything less pays homage neither to the polity nor to the ethics of one's profession. If such pursuits create tension, then perhaps the best way to relieve the stress is to educate the public about the necessity and utility of free inquiry.

Objectivity in Education

Marvin Zimmerman
SUNY, Buffalo

For the teacher, the pedagogical choice is not merely between opinion or fact. There is a third choice consisting of both opinion and fact. There are some who settle for fact alone, on the theory that this avoids controversy or indoctrination. Avoiding indoctrination may be a necessary condition for sound teaching but hardly a sufficient condition. It is a mistake to suggest that indoctrination and opinion are the same and thus eliminate all opinion from the classroom. Though all cases of indoctrination may well be cases of opinion, the converse, i.e., that all cases of opinion are cases of indoctrination, is blatantly false. Where the teacher presents his own opinion and criticism of same, this is preferable to prohibiting his own opinion (and others as well). Excluding opinion from the classroom withdraws valuable blood and muscle from any course worth teaching and taking. Indeed, one of the significant parts of the learning process consists of making everyone aware of the problem of indoctrination, objectivity, and related issues.

In the strong desire to avoid indoctrination, one may eliminate all reference to opinions of any kind. On the other hand, in the strong desire to make the subject-matter digestible, interesting, meaningful, one may go to the other extreme and provide huge doses of opinion, attitudes, biases, etc. Both groups above have picked up a half-truth and made it a whole truth. Ironically, if students were subject to both kinds of teaching in equal amounts, the combination might be desirable. The most desirable state should consist in being taught by faculty members, each of whom presents a balanced curriculum—both opinion and objective truths.

The virtue of sparing students the anguish and shock of new ideas clashing with traditional pieties and loyalties may be commendable. Here, however, I suspect the disease may be better than the cure. One hopes that students will recover from the "cure" of having been spared any intellectual or emotional agony. One must distinguish between being indoctrinated or being shocked by *new* ideas. It is not at all rare to discover students who are shocked by *old* ideas. However, there is no excuse for cruelty or sadism in teaching controversial ideas, old or new.

There are many who blame our educational and social problems on the widespread advocacy of relativism and the rejection of absolute or eternal values. This, they maintain, leads to belief in indoctrination and rejection of absolute values.

A critical view of absolute values should not interfere with being objective and eschewing indoctrination. Even belief in absolute values does not assure objectivity. Objectivity requires giving a fair hearing to many points of view, including those who advocate indoctrination and those who deny the existence of absolute values.

Historically, absolutists in the Church and Government frequently employed doctrinaire methods, just as many contemporary relativists have done. Even an advocate of indoctrination might feel obligated not to engage in it in class, as fulfilling a professional or contractual need. Neither the absolutists nor the relativists have a monopoly on virtue. This is not to deny the need for adequate machinery to judge cases of indoctrination. The last decade cries out for this need.

One must distinguish between immoral means used in research, and the use of research to achieve immoral ends. Clearly, to forbid all research which *could* be used for immoral purposes, would, in effect, require closing down or forbidding all conceivable experiments. Even aspirin can be employed to kill human beings. Furthermore, where questionable means are used, e.g., experimenting on terminal patients, a case may be made that this is the lesser of two evils, not only for patients but others in the future.

One must distinguish the role of scientist or teacher, on the one hand, and that of citizen on the other. One may as citizen oppose research which could lead to harmful consequences. Indeed, it would be a moral obligation for one so convinced to use all legal machinery, including resigning one's post to inform the public. But it must be conceded that even scientists have difficulty in making social, political, or ethical decisions involving scientific knowledge, let alone average citizens.

Both teaching and research have a common denominator, i.e., they are used in arriving at truth. They are thus characterized at best as being committed to objectivity and avoiding indoctrination and bias. It would require danger of the highest sort to justify restrictions on teaching or research. References to Hilter's barbarism as basis for restriction could justify abolition of knowledge in almost any area of chemistry, physics, medicine, biology, etc., inasmuch as Hitler employed knowledge in these and other areas to carry out his evil goals. Virtually all tools we possess can be used for evil as well as good. It is better to risk evil results by encouraging unrestricted investigation and research than risk evil results by curbing the search for truth. Some ignore or forget that "unilateral" restrictions may actually encourage misuse by other powers in the world. Knowledge of "treatment" or "cures" requires research, e.g., nuclear radiation, poison gas, and germ warfare.

Objectivity and Indoctrination

Fred Baumann
Assistant Executive Secretary of UCRA

The ethical problem of distinguishing between objectivity and indoctrination in teaching rests on some presupposed, traditional arguments. Objectivity and indoctrination are names for methods; and, obviously, they are terms of praise and blame. But what is praised in the method of objectivity, and what is blamed in indoctrination?

Indoctrination evidently means teaching what is not actually known to be true as though it were known. In terms of effect, indoctrination need not be conscious. By contrast, objectivity means strictly refraining from teaching as known that which is unknown. The distinction between methods thus rests on the difference between knowledge and the appearance of knowledge, that is, opinion.

Telling the difference between knowledge and opinion is a perennial difficulty. Opinion is thought that stops short and draws conclusions prematurely. Passion, laziness, and prejudice encourage one to settle for opinion rather than knowledge. Even knowledge of only a small part, rather than knowledge of a larger part or the whole, may prove to be fundamentally defective. Thus it did not appear, prior to the Scientific Revolution, that any *method* could ensure the separation of knowledge from opinion unless that method was founded already on knowledge of the whole.

The introduction of politics into the university curriculum a century ago was not the first time that the problem was raised of distinguishing the teaching of knowledge from the teaching of opinion. One Renaissance university made dual appointments—e.g., hiring a Platonist for every Aristotelean—to cancel out bias. The same remedy currently is adopted in certain American economics departments that hire Marxists to balance liberals. The difficulty in both cases is the same. As laissez faire economists will point out, it is false to assume that the truth must lie between the positions of those antagonists who are hired.

Since Descartes' time, natural science has claimed knowledge of a research method that solved the dilemma of having to know the whole before being certain of a part. This method produced infinitely replicable facts and concepts and was, thus, most suitable for use in teaching. The essence of the method was the use of a universal standard of measurement, external to the objects of study, that reduced all things to relationship with each other in terms of the standard. That standard was mathematics. No longer was the question asked, "What is gravity?" What effect it had, measured mathematically, was answered.

The effort to apply this objective method to the study of humans predated the twentieth-century developments to which Charles Frankel refers. His praise for the objectivity of nineteenth-century historical scholarship, which left "the implications for the present tacit rather than explicit," refers to an understanding of the discipline that saw it as scientific. Dealing with fairly narrow source material and accepting a positivist epistemology, Rankean historiography claimed to report "how it had actually been." However, reality was somewhat less halcyon than Professor Frankel indicates. In Ranke's heyday, German historians fought bitter struggles about the role of the Holy Roman Empire in German history. The implications for the contemporary problem of German reunification with or without Austria were clear enough without having to be made explicit.

Frankel is right to see in modern social science a more rigorous effort to follow the methods of natural science in studying human beings. One great difficulty arose in this project, however. Following the method of natural science meant using a standard external to the subjects of study. In this case the subject, the human being, was at the same time making the study and was vitally interested in the answers. The answers were not available in relation to the subject but only in reference to the external standard. Thus, a correlation might be demonstrated between the price of corn and the marriage rate. This fact, and any others of that kind, could not answer a question about the value of the institution of marriage as an aid to human felicity. This incommensurability between the answers that scientific method provides and the questions that human beings want answered is reflected in the so-called fact-value distinction.

As the term is frequently understood—though apparently not as Frankel understands it—it symbolizes a limit to the claims to knowledge of social science. Opinion is not, as it was for the early positivists, to be eliminated altogether. Rather it is to be driven beyond the gates, to ultima Thule. In exile, opinion changes its character and name and becomes "value." That is, in the past, opinion was understood as accurate calculation; it is now understood as separate from calculation altogether and as being pure, groundless assertion.

Professor Diamond's paper is directed to the consequences of understanding that distinction. He fears that the citadel of intellect may not be stronger with opinion outside and science within. In fact, much of the argumentation of those who openly desire to destroy the traditional privileges and structure of the academy is directed at the difficulties inherent in understanding the difference between facts and values. In German universities (and no doubt in gymnasia as well), leftist students and faculty recite the view *ad nauseam* that—if ultimate values are separable from rationality and not grounded therein, and if they determine fundamental loyalties—then it follows that science itself is merely a product of a set of irrational values and choices. It is thus argued that the pursuit of science and the preference for objectivity over indoctrination are themselves not rationally justifiable but products of the desire to preserve the status quo. Indoctrination that leads to what such critics consider to be benign social consequences may be preferable, given the ultimate value, to the search for truth. These critics also may argue that if ultimate values determine ends and science merely discloses consequences, then science is merely instrumental and equally as well adapted for use by those interested in power as by those interested in truth. These opponents' attacks on the university require an answer from those who teach about humanity, if the latter are to justify the seriousness of their professions.

Professor Frankel's answer is to argue that the understanding of the fact-value distinction outlined above and shared by Diamond and the New Left critics of objectivity is incorrect. According to Frankel, Max Weber, who originated the distinction, meant only that the ethics of ultimate ends lie beyond scientific jurisdiction "simply because the people who are guided by such an ethic refuse to submit it on principle to scientific inquiry." This implies that science can offer a rational account not only of the consequences of holding ultimate ends but of whether one should pursue those ends. Frankel strengthens this implication when he states that he believes Weber was proposing "a general program of scientific inquiry into the legitimacy of our notions of what ought to be." Thus for Frankel, Weber encourages science to determine the ought.

At the level of science, if not of prudence, there is hardly any issue between Frankel and Diamond. Diamond is surely not arguing that the truth can be made convincing to everybody. If what Weber meant is that fanatics cannot be persuaded to use the tools of reason, he would have agreed generally with the tradition of political thought. But it would be quite unclear then why that insight need be called a fact-value distinction, when a "knowledge-ignorance" or "reason-passion" distinction would seem more accurate. It is not evident why, on Frankel's account, science should be debarred from judging ethical systems that are based on and compounded of error merely because one of the systems' errors is that they refuse on principle to accept the judgment of reason. In what way is science not empowered to judge error when a way of life is at stake?

Since Frankel's account of the fact-value distinction seems to leave nothing that cannot be mastered by scientific reason, it seems fair to conclude that he saves this distinction from its nihilistic consequences by defining away its essence. But he raises something that should be explored further—namely, what it would mean to have a science that investigated the legitimacy of one's notions of what ought to be.

The method of the social sciences, which applies to the study of humans the method of natural sciences, will not be adequate. One can, for example, trace the political consequences of choosing to start a bloody war or to submit to an odious tyranny. Yet, determination of what one ought to choose can be known only if the political consequences can be traced further to the well-being or misery of human beings. The difficulty would be that no external measure could tell one what he or she wants to know.

To take a more extreme example: when faced with the argument that "a good war justifies any cause," showing that wars cause bloodshed will not be a sufficient refutation. The war-lover making the argument already knows that. Nor can one simply assert that the evils of war are self-evident and that only someone who refuses to submit to the ethics of responsibility or the standards of science could fail to be convinced. The argument must be met on its own terms. Is the supreme good that of being a warrior? What is it like to be a warrior, and what does being a warrior do to a person? What basis might there be for a warrior to foresake the alleged good of war on account of other people? And what aspect of human nature might obligate one to forsake war?

Scientific inquiry into the nature of the *ought* should begin with human experience and not with any standard external to experience. A crucial element of that experience is opinion about the ought. But will such inquiry prove amenable to the separation of knowledge and opinion and, thus, of objectivity and indoctrination?

The essence of this kind of inquiry is to separate knowledge from opinion. After all, it starts with opinion and articulates its unacknowledged assumptions and consequences, and eventually discerns the self-contradictions of opinion. The inquiry seeks to thresh out from the chaff of opinion the grain of a rational, consistent account of what human beings ought to be and do, on the basis of what they really are and want. This is, of course, not the method of modern natural or social science, which starts from the undoubtable and builds from there. Rather, the inquiry starts with the unsure and cannot reach certainty until the nypothesized end, in the method of ancient dialectic.

Such a method, therefore, would be thrown back to the problem of telling knowledge from opinion, proper teaching from indoctrination. Since the teacher admits that his approach, questions, and provisional formulations are not solid and unquestionable, he faces afresh the challenge of the ideologue, the partisan, and the principled fanatic. Clearly, the treatment of democracy offered by a wise political philosopher differs from that offered by a street-corner demagogue. But that difference cannot be so easily described, for it is possible that the more advanced stage of the philosopher's opinion has led him farther astray than the primitive notions of the demagogue.

Teaching about human beings has its problems. Whereas it is fundamentally distinct from politics because it is about the search for truth—and not for power, public morality, or the common welfare—from the point of view of politics, teaching about humans is only a fancy, disguised and therefore insidious way of carrying on politics. Of course, the political perspective on teaching need not confine itself to the teaching of politics. One need only see how totalitarian regimes control academic disciplines that have only the faintest connection to the study of human beings. In such cases, the political view unlimited by other considerations treats everything human as political.

Teaching about humanity is involved willy-nilly in a relationship with politics in a way different from that discussed by Frankel. The issue here (and it is this issue to which Diamond's remarks about prudence are addressed) is the intrinsic and necessary, if involuntary, political character of teaching about human beings. It would be a mistake to take the political view of teaching as simply correct, since such a view sees only a part of what teaching is and takes it for the whole. Nonetheless, some account of the political element in teaching must be given to the political world. It is not merely a question of basic prudence; rather, it is a matter of articulating an important difference that is basic to how teachers understand themselves.

The attitude of calculated inattention is offered by Frankel. He is more ready to take this route than I am, partly because his confidence in social science is unshaken. He criticizes Diamond for dividing politics and teaching into different realms. But Frankel's own account of their mixture is, as I have argued, one of purely extrinsic coincidence of purpose. In fact, he would subscribe to a radical separation of the realms if he were willing—as I believe he would be—to characterize the difference between the methods of the political philosopher and the demagogue, as that between objectivity and indoctrination. Therefore, he does not see much of a challenge in the political perspective that claims to find a fundamental similarity in the activities of the philosopher and the demagogue.

But Frankel offers a plausible political argument as well. Readily conceding that honest teaching is not possible in nonliberal societies, he contends that the best due one can pay liberal society is to partake of the privileges it offers. To behave more timidly could lead precisely to doubts about the propriety of the privileges.

There is surely much to this argument, but it neglects the possibility that pursuing truth wherever it leads may undermine the self-confidence of the liberal society in which that teaching takes place. R. G Collingwood's *Autobiography*, for example, makes a strong case that the irresolute, cynical generation of English politicians who sought to appease the Fascist powers, was a product of a new education that taught that philosophy was merely a game with no relevance to moral questions. If the pursuit of truth produces the common teaching that ultimate values are not rationally discussable, then the educated citizens will probably believe that there are no reasons to think that the liberal society in which they live is preferable to any other kind. Given the degree of self-discipline and tolerance of disagreement that liberal society requires, a disbelief in the rational superiority of itself is likely to have damaging effects in the long run.

To recognize that this possibility exists is, of course, not to recommend any particular course of action. It is merely to insist that there is a problem that cannot be wished away. One may conclude that liberal society is not threatened by the belief in the irrationality of ultimate values; but it would take a serious political assessment to bring conviction, not merely an assurance that there is a harmony between *Lehrfreiheit* and a free society. One may also arrive at the view that Robert Goldwin suggests: that the search for truth must take precedence over all political considerations. But, Diamond argues, that conclusion depends on a judgment that takes the political world into account. After all, if one is to argue *fiat Scientia, ruat coelum,* there must be a good rationale for it. Imagine a technocratic argument being made that sees in the material blessings of science a fair trade for loss of political liberty. A far more promising path is the effort to articulate the excellence of the scientific pursuit. That account, however, would have to be of the kind discussed earlier in the example of the warrior. It would have to articulate what the scientific life was like, how the life of the scientist made use of or neglected human capacities, and how it compared with other lives. It is an open question whether or not such an account would give us a reason to prefer the political philosopher to the demagogue. But the effort to articulate the difference is a proper task for students who study human beings. If a justification of the scientific pursuit taking precedence over all questions of political prudence were to result, then much of the challenge of those who see only indoctrination and politics in the study and teaching about humanity would have been met.

The main question remains and can be formulated: to what extent, if any, may the academy compromise its strict devotion to the pursuit of knowledge to ensure its continued preservation? The answer seems to be that it cannot, because such a compromise would destroy the academy as surely as any outside imposition of limits. Either one is after the truth or something else; there is no third possibility. However, since it seems to me that both Frankel and Diamond would agree to this, the question seems to be misstated.

The reason for this is, I believe, that the teaching method Diamond suggests follows and mirrors what he understands to be the proper method of pursuing knowledge. He recommends starting with conventional opinion and articulating it as sympathetically as possible before coming to the limitation of that understanding. Surely this is the procedure one would follow in moving from opinion towards certainty in the study of human beings. How can one claim to have discovered the self-contradictions in a set of beliefs, if one has not given them an opportunity to speak for themselves? The method thus has the value of teaching students how to inquire into these subjects themselves. This strategy also highlights the difference between the political advocate, who is a philosophical dogmatist applying his formulas to every exigency, and the teacher. The teacher dispassionately strives to give due weight to every contending opinion and does not begin with the class prejudice of the intellectual against whatever is merely conventional.

Neither corruption of the students, nor fear of Archie Bunker, is the real issue here. In a world in which the zaniest doctrines are given universal currency and paid as much serious attention as everything else, it is hard to know whom one would be protecting and against what. Nor may the fear of the imposition of crippling external restrictions lead the university to levy them on itself. The real issues remain the justification of teaching as something higher than political advocacy and the discovery of a method of teaching about humans that is at once directed to the questions people want answered—and that can distinguish between knowledge and opinion.

Objectivity and Biased Skepticism in Higher Education

Henry Novotny

California State College, Bakersfield

As it perhaps should, the present UCRA conference on the Ethics of Teaching and Research has raised more questions than It has answered. The papers and ensuing discussions suggest that much of the practical ethical perspective which we have developed in clinical psychology applies to the teaching of professionals and researchers in general.

Let me cite some principles of general validity. One must account for the ethical adequacy of one's decisions in the light of competing values and considerations of their consequences. One should be more concerned with conflict resolution than with the advocacy of any one value taken as an absolute. It is ultimately the ethical quality of the overall decision which should be judged rather than the particular components in isolation.

Nonetheless these principles are not sufficient. The researcher whose aim is the development of knowledge and its intelligent application to appropriate problems faces, on the one hand, the ethical imperative to pursue research as objectively as he can and, on the other hand, the recognition that efforts to reduce the ambiguity in causal inference to a minimum, may conflict with values flowing from concern for the welfare of the research participants. Scientific knowledge and techniques which may be used for human betterment may also be used for manipulative and exploitative purposes. The consequences of scientific theories and inventions derived in strict accordance with the ethics of research may on occasion be socially harmful.*

I shall limit my remarks first to a response to several propositions offered earlier at this conference, and then submit several propositions of my own. I shall suggest that universities should be held accountable not so much for their activities as for the intellectual capacities and outlook of their students. I shall argue that learning institutions should impart to their students, as a curricular "minimum indispensable," a realistic, *functional* description of the world, of the social and physical reality with which students will have to deal, and that the oft-lauded "attitude of radical skepticism" should be developed by the academy in a more even-handed manner so that students would be less likely to succumb to the twin evils of much modern pedagogy in social affairs, viz; gullability and despair.

Let me start by recalling the remarks by Father Francis Canavan of Fordham University who rejected the view that only a university organized as a free marketplace of ideas is justifiable in a pluralistic society. Father Canavan suggested that "The real premise of the charge that a Catholic university is incompatible with a free society is not a pluralism but a radical individualism according to which the rights of the group and its institutions must always yield to the individual's claim of freedom." Father Canavan suggested that a pluralistic society should accept the existence of groups and institutions which differ in their fundamental assumptions.

One must agree with Father Canavan that, in a pluralistic society, individuals may have to seek expression through an existing multiplicity of social groups, organizations, and institutions. One must also remember, however, and I am certain he would agree, that even in a pluralistic society a number of individual "rights" should still be guaranteed, as well as the preservation of the pluralistic framework itself. It would follow, however, that one would have to set some limits to the kinds of institutions permitted to operate. Discouraged, for instance, would be the formation of undemocratic institutions by intolerant, undemocratic groups aiming to subvert the democratic social structure which makes possible the very existence of the plurality he extolls.

Accepting such limitations, Father Canavan's proposition has much to recommend it. With the admission that a typical university hardly represents a "free market place of ideas," anyway, and in the face of the persistent efforts by governmental agencies to homogenize the citizenry culturally, racially, and even intellectually—the concept of local autonomy and neighborhood schools is becoming a nostalgic memory of the past—it seems imperative to establish a mechanism for the preservation of cultural and philosophical pluralism in the U.S. Perhaps it is possible to establish "institutions which differ in their fundamental assumptions" without creating convenient vehicles for totalitarian, power-seeking, and action-oriented "isms." This might hopefully lead to a more meaningful competition between conflicting philosophies which would then, I presume, have to seek their confirmation and disconfirmation at least partly in the general public arena from which the students are recruited. Such a pluralism of learning institutions would force additional issues into focus such as the need for a clear and unambiguous definition of goals, methods, and procedures adopted by the university. This might be viewed as an educational "service provider" competing in the free market for student-customers. To give the necessary free and informed consent, prospective students (and perhaps parents) would have to be thoroughly briefed about the philosophy and social values embraced by the institution and its faculty, as well as about the departmental views bearing on the students' field of interest. "Truth in packaging" regulations might be required to guard against academic efforts at obfuscating the issue of values and smuggling the latter in under misleading labels.

The issue of values brings up Professor Diamond's suggestion that the disciplines dealing with human choices should free themselves from the "self-denying ordinance of the fact-value distinction" and "avoid the defect of making science sterile" by turning to the question of what is "healthy" and what is "diseased" in society. That, in my judgment, is very ill-conceived advice. One can only shudder at the specter of a therapeutic society in which what is mentally "healthy" and socially sane is decreed by the powers that be.

How to improve the relations and communication between the university and the society at large is an issue which comes up at virtually all academic conferences. Thus, of the three "ethical standards" which Professor Diamond suggested for teachers, one is based on the "necessity" to "find the just principles and the rhetoric" to "win for education, as we in our wisdom see its need, the public consent without which our enterprise is at an end." Father Canavan suggested that the academy should persuade the surrounding political community to protect academic freedom.

What sometimes disturbs the public, and perhaps rightly so, is the academic attitude expressed by such propositions. It is both ethical and logical to expect that the university, whether it desires to improve its public image or not, should try to do more than carry out an efficient public relations campaign. At the very least, institutions of learning owe the general community from which they derive support, the maintenance of a functioning, two-way communication process by which the general public and its spokespersons can express their concerns to the institution, and receive non-patronizing explanations in return. Not only are questions of ethics and courtesy involved, but also the humbling thought that the academic scholars may not possess a monopoly of knowledge and wisdom.

At present, there are really very few avenues through which a non-academician can initiate a meaningful dialogue with the university (unless he is a trustee or a financial supporter), especially so if he intends to be critical. How easy it is to label him an anti-intellectual with fascistic tendencies intent on stifling academic freedom! Would it be perhaps possible to establish standing faculty committees, with appropriate official status, to deal with interested outside groups in the name of the institution? If properly organized such an arrangement might result both in a more understanding and supportive public and a more realistic academic attitude.

I return to the first of my propositions which is that all learning institutions should be held in a clearly specified way accountable to the general public for their products. I am not implying in the least the slightest abridgement of academic freedom. I am not referring to the academic processes as such, nor am I suggesting that academicians would always have to agree with public opinions. They may have excellent reasons for disagreeing with public opinions. I merely suggest that formalized public feedback is overdue, and that the institutions of learning should bear not only an ethical, but also an objectively formulated, responsibility for the gross cognitive, emotional, and behavioral changes which they induce in their charges.

By way of illustration, let me recall an incident which was reported two or three years ago. A student was ejected from (of all places) Antioch College following a seven-week student strike. Notified by her son of his expulsion, his mother exclaimed: "It doesn't seem fair that the college which made you a radical should now throw you out for being one." How many would question that the mother of the student had excellent grounds for complaint?

It is obvious that our limited understanding of human responses does not always allow us to judge accurately complex human interactions and predict reliably their consequences. On the other hand, we can and have learned by experience and can often make quite valid conclusions, at least on a statistical or even common sense basis. Epistemological and pedagogic difficulties have never stopped us from defending the worth of what we do. Why should we now fear evaluation? Attempts to escape responsibility for one's actions and their consequences are, of course, as old as mankind. The presumed sophistication of our age has changed little in this respect. To some degree we all share this tendency whether acting singly or in groups. Perhaps one of the great contributions of our civilization is to insist on finding objective criteria by which to define goals and to measure performance, progress, and achievement. Because of traditions and the nature of the processes involved, such formalization does not come easy. For instance, we have had our share of difficulties in clinical psychology, a field in which many have claimed an exemption from the requirements of objective assessment because the presumed uniqueness of the process and the special genius of the claimants allegedly render objective measurements inapplicable. If so, how does a psychotherapist justify his claims of therapeutic success? I believe institutions of learning should lead the way and establish the criteria and the procedures by which their educational performance can be more meaningfully assessed and appreciated by the general public. How does the institution of learning objectively measure the growth of perception and intellectual maturity among those who take assorted courses for four years?

My second proposition is that, as part of general education, the university should familiarize the students with a modern, representative, and practical *functional* description of the world, and of the social and physical phenomena with which they will have to cope. The students should also acquire at least the requisite fundamental technical and social skills. They should learn not only how to deal with everyday technical problems but how to approach human problems that do not yield to the techniques successfully applied in dealing with impersonal affairs. They should be impressed enough with the unavoidable intricacies of social existence to avoid the simplistic, pseudo-scientific social schemes that promise power to the elect and a utopia to everyone. They should also learn enough civilizing social skills to convert their cocksure ignorance into tentative knowledge of social structure. The students should leave the university aware of the world and the social environment as a complex of orderly and lawful mechanisms which we still understand only poorly but whose functioning we can discover—at least on a piecemeal basis—through persistent, systematic, and methodical efforts. The students should not graduate with a bewildered feeling that they live in an incomprehensible and illogical jungle of events in which strident rhetoric and party slogans can help them make their way rather than dispassionate dialog, empirical research, and experimental verification.

Some of my humanistically oriented critics might charge that the emphasis on functionality, which presupposes objective and operational definitions of variables, deprives students of intellectual pleasures by scanting the humanizing subjective experiences which can occur only in formally unstructured frameworks. Two points. First, my proposition is limited to that area of personal and social life in which definable skills and effectiveness can demonstrably facilitate more satisfying social experiences for all of us. Second, it is precisely the apparently deplorable condition of students' present subjective life on the campus, their widespread unhappiness and despair in a hostile unintelligible world that moves me to suggest changes.

I believe that the magnitude of students' frustration and discontent is clearly correlated with the degree of "softness" and subjectivity in their area of specialization. Most of the psychologically integrated students can be found either in the professional schools or in departments devoted to the hard sciences whereas the social sciences and humanities are seats and seas of discontent. One might argue of course that discontent is healthy or that it is the nature of the subject matter as such, or perhaps even selective enrollment, that accounts for the observed correlation. While these propositions may have to be qualified, I still believe that there is an undesirable, surplus effect attributable to a selective, biased and intellectually easy "attitude of radical skepticism" in the academy.

The skeptical attitude and a predisposition to question what we see and hear is, of course, the cornerstone of sophisticated life. The difficulty starts when it is applied selectively and results in self-hate, self-doubt, and general frustration. Skepticism is healthy when it is basically constructive, not when it encourages suicide, whether individual or collective. There is no ground for believing that the skeptical attitude must necessarily make living an aversive experience.

I do not question that the "attitude of radical skepticism" may be the hallmark of good teaching if it becomes part of the process of rational inquiry. But as it is imparted in many classrooms it is developed primarily with respect to democratic values. On one hand, it generates gullibility among students concerning alternatives to democratic policy; on the other hand, it seems to produce a radical disbelief in the achievements, potential and promise of the democratic prospect in America.

The problem of gullible students has been noted before. "Is it expecting too much of effective general education that it develop within students a permanent defense against gullibility?" So asked Sidney Hook in his address at the last UCRA conference. "It is astonishing to discover," he continued, "how superstitious students are, how vulnerable to demagogic appeal, to empty show and eloquence." Professor Hook then illustrated his charge by citing a "bizarre experiment" in which a professional actor was hired by a medical team to teach "charismatically and nonsubstantively on a topic about which he knew nothing." Results indicated that 55 educators, psychiatrists, psychologists, social workers, and administrators in courses in educational philosophy were "very favorably impressed" by his hour-long presentation which consisted of "nothing more than a goulash of double-talk, neologisms, nonsequiturs, and contradictory statements." The only criticism offered was that the presentation was "too intellectual."

Radical skepticism as now developed in higher education seems to focus only on certain targets. It results in an anti-western, anti-American critical orientation which, in its viciousness and mendacity, is reminiscent of the Nazi propaganda I used to hear in occupied Czechoslovakia during World War II. The students always seem ready to question the motives and actions of the defenders, often the democratically elected representatives, of western interests (which of course in the proper context is desirable). They are, however, seldom ready to exercise the same kind of skepticism with regard to the purity of motives and humanitarian intentions of those that propose dictatorial alternatives to democracy as long as they espouse radical-left objectives and use radical-left rhetoric. It is amazing how many students who were hypercritical of the rhetoric of democratic statesmen and politicians swallow without even a critical burp the inanities and absurdities of Mao-tse-tung.

Education of any kind may be viewed, at least in part, as indoctrination, however one defines the term. Most of us might also concede that such indoctrination is inevitable and that the most we can do is to bring as much objectivity and unbiased methodology into the classroom as possible. Under these circumstances, how should we feel about underhanded and unauthorized processes of conditioning? I submit that, as the terms we employ become more and more obscure and subjective, and less and less grounded in observable events, and as they lose more and more ties with objective referents, the educational process becomes progressively a case of "mindless" conditioning. I mean a conditioning without the student's awareness of what is going on, a process of conditioning certain negative verbal, emotional, and overt physical responses to stimuli that objectively are empty expressions. This absurd process becomes really unethical and dangerous when carried out in a purposely biased manner, using carefully selected expressions which possess carefully selected emotive connotations. Since our actions and sentiments are very much determined by the semantic environment we live in, it is obviously of the highest priority that we teach students to be on guard against such illicit manipulations.

Of the many superstitions and emotively biased constructions that haunt the academy, few are more influential and more damaging than the conclusions and interpretations of The Authoritarian Personality study by Adorno, et al. I do not question many of the component findings of the study and I do not doubt that the developed scales measure something. What I question is the validity of some of the assumptions and interpretations which seem to result in unwarranted labeling. That there would be methodological flaws in an undertaking as ambitious as The Authoritarian Personality is to be expected and I am not overly concerned with such shortcomings as pointed out, for instance, by Christie, Jahoda, Hyman and Sheatsley. Much more serious to me is the fact that Adorno et al. first set out to measure "fascistic tendencies," proceed to develop scales that presumably measure fascistic authoritarianism, and then without apparent justification treat the scales as if they measure "authoritarianism" in general. In that way the authors foster the implication that a non-fascist cannot be an authoritarian while the individual who dislikes ambiguities and is committed to law and order, i.e., is "rigid," is "authoritarian" in the sense that he may be justifiably suspected of at least latent fascism.

Much of the bias, I believe, is brought into the study by the use of the "Politico-Economic Conservatism" scale which the authors identify with the "Right-Left (R-L) dimension." I suggest that the R-L "dimension" is a scientific and logical monstrosity. While the progression ranging from "reactionary-fascist" through "conservative, liberal" to "socialist-communist" was used previously in political and ideological discussions only, the R-L scale has been now given the cloak of scientific respectability. Demonstrably insensitive to basic social—one may say human—concerns, the scale is nonmonotonic on such variables as, on the one hand, tolerance of opposite viewpoints, acceptance of empirical findings, reliance on corrective feedback, and espousal of a liberal and pluralistic philosophy and, on the other hand, to the tendency of individual and collective oppression and exploitation, and to mass murder. Never having tested a known Communist or Fascist, the mindreading authors of *The Authoritarian Personality* employed the R-L scale to "extrapolate" their findings from conservatives and liberals to the respective extremes. By further implying that the detected fascistic syndrome is in fact a syndrome which characterizes all "authoritarians" in general, reasonable and tolerant conservatives acquired fascistic tendencies while fanatical Communists became "extreme liberals." The main consequence of the scale as used in the study then seems to be a process by which undeserved, negative connotations are attached to groups and individuals of a particular economic and political (especially anti-left) persuasion.

It is not surprising therefore that the intentions, methods, tactics, and objectives of extremist "left" movements (where "left" is a euphemism for Communist) are so often misunderstood. It explains why in a free and presumably informed society such as ours, what Solzhenitsyn reports about the Gulag Archipelago is often greeted with surprise, not to mention disbelief. I realize that discussing "cadres and corpses" is seldom an edifying intellectual task. But to discuss extremist "left" theories in terms of their abstractions and slogans without assessing their costs and consequences in human suffering—which is invariably and properly done when the ideologies of Fascism are considered—is an inexcusable breach of scholarly integrity.

I suggest that it is an ethical and social obligation of university faculties not to temper their teaching and application of skepticism but to universalize it so that it is directed against *all* forms of dogmatism and extremism. But the choice of intellectual and emotional alternatives is not between skepticism and dogmatism—it is possible to have knowledge which, if not certain is reliable and to be skeptical without being paralyzed by doubt. One can accept the challenges of experience with hope without credulity and an awareness of the imperfections of man and society without despair.

NOTES

*The interested reader is referred to two booklets issued by the American Psychological Association: *Ethical Standards of Psychologists,* and *Ethical Principles in the Conduct of Research with Human Participants.*

The Ethics
of Teaching

Faculty and Standards
of Ethical Conduct

Robert M. Rosenzweig
Stanford University

From time to time issues involving the standards governing the conduct of college and university faculty come to public attention, are debated—sometimes heatedly—inside and outside the profession, then slide from view. It is a natural history that describes a large number of matters in a society in which institutions are dispersed and fragmented, producing heavy reliance on a notoriously flighty set of communications media.

We are now in a period of high saliency about the issue. It would be hard to recall a time in recent memory in which so much public and professional attention was devoted to the ethical standards of the teaching profession. The McCarthy period was perhaps one such, but the issues in contention then, while of central importance to the academic world, were narrower and much less varied than those now before us.

It is not hard to find reasons for the current interest in ethical matters. One set of reasons was self-imposed—perhaps *self-inflicted* would be a better term. University people, including faculty, have been among the most articulate advocates of the "politics as moral crusade" school of thought of the 1960s and early seventies. The Civil Rights Movement, the Free Speech Movement, the Vietnam and Cambodia protests, the "restructuring" of the University, classified research, ROTC, and a host of other issues were argued not as issues of public or institutional policy on which reasonable people of equal integrity could differ—surely an essential premise of democratic politics—but as matters whose essence was a moral imperative dictating a single answer. Those who did not happen to share that answer were simply in error, and in the climate of the times error had no rights. It should be added that a special place in Hell was reserved for those truly immoral souls who believed that preserving political and intellectual processes that are open and free from coercion will produce greater social benefit than the "right" answer to any particular policy dispute. It was Alex Bickel who in 1969 best captured the atmosphere of the times when, in answer to the question, "What is happening to morality today?" he replied, "It threatens to engulf us."

In many respects we deal today with the legacy of those not very distant times. In one sense, having articulated a standard for the judgment of others while at the same time helping to break down the processes by which reasonable standards can be applied, we now find ourselves being judged in the same spirit. It is in no way a defense of the conduct of the Nixon Administration to observe that its own lawlessness may have been given the color of legitimacy by lawlessness justified on so many campuses as a higher form of morality.

In another and more important sense, the events of recent years have produced changes in attitudes and behavior among some faculty that must be attended to. To take but one example—one to which I shall return later—it was not too long ago that one would have found substantial if not complete agreement among faculty that there was an important difference between education and indoctrination, and that the former is the teacher's province. Today, one hears far more often about the centrality of value questions to education expressed in formulations ranging all the way to the obligation of the teacher to produce value changes in his or her students. Without, at the moment, passing judgment on the merits of such a formulation, I will simply observe that it is about 180° away from the position that formed the core of the academic defense against McCarthyism only twenty years ago.

Still, if it were only the legacy of recent events that has produced our current concern with the ethics of teaching, it might be reasonable to predict that the concern will prove to be as transitory as were the events that produced it. I think that no such comfort, if it be that, is warranted, for there is ample evidence that we are not alone. Indeed, if anything, the academic profession has been somewhat less subject to ethical challenge than its sister learned professions of law and medicine. The three professions have two characteristics in common that account for this challenge. The first is simply numerical: more people than ever before, both in absolute numbers and as a percentage of the population, actually use or believe they need to use the services of the practitioners of those professions. Law, medicine, and higher education are no longer the property of the well-to-do. Second, and even more important, each of those professions is now seen to be critical to the functioning of the society and to access to society's benefits. Small wonder, then, that those who practice find the standards that guide them increasingly subject to public scrutiny, up to and including demands for public regulation.

It seems unlikely that colleges and universities will decline in importance in America. It is equally unlikely, therefore, that the conduct of those who are at their center—the faculty—will be treated as wholly private behavior. Thus, even if there were no reasons internal to the profession itself for thinking as carefully as we can about the matter of ethics, it seems probable that others will force this task on us. As I shall make clear, I view that prospect as very much of a mixed blessing. The mixture may be more palatable, however, if a serious effort is made to distinguish trivial issues from those of consequence, to be as clearsighted as possible about our expectations for the practitioners of the academic profession, and to scrutinize proposed remedies in the light of the common phenomenon in social affairs that the cure can be worse than the disease.

What, then, are the issues? What kind of behavior or misbehavior has led academic people, public officials, and the communications media to their concern for the ethics of teaching? As an approach to this question, I have scanned the public and educational press for examples of alleged ethical misconduct that some editor thought important enough to put in print. Here is a sample:

1. allegation that a faculty member conditioned grades in his course on the amount of food or money students were able to raise or contribute to a particular group.

2. a number of charges of faculty "moonlighting"; that is, holding two or more jobs simultaneously, often without the knowledge of either employer.

3. charges that sexual relations between teachers and students are widespread, both at particular institutions and in general. The implication of these stories usually is that this condition has become worse (or better) in recent years, although I have seen no time-series data to support the implication.

4. charges that teachers who purport to be objective and value-neutral in their teaching are dishonest and doing a disservice to their students.

5. charges that teachers who renounce the possibility or desirability of objectivity and value-neutrality are dishonest and doing a disservice to their students.

6. charges that teachers trade grades for what I have seen called "sexual favors." This is different from item three, above, which presumably rests on attraction rather than coercion.

7. a variety of charges under the general heading of "neglect of teaching"—inadequate preparation, excessive absence from class, careless advising, and so forth.

8. racial and sexual prejudice, and more broadly what one writer called a "patronizing and discourteous manner toward students and staff."

What is so striking about this list, which is quite random and which I could easily extend, is its ill-assorted quality. It is not simply that in listing them I have not attempted to assess the seriousness of each; more to the point is that they come to us as an audience with no such assessment. The dominant impression I draw from my scanning of items is that of an incredible jumble, the net effect of which is to make every alleged transgression as serious as every other and whose gross effect is the conclusion that things are terribly, terribly wrong.

I want to challenge both of those conclusions. The first is pernicious and the second is at best unproved.

It seems to me essential if we are to have anything useful to say about important matters that we agree on what is important. As a beginning proposition, therefore, I would assert that private behavior is not public business. Thus, it seems to me that the sexual conduct of college teachers, although it is guaranteed to titillate newspaper readers and therefore is a hardy perennial, can be dismissed as having no greater ethical meaning than the sexual conduct of businessmen and their secretaries, doctors and nurses, or pilots and stewardesses. I, personally, have never seen a documented case of a teacher coercing sex from a student in exchange for a good grade, but if there are such cases, they are essentially no different in principle from charging money for a grade. In substance, such a practice would be a form of extortion and I have no doubt that it would be punishable as professional misconduct under even the most loosely drawn tenure statement.

Similarly, "moonlighting" seems to me to have minimal ethical content. It is a matter that is properly handled in contractual relations between the teacher and his employer, and a wide variety of arrangements all equally ethical can be imagined.

The governing principle surely is that not every transgression of someone's or some group's notion of right and wrong conduct is, *ipso facto,* a violation of professional ethics. If we act otherwise we are headed for trouble, for it is humbling to remember that college teachers, far from constituting a small elite of moral exemplars, in fact number more than 875,000. I invite you to ponder the variety of behavior that is likely to be found in so large a group.

There are, after all, real and important issues aplenty. The one on which I wish to focus is, I believe, the most enduring, most vexing and least tractable question facing a thoughtful teacher and a concerned profession. It arises at the point at which the ethics of teaching meets the teaching of ethics. It is "the teacher's moral and professional responsibility in influencing the value judgments, the moral attitudes and basic emotional commitments of the students." To put the issue in the form of a question, "Is it part of the teacher's duty to attempt to change student values in the direction that the teacher believes desirable?"

I should point out that I have intentionally put the question in active, volitional terms in order to make clear what I take as given, namely that any sentient being has a system of values which informs his behavior, which is communicated in one way or another to those with whom he interacts, and which may have the effect of changing their values in the direction of his. Perhaps even more to the point, it strikes me that the words "teacher" and "preacher" are related in fact as well as in sound. The teacher who does not have a moral stance toward his subject—a set of values which places his small part of the intellectual universe into a larger context of knowledge and principle and that thereby defines his relationship to his subject—is as bankrupt as a preacher whose only tool is the collection plate.

The question I have asked, then, does not yield to a categorical yes or no, if only because there are values and there are values. No doubt a very substantial majority of faculty would agree that their duty extends at least as far as encouraging adherence to those values commonly thought to be essential to the processes of intellectual inquiry, itself—rigor in gathering and interpreting evidence, and readiness to change conclusions when confronted with contradictory evidence. It is interesting to note that a recent survey of more than 42,000 college faculty, conducted by the American Council on Education, did not include what might be called the values of the intellectual process among a list of undergraduate teaching goals which those surveyed were asked to rank. However, I take it that some such notion lies behind goals like "master knowledge in a discipline," and "develop the ability to think clearly." More than 90% thought the first was essential or very important; more than 95% gave equal rating to the second.

But the matter does not stop there. In the same survey, about half the respondents considered the development of moral character to be an essential or very important goal in their teaching of undergraduates, and more than sixty percent felt similarly about their duty to develop responsible citizens.

As with so many surveys, this one tells us only enough to pique our interest. What moral values should be taught? Is there agreement on that question among those who think they should be teaching them? What is a good citizen? How does one teach moral values and good citizenship? And what do those on the receiving end think of all this? We shall never know the answers, but the questions beg for answers because they lie at the heart of any assertion that it is a teacher's duty to change and improve his students' value systems.

It should be clear that, while the terms that are used to discuss these matters are often abstract, even uncomfortably so, the issues are quite real. The most dramatic recent evidence of their reality, although in the long run perhaps not the most important, has been the campus reaction to corruption of the Nixon Administration. There has been, of course, the predictable silliness: the University president who proclaimed "values year" on campus because, according to the *New York Times,* "he was disturbed by the number of ostensibly well-educated young people implicated in Watergate." And the college dean who asserted about his institution, "It is impossible to go through four years here and come out with the rather crude notions about the political process that were apparently at the core of Haldeman's and Ehrlichman's thinking." (To which one faculty member responded, "Who fostered the Spanish Inquisition?—good people from the finest Catholic universities." And to which a student, just returned from a year's internship in Washington, said, "I wouldn't say our men wouldn't do things like that. No matter how much of this education you devour, when you get back there and see you're rewarded for the kinds of plans and schemes Magruder and Liddy came up with, well, gee, that's hard to deal with.")

More serious has been the curricular soul-searching in schools of law. It is beyond my purposes here to discuss the current debate over the teaching of legal ethics. My general view of that debate is the fact that it is occurring is healthy, but in the end it will produce little in the way of substantive change in law school curricula. The main reason for my skepticism *is* relevant to my purpose because it bears directly on a question that must be addressed by those who seriously wish to *produce* higher ethical standards in the teaching profession: namely, are those standards to be enforced, and if so, how? The point has most clearly been made recently by Dean Murray L. Schwartz of the UCLA Law School. Dean Schwartz addresses directly the possibilities of the educational institution attempting affirmatively to change the values or preferences of the students. "That undertaking," he says, "would not only require a radically different approach to legal education from the current one; it also suggests that faculty members should be appointed not only because of their traditional competence of scholarship and teaching but also because they possess the 'right' values to be transmitted to their students. One wonders about the dimensions of the struggles among the university boards of trustees, administrations and faculties were this criterion for appointment to be accepted."

I hardly need point out that the prospect that Dean Schwartz holds before us would, if it were to become real, reverse fifty years of effort by the AAUP and like-minded groups to remove the question of "right" values from decisions about faculty appointment and promotion. Some might think that a good thing, but I daresay the prevailing view is to the contrary.

Still, it might be argued that there is no necessary reason why the articulation of a set of ethical standards or expectations for the profession needs to be enforced; that it is sufficient if a set of standards exists, is clear, and is widely agreed to. In principle, no doubt that is true; in practice it seems to me quite unrealistic, for it ignores what appears to be an almost irresistible contemporary drive to turn standards into codes, to establish machinery to enforce the codes, and adjudication processes to interpret and apply them. If we have learned anything from the experience of Affirmative Action, the reform of political campaign practices, the Buckley Amendment and other recent attempts to turn ethical standards into enforceable behavior, we should have learned at least that much. We would do well, I believe, to devote some effort to examining the cost to the profession of trying to make explicit the standards of behavior that have implicitly guided the best of us—however, one wants to define "best" in that context.

Perhaps the experience of one institution, Stanford University, can be instructive. I choose it as an example partly because I know it best, partly because, if it is a deviant experience, it is only because the quality of thought that guided it was perhaps higher than one would find at most institutions, and partly because it illustrates well the kind of drive to which I have referred, as well as the ambiguities of the outcome.

The Stanford experience began in 1971 when the President of the University brought charges against H. Bruce Franklin, a tenured member of the faculty, and asked for his dismissal for four separate incidents, the first of which took place on January 11, 1971 and the last three on February 10, 1971. The grounds on which the sanctioning of a faculty member were permissible under the existing tenure statement were "substantial and manifest incompetence, substantial and manifest neglect of duty, or personal conduct substantially impairing the individual's performance of his appropriate functions within the community." The last of those was chiefly at issue.

As provided by the tenure statement, a hearing on the charges was held by the elected Faculty Advisory Board. The proceeding was public; it began on September 28, 1971 and ended on November 5. There were 33 days of hearings. One hundred and eleven witnesses were heard in 160 hours. The transcript contains about 1,000,000 words.

On January 5, 1972 the Advisory Board upheld three of the four charges and a majority recommended dismissal. One aspect of its decision is of particular interest here. As a premise to its conclusion it was necessary for the Board to satisfy itself that the grounds for dismissal stated in the tenure statement were neither so broad nor so vague as to constitute inadequate warning to faculty about the kind of conduct that would fall within their net. It did so in the following words:

> . . . . The faculty of the University is a small community, characterized by face-to-face contact and personal interaction. Legislation proscribing conduct in a disciplinary context is rare; when it occurs, it merely codifies previously shared understandings.
> . . . . Plainly it would be intolerable for the state to provide that a citizen could be imprisoned for "substantial and manifest incompetence, sub-

stantial and manifest neglect of duty, or personal conduct substantially impairing the individual's performance of his appropriate functions within the community." The situation is different, we believe, when the public to which similar regulations are addressed is the faculty of the University. In the more restricted setting, the regulation invokes a web of largely unwritten rules as tough and living as the British Constitution. Powerful traditions, modified by contemporary practice, furnish a reliable guide to faculty conduct. . . .

Two points are especially relevant about these words and this case. The first, and most obvious, is the generality of the standard on which the decision rested, and the second is that the conduct in question did not involve the faculty member's teaching or research, but his behavior in activities involving the University and therefore calling into question his fitness for continued membership in the University, notwithstanding his performance as a teacher and a scholar.

The first of those—the generality of the standard—had begun to concern the faculty and the administration even before the case was brought, and a committee formed under the auspices of the local AAUP chapter, had made recommendations for a more elaborate code of conduct and system of discipline. The decision in this case gave even greater impetus to the movement in that direction, and efforts went forward to amend the tenure statement to provide greater specificity in certain areas of conduct, and to provide enforcement and adjudication machinery that would be more expeditious and less cumbersome than the one that had just unfolded.

Much of 1972 was devoted to this effort, and the resulting Statement on Faculty Discipline which took effect in January 1973 is an interesting document. The key to understanding it lies in its opening paragraph:

In the interest of preserving academic freedom within the Stanford Community, all members of the Academic Council are expected to maintain standards of professional behavior. However, no member of the Academic Council may be subject to disciplinary sanctions by the University unless his conduct falls within one or more of the following categories:

Then follow nine categories of conduct ranging from such a general one as "professional misconduct in the performance of his duties" to such a specific one as "refusing to appear and testify when summoned in connection with, or giving false testimony in, any proceeding governed by this Statement."

Two points are of special note. The first is that no terms are defined. "Professional misconduct" and "neglect of academic duties" are given no more precise content by this statement than they had under the old tenure regulations. Some specific acts were made clearly punishable, but after almost two years of work the faculty found that where the heart of a faculty member's responsibilities were concerned it was unable to improve on that "web of largely unwritten rules" which had been the foundation of the earlier dismissal action.

The second important point has to do with that peculiar sentence which says that no faculty member "may be subject to disciplinary sanctions . . . unless his conduct falls within one or more of the following categories: "That sentence was intended to say to the faculty that it was not adopting an open-ended instrument for its own repression; instead it was agreeing to a more precise statement of unacceptable kinds of behavior, and in return was receiving a commitment that no one could be sanctioned in any way by the University for other conduct.

I confess that even after two years I am unable to think of a better way to blend rights and obligations in a single organic statement. But the ambiguity is evident. To some members of the faculty the very lack of definition of key terms posed too great a threat to bear. Whatever the degree of mutual trust among members of a community that is required in order for them to tolerate ambiguity in such matters, it was lacking in the Stanford faculty at that time. The Statement was adopted by the faculty, but in the process of adoption a pledge was demanded and given to begin work on a corresponding Statement on Academic Freedom.

A year and a half was consumed in the effort to produce an acceptable statement. The Statement that was finally adopted in April, 1974, is surely one of the more inelegant declarations of faculty rights on record. That is not because the people involved were incapable of writing perfectly sound English prose but, I believe, because they had been given the essentially impossible task of producing a statement of rights that appeared at least as binding and specific as a statement of proscribed conduct. They key paragraph read:

Decisions concerning
1. the search for, and appointment and promotion of, faculty;
2. the assignment of teaching and other primarily academic responsibilities;
3. the support and sponsorship of scholarly research; and
4. any other granting or withholding of benefits or imposition of burdens, shall be made without regard to a person's political, social, or other views not directly related to academic values or to the assumption of academic responsibilities; without regard to the conduct of a person holding an appointment at Stanford unless such conduct is directly related to academic values or to the assumption of academic responsibilities or is determined, in a proceeding pursuant to the Statement on Faculty Discipline, to come within the provisions of Section I of that Statement; and without regard to an individual's race, ethnic origin, sex or religion. Nothing in the foregoing shall be deemed to affect the Univesity's application of affirmative action policies in its faculty search procedures.

Once started in this direction, the slope becomes slippery, indeed. The lawyers tell us that there is no right without a remedy. The Statement therefore provides for a grievance procedure for those who believe that they have been wronged. It took two and a half pages single-spaced to describe the general outlines of such a procedure, and shortly thereafter another document was issued, this one six pages long, also single-spaced, to spell out the procedure in detail and the end, I am sure, is not yet in sight.

I do not intend by these comments to denigrate almost three years of intense effort by some of the best people in the faculty and administration of the University. The Statement on Faculty Discipline provides a sounder basis and better procedures than had existed for dealing with certain kinds of faculty transgressions, especially those against the peace and order of the institution; and there is nothing in the Statement on Academic Freedom with which I disagree. Furthermore, from what I have seen of comparable efforts elsewhere, ours at Stanford bear up well by comparison. In short, I do not believe the job can be done more honorably, more intelligently, or with very much better results.

But let me return to the point at which I introduced this case history. What we have seen at Stanford is a progression. Each step appears valid on its merits and appears to follow naturally, indeed almost inevitably, from the prior step. But the sum total is a web of regulation and procedures for litigation that can confound the institutiuon, and that may in the end prove less durable than the "web of largely unwritten rules" whose perceived inadequacy had set the process in motion.

My interest here is not in observing or predicting unintended ironies; rather it is to underscore a conflict. One side of the conflict is that it is widely believed that there are important issues of ethical standards and lapses in conduct that the teaching profession must attend to. The other side is that even the best intended and most intelligent effort to attend to them may produce gains, and those at an exorbitant cost in new regulations, elaborate procedures, and the bureaucracy that inevitably attend both.

I believe that the answer does not lie in codes, whether they consist of broad exhortations or specific injunctions. The profession is obliged to keep alive and under consideration, in its many forums, issues of which it is aware, either because they concern the public or because they are known to practitioners. I make the suggestion knowing that it is unlikely to appeal to the large and growing number who look to the law—or its equivalent—as the weapon with which to attack every contentious social issue, the means to right every wrong and to repair inequity. Should that view prevail in the end, those who inherit its consequences no doubt will learn to live with them. But some will look back to the disorder of an earlier day and yearn for the ambiguities which their forebears, for some reason, thought were intolerable.

Faculty Codes and Professional Responsibility

William W. Van Alstyne

Duke University
President, American Association of
University Professors *

A fetish for legalism and a preoccupation with the provisioning of campus codes are not adequate substitutes for a sense of professional responsibility. I agree also that efforts to prepare codes full of exquisite detail may even tend to work at odds with their best purposes. Those purposes are generally to avoid confusion and minimize dispute by more perfectly specifying institutional standards of accountability. Yet, in the process of attempting to eliminate all possible vagueness, three dysfunctional consequences may occur simultaneously. First, so far as the common law of the campus is to be wholly abandoned to the exclusion of written standards, earlier disputes will nevertheless reappear over the precise meaning of these standards. Second, as such quarrels may tend to become quibbles and phrase-parsing contests, they may also be more degrading to the participants by making trivial the larger concern of professional responsibility. In short, badly drafted or merely overdrafted codes do not necessarily reduce disputes, even while they may sink to the level of picayune words over academic values. Third, in the quest for completeness, the codes may waste innumerable hours of faculty, student, and administrative time trying to anticipate an almost infinite number of "what if" situations. Once embarked on a codification, a committee tends to experience the same problem as a person who starts out to spell "banana." We all have a clear notion of how to begin; the problem is figuring out where to stop. Professor Rosenzweig's paper makes these points quite well, and I find little basis to disagree.

Specifying at least the principal rules for a polity (including an academic polity), however, may be well worth the effort. To a considerable extent, formulating a rule that allegedly merely restates the common law of the campus may apprise one of his own illusions. As long as there were no particular confrontation and no rule, but only a common law, one could ignore the fundamental differences that exist entirely in mutual good faith. Teachers, students, and administrators frequently assume different notions about academic freedom and responsibility. Waiting until a specific episode develops that brings out latent allegiances, divides loyalties and overwhelms one's detachment is by no means a safe or desirable way to administer justice—whether on a campus or in a larger community. With the immense growth of higher education since World War II, moreover, those drawn into university teaching and administration may well have less in common than one supposes—and, correspondingly, may have less in common as to what they suppose a good academic common law contains. Thus, there may be great educational value in forcing an occasion on campus to address the content of its alleged common law. Considerations such as these may have accounted, at least in part, for the sheer length of time Stanford gave to its own undertaking. I think one would be shortsighted in counting the time spent in Stanford's effort as being wasted or of no account. The reestablishment of even a modest consensus on a campus common law is no trivial accomplishment.

The functions of rules are understated, if only their "fair notice" functions are emphasized. I agree that a person ought not be held accountable for conduct that he was unable to ascertain as forbidden when he did it. But I think Rosenzweig understates the purposes of rules when he observes that, in many situations, a member of an academic community does have a reasonably good impression that what he proposes to do may be regarded as offensive to the campus common law—even without benefit of a precise, written rule. And there are additional hazards of operating with gratuitously vague (or no) rules.

When a borderline incident involves a widely admired person or a widely shared cause, the absence of a rule invites the unequal application of the campus common law vis-à-vis the less well-regarded actor and the more despised cause. This is a familiar phenomenon in regard to the banning of certain speakers on campus. Under circumstances where an ad hoc decision is made on who may be invited to speak on campus, it is our common experience that such a decision is often made with an alarming lack of ideological neutrality. The acceptability of a speaker often depends less on a fair assessment of whether he or she will incite disruption, than upon a craven assessment of whether the speaker's appearance will identify the college with the ideas the speaker will probably present. We are often charitable to ourselves, our students, and our colleagues when a particular cause strikes us as good and compelling. One tends then to excuse excrescences of misconduct, discourtesy, and disruption, even while becoming immensely conscious of law and order when disagreeing with a cause or a speaker. The sheer shapelessness of a common law ineluctably encourages such a double standard, whereas the provision of a general rule may help one account more honestly for his or her responses.

Of course, not everything that one worries about as being possibly punishable by a common law will merit such action. Yet, the uncertainty of a situation is a compelling reason why each person may be induced to steer a wider course around doubtful areas, than he would need to do if a standard law had been stated. Surely if one assumes that any conduct even approaching the kind that would be properly punishable is also undesirable, then, one will rejoice in the marginal vagueness of the common law—because it has this gratuitously discouraging effect. But the assumption is by no means a safe one. In certain areas at least, the inessential vagueness of a common law, or unwritten rule, will depress the exercise of protected and important freedoms—e.g., academic freedom and the freedom of speech and the press. To the extent that one is intimidated by uncertainty and withholds an unpopular critical thesis or fears association with a minority cause, the polity as well as the individual may obviously lose what it should have desired to receive—even against its superficial will. For this reason, among others, the Supreme Court has been most critical of "nonrule" or "vague rule" or "overbroad rule" cases involving the First Amendment; and I think there may be something for us to learn from these cases as well.

It is uncommon, of course, that ordinary statutes and ordinances are cast in terms of what is permitted, rather than what is forbidden; but there are occasions when this may be immensely useful in light of the chilling effect resulting from the absence of such affirmative statements. Thus a rule reiterating the protection of academic freedom—similar to the rule specified at Stanford—may be a welcome complement to a common law within a tolerable boundary, or to negative, destructive implications that might otherwise arise from other rules purporting to describe improper or sanctioned conduct.

The last point may seem perverse to offer because it is so rudimentary and even contradicted by the examples given in Rosenzweig's paper. Yet, one ought not to overgeneralize the professor's examples. In many areas, when done well and conscientiously, moving from a campus common law to a basic set of published rules does advance the common interest. One can imagine how much more hectic and disputatious campus life would be, for instance, if one relied only on a common law regarding parking space! One trades away *ad hoc* virtues of a common law and willingly puts up with marginal, arbitrary parking rules, because the need for certainty and reliability is so great that it is intolerable any other way.

Moreover, one understates the value of a rule if one praises it only for its superior efficiency, for that suggests that one has been compelled to trade off a higher value for this inferior, merely economic one. But that is not a fair statement of the matter. The unpleasantness of uncertainty, the bitterness of having no rule at all—with each case suggesting that issue must be joined—are intensely divisive influences that may seriously, corrosively disrupt a campus. The formulation of standards on academic conduct may be harder and more elusive than mundane matters such as parking, but the effort may nonetheless be entirely worthwhile.

I am inclined to conclude these brief comments on Professor Rosenzweig's paper by disagreeing with him after all. What is good about his paper is his important reminder that no community can function well without the mucilage of some common respect and shared values. What is deficient is found in the clear implication of either/or: Either an academic polity has that common commitment, in which case no published rules are necessary; or it lacks that common commitment, in which case no published rules can save it. Rather, one may yield to the importance of a common commitment, while holding also that the articulation of published standards—at least in areas of recurring, doubtful, and divisive uncertainty—may be wholly complementary. The exercise of undertaking the effort may be the best test of whether there is the substance of a common respect and common values after all.

NOTES

*These comments are personal and do not necessarily represent the views of the AAUP.

Legal Ethics and the Ethics of Law Teaching

Marvin E. Frankel
Judge United States District Court

As Dr. Rosenzweig's paper reminds us, the law schools' concern with legal ethics is indeed the center of much talk and debate these days. One might suppose this would always have been so. Felix Cohen wrote over 40 years ago: "every final valuation of law involves an ethical judgment."[1] Lawyers, whether they know it or not, are—like Molière's gentleman—doing ethics all the time. It might be expected that the supposed academic experts in the administration of norms and normative judgments would be deeply and steadily concerned with their own ethical questions. But the fact, at least until the last decade or so, has been otherwise.

Legal scholars have tended, as Cohen also observed, to shun explicit dealings with ethics.[2] Ethical questions were not discussed much in studying and evaluating either substantive or procedural law problems. The same, until lately, was true for the subject of a lawyer's ethics, or professional responsibility as it is commonly called these days.

The attitudes of the legal academy toward this subject have included an interesting mixture of disdain and conformity. The specific, announced rules of legal ethics—especially as embodied in the bar's Canons of Ethics (as they were known until the 1970 revision published as the Code of Professional Responsibility)—tended to be beneath scholarly notice. Courses in legal ethics were totally absent from the curricula of many great schools. When they were taught, more often than not a lower-level instructor—even descending frequently to a dean—took the assignment.

The contempt, which is often the case, may have reflected in part a measure of insecurity or at least diffidence. Many law teachers nurse some self-doubts about their isolation from actual professional practice. For at least a fair number, the doubts are not lessened by an awareness that they chose teaching not merely for its own sake but as a role preferred to practice, which either they do not like or, sometimes, about which they do not feel competent.

Whatever its full explanation, the overall lack of interest among academicians in the rules of the lawyer's professional game has had one clearly regrettable consequence. The teachers have on the whole accepted that game, with all its dubieties, as a fact of life that is subject to little critical scrutiny and scarcely imagined as a possibility for creative scholarship. On the one hand, the approved canons have been viewed with scorn.[3] On the other hand, there has been little effort to study these canons, revise them, or generally scrutinize the profession's ethical premises.

The upshot has been that the academies have served, by default if not more positively, as supporters of the ethical status quo. The teaching of ethics has followed mostly the analytic, manipulative, allegedly Socratic designs of the law teacher's art. The academicians have borne all of the profession's ethical ambiguities, tensions, disgraces, and miseries with the composure of untouched bystanders.

The tendency to neglect legal ethics is often explained and justified on the proposition that one cannot do much, and ought not to try, to dictate the morality of the young adults who enter law schools. How do you train or encourage a student to fight with all his skill for the vindication of a crooked client and, at the same time, to cherish honest and fair dealing as prime values? Do lawyers or legal scholars genuinely believe that the truth is best discovered by contending adversaries, each equipped with approved devices for concealing and distorting the facts? Can it really be part of a learned profession to negotiate for a client using the time-honored techniques of exaggerating his side, lying about what he is prepared to accept, and concealing the defects and weaknesses in his position?

Questions like these are not often confronted in the legal academies. They have been answered by default, however. Legal scholars have accepted that the lawyer must seek victory for his crooked client over the wronged opponent, must use the tricks of cross-examination to make the truthful witness on the other side look like a liar, and must be his client's paid huckster to settle auto accident cases or labor-management disputes. When such propositions are treated as settled axioms, it should not be astonishing that my friend, Dean Murray L. Schwartz, and others are pessimistic about the genuine benefit from teaching legal ethics.

However, my main point is that the axioms themselves ought to be the focal subject of scholarly attention. I urge professors of law to take, as a primary assignment, the skeptical study of legal ethics to seek a basic core of values that are intelligible, worthy, generally accepted, and reasonably consistent.

As a fundamental beginning, the academics should study critically and teach about the system — about lawyers' roles and responsibilities, about the extent to which these responsibilities may inevitably collide with the community's espoused moral values, and about the kinds of basic reform needed to move toward a more acceptable, harmonious scheme of legal ethics.

I have brushed already against what I view as first-priority questions in this undertaking. More explicitly, our existing Code of Professional Responsibility makes clear that there are two bedrock principles that are corollaries by which the lawyer should be guided.

First, that ours is an *adversary system* — most clearly in the courthouse but generally throughout the range of the lawyer's activities — as counselor, negotiator, planner, even as public functionary. The premise of the adversary ideal is that, if two sides try with all their might to prove contradictory or at least sharply inconsistent propositions and both seek to discover helpful evidence and block hurtful evidence, then what emerges should be as close as possible to the truth on questions of fact as well as of law or value.

Second, as a corollary, the lawyer is to be the client's loyal champion, not only preserving his confidences but seeking at almost any cost to crown his efforts with success. That may mean the lawyer must shield the guilty, confound the innocent, and thwart deep interests of a wider public. A classic statement of this position was made early in the last century by Lord Brougham, who said:

> An advocate, in the discharge of his duty, knows but one person in all the world, and that person is his client. To save that client by all means and expedients, and at all hazards and costs to other persons, and, amongst them, to himself, is his first and only duty; and in performing this duty he must not regard the alarm, the torments, the destruction which he may bring upon others. Separating the duty of a patriot from that of an advocate, he must go on reckless of the consequences, though it should be his unhappy fate to involve his country in confusion.[4]

I am suggesting that basic assumptions of this kind have gone for too long unexamined and, therefore, have been uncritically accepted in the academy. Not surprisingly, some lawyers have followed a similar pattern of inert conformity. Questions that one would think were settled long ago are subjects of confusion and dispute within the profession. Following are a few examples from what could be a long list:

1. What should a lawyer do when his or her client proposes to take the witness stand and commit perjury?

2. What are the duties of a Wall Street lawyer when a corporate client has published statements affecting the sale of securities, and those statements are likely to mislead investors?

3. To what extent is a lawyer entitled to avoid listening to a client's tape recordings of key conversations, while maintaining the innocence and purity of the client's part in those conversations?

4. Must a lawyer report what he knows—or is he forbidden to report what he knows—For example, when his client takes him to the buried bodies of young people whom the client says he has murdered, while the families of the dead have for weeks been trying frantically to learn where and how they are?

For myself, at least, I have tentative answers to these questions. My point, however, is simply that the legal profession—for all its canons and codes—lacks agreed answers to the above questions and to a considerable list of similar ones. And the law schools have neglected a cardinal responsibility for leadership, in failing to appraise, revise, and lead students in sorting out their ethical ideals.

I believe that the ethical premises of the legal profession must be reexamined and revised. I do not urge scrapping the system. But I do believe in giving a higher place than we have to truth, fair dealing, and wide community interests. This would entail serious revisions of the present legal system. Specifically, I recommend restricting the authority that is now left with partisan contestants to define the issues, investigate the evidence, and present only what they want, to resolve legal disputes in court. For similar ends, we need to rethink and recast the attorney-client relationship by modifying the lawyer's role as hired gun and adding to his obligations as an officer in a learned, public profession.

There is an interesting manifestation of the leadership failure of law teachers in a public issue that lately has engaged the law schools, the bar, and the bench. Chief Justice Burger of the U.S. Supreme Court and Chief Judge Irving Kaufman of the Second Federal Circuit Court have complained for the last couple of years about what they perceive as the low level of competence among advocates, and about the law schools' responsibilities for this condition. Kaufman has pressed vigorously and with measurable impact for the requirement of specific kinds of law school courses as prerequisites for admission to the bar of the federal court. The law schools' reactions have not been altogether uniform, but the preponderant stance has been to resist Kaufman's recommendations as unwarranted interference for which no sound reason has been shown. By and large, I agree with the schools' resistance. Yet, I feel this position of resistance is unnecessarily weak and vulnerable, at least in the general form of its expression.

When one examines what the Chief Justice and the Chief Judge are talking about, one discovers that a large part of their indictment of law schools is for failure to teach effectively the skills lawyers use as adversary champions in the courtroom. High on the list for Burger is the skill of cross-examination—how to destroy a hostile witness, whether or not he is truthful. Similarly, the Chief Justice stresses the art of asking questions and learning when not to ask questions, so that one gets only the truth he wants, avoids the truths he does not want, and ascertains at all costs that witnesses do not plunge ahead and tell the whole truth and nothing but the truth. If the facts are faced, law schools do not do much in the way of teaching such things. It is doubtful how well they could, or more importantly, whether they should.

However, these thoughts are not being expressed in the statements of opposition to Burger and Kaufman. There is much talk of keeping the law schools free. But if they are supposed to teach practitioners of a learned profession, *from* what or *for* what are they to be free? Some of the protesting deans and teachers seem to tacitly accept the adversative premises of Burger and Kaufman. Sometimes, but much less often, the propositions are positively espoused by those who are fighting an attempt by the bench or bar to dictate aspects of the law school curriculum.

For reasons I have touched on, I have some doubts about the overall soundness of the law schools' positions if the existing rules of the adversary game are accepted. Minimally, a conscious evaluation of those rules is essential for an informed, fully principled stand on the particular curriculum battle I have mentioned.

Law schools have always taught ethics, mainly by setting bad examples of inertia or confusion. They must do better, not by the preaching of virtue, but by leadership toward a central set of coherent, ethical precepts suited to a judicial system in the kind of society we strive to be. At a minimum, I believe the law schools must devote concerted energies to this vital work before allowing themselves to deem it useless.

NOTES

1. Felix S. Cohen, *Ethical Systems and Legal Ideals* (1933), p. 7.
2. Ibid., p. 2.
3. See J. Sutton, Jr., "Summary and Evaluation Report on the Legal Profession Course," in *Education in the Professional Responsibilities of the Lawyer*, ed. D. Weckstein (University Press of Virginia, 1970), pp. 54, 57.
4. Trial of Queen Caroline (1821), p. 8.

Legal Ethics:
A Problem of Role Definition

Norman Redlich

New York University Law School

For too long, legal ethics have been in the backwater of American legal education. While law schools expanded their course offerings in response to the realities of business regulation, the civil rights movement, international economics, the war on poverty, environmental interests, and the urban crisis, it took the shock of Watergate to force lawyers—and the law schools that spawn them—to question whether lawyers were being properly trained in the ethics of their profession.

Many in the profession have argued rather defensively that Watergate was an aberration, that the former president's men were not acting in their professional capacities, that no amount of ethical training will cure the inclinations of thieves and liars, and that it was the legal system that finally drove Richard Nixon from office.

All this is true. But I believe that Watergate did highlight a critical deficiency in legal training: the failure to define a lawyer's role in the various situations in which he may find himself. Certainly lawyers cannot brag about the multi-optioned career that legal training provides and then claim no responsibility for their conduct when they exercise one of these options, such as being an advisor to a high government official.

The teaching of legal ethics means teaching role-definition. When viewed in these terms, the subject becomes quite teachable. It is true that teachers cannot, in the course of legal training, teach a liar to tell the truth. In that sense the cynics are correct when they argue that, if a person does not know right from wrong by the time he reaches law school, there is not too much that law teachers can do. But they can teach students that a lawyer's role is not merely to be an advocate. A lawyer, particularly a government lawyer, has a responsibility to guide and even force his client to act in a certain way. If only one of the many lawyers around Nixon had understood that they had responsibilities to the presidency, to the Department of Justice, and to the United States government that transcended their responsibilities to the president as an individual, then they would have not only been serving their professional standards but also would have better served the president.

Can a student be taught how to weigh these seemingly conflicting responsibilities? How can one teach a course in corporation law without posing these identical questions to determine whether the lawyer has a prime loyalty to the shareholders who own the company, the board of directors that represents those shareholders, or the management that hired the lawyers? Should one teach constitutional law without considering how a government lawyer should act when he believes that the government he represents has acted unconstitutionally, even though a court may not have ruled specifically on the facts in his case?

I have, for several years, taught about the most famous constitutional law case in American jurisprudence—*Marbury* v. *Madison*—as an exercise in legal ethics. In that case the question was whether Secretary of State Madison could be compelled to deliver a judicial commission to Marbury, a "midnight judge" appointed by outgoing President John Adams. Traditionally, the case is taught in terms of whether Congress had the power to pass a law that argumentatively gave Marbury the right to bring his suit to the U.S. Supreme Court. The case is best remembered for the decision that the congressional statute was unconstitutional, and that the Supreme Court could invalidate an unconstitutional statute.

Suppose Secretary of State Madison had asked his lawyer for advice as to whether he should deliver the commission in the first place? After all, it was by pure accident or negligence that the commission had never been delivered. Should this happenstance have been used as the basis to deny a judge his position for purely political purposes? If the Supreme Court had ever ordered the secretary to deliver the commission, and the president had chosen to test the Court's authority by telling the secretary to ignore the order—should the government lawyer have attempted to defend this position or resign? These and many more questions emerge from a case that lawyers, political scientists, and historians view exclusively in terms of the substantive legal and political issues that were involved.

There are a few more examples of how pervasive the subject of legal ethics can be in teaching substantive law. In 1960, the Supreme Court decided the famous case of *Communist Party* v. *Subversive Activ-*

ities Control Board. The Court upheld the registration requirement in the 1950 McCarran Act, which compelled certain organizations, after appropriate hearings, to register with the Subversive Activities Control Board as communist-action organizations. The government successfully argued that the only issue that the Court should decide was the narrow question of the validity of the registration requirement. However, the statute raised many other issues. Did it violate the privilege against self-incrimination of those compelled to register? A member of a communist-action organization could not apply for passport or work in a defense plant. Were these provisions constitutional?

These issues were "premature," said the Court. Everyone, including the government lawyers who made this argument, were fully aware that ultimately these issues would have to be decided by the Supreme Court, as in fact they were several years later and all to the government's disadvantage.

There is an obvious question of professional ethics here. Was it proper for the U.S. to postpone consideration of these issues, at considerable cost to those challenging the statute, to win its case on the narrow point that was actually decided? I think that the government did act in an ethical manner; but a discussion of that issue raises serious questions about a lawyer's responsibility to his client, the administration of justice, and to the public generally.

Every law school has a moot court program generally for first-year students, in which they write an appellate brief and argue the appeal, simulating an actual appellate case. What should a student do if he or she comes upon a case, during the course of research, that is contrary to the position the student is asserting? The Code of Professional Responsibility clearly imposes a duty on the lawyer to bring this adverse authority to the attention of the court. Probably few students are so advised by their instructors.

Problems of representing potential conflicting interests must also be considered. In teaching matrimonial law, one should instruct students on how to deal with the common occurrence where a lawyer has been representing a family that encounters domestic problems. Should the lawyer represent the husband when he has been the lawyer for the complete family unit, including the wife? I doubt it.

The law of evidence is, of course, replete with questions of legal ethics and professional responsibility. How broad is the lawyer's duty not to reveal facts about his client—even if they came to the lawyer from a third party and, therefore, are not technically within the scope of the lawyer-client privilege? What are the limits to trickery in attempting to destroy the witness who you believe is lying? And, even more troublesome, how far should a lawyer go in destroying the credibility of a witness who is known by the lawyer to be telling the truth?

I have raised all these issues in my classes in legal ethics; the discussions that are generated force students to think about their relationships to their clients, their adversaries, the courts, and other parties.

If the issues are interesting and important—and if they pervade all aspects of the study of law—why have they been so largely ignored in our law schools? Unfortunately, few academic careers are built on training students to understand their roles as lawyers. The path to academic recognition is more easily travelled by writing in substantive areas of the law. More importantly, to teach legal ethics effectively, one must have had some experience in law practice, particularly at a level of direct client responsibility. Too many able young men and women enter law teaching after a stint as a law clerk to a prominent federal judge, and possibly a few years in large law firms or government agencies where they do not have the direct responsibility of representing clients.

Perhaps the major reason why the subject has not attracted major attention in law schools is the lack of relationship between the teaching tools and the interesting problems that should be taught. The case method of teaching law, originated by Dean Langdell almost a century ago, was an attempt to teach with reference to the problems that actually arose in litigation. The method still has validity despite the criticism that it focuses entirely at the appellate, rather than the trial, level. Whatever its faults, the case method of teaching substantive law does focus on the major problems that are litigated up to the appellate courts.

That is not the case with the major issues of professional responsibility and legal ethics, however. I do not know of any decided case that deals with the question of whether a lawyer should knowingly put on the stand a defendant who will deny his guilt and thereby commit perjury. Yet this is one of the most troublesome situations that a defense lawyer must face in his daily practice. It is necessary, therefore, to develop new teaching techniques, such as recording and playing tape cassettes, to bring the classroom closer to the reality of the ethical problems in the practice of law.

I am pleased to note that, under public prodding, a requirement from the American Bar Association that mandates the teaching of the Code of Professional Responsibility, law schools are rapidly expanding their offerings and using imaginative teaching techniques to deal with some of the ethical problems.

If legal ethics are to be a permanent part of the American legal education scene, how should the teachers' qualifications be judged? As a law dean who must ultimately decide whether to offer a position to a teacher after appropriate committee clearances, I find this question rather troubling. Normally one is only marginally concerned with the prospective teacher's position on substantive issues in the law of contracts or property or corporations. One considers the candidate's effectiveness as a teacher and his or her productivity as a scholar, expecting him or her to be fair in exposing the students to differing viewpoints. But I have wondered how I would react to a prospective teacher of legal ethics who told me that he felt that he had no obligation whatsoever to influence the moral judgments of his client, that he would confine himself to the narrowest scope of the job of providing legal advice, or that he had no concern about the type of person he was representing as long as he could pay the fee. None of these positions is necessarily fallacious. I simply do not agree with them. Fortunately, I have not yet had to face this problem; but there is no doubt that when one hires people to teach students to make ethical judgments, one is forced to make ethical judgments about the candidates before hiring them. And these are the kinds of judgments that administrators and faculty colleagues have normally shied away from making.

Within the past year, scholarship has grown and there is a greatly renewed interest in the teaching of legal ethics and professional responsibility. It is a good sign that law schools are now addressing some of the most critical issues in the practice of law.

Legal Ethics and
the Adversary System

Gray Dorsey
*Washington University School of Law**

Judge Frankel asserts an ethical obligation of law professors to develop and teach the ethics of the profession, as well as the substantive and procedural law. He indicts the legal professoriate for condoning an unsatisfactory ethical *status quo* by failing to lead in the critical study, constructive revision, and teaching of legal ethics.

FAILURE TO
TEACH LEGAL ETHICS

Undoubtedly the law schools have only recently begun to give serious attention to legal ethics. There are now five books intended, or suitable, for use as the principal resource in a legal ethics course. This is about the same number of books available for adoption by the teacher of a standard course such as contracts or torts. The legal ethics books are by able persons and present the hard questions raised by Judge Frankel in his remarks. The earliest copyright on these five books is 1966, although three are successors of earlier editions or books.[1] In many law schools the legal ethics course has recently been introduced, or efforts have recently been made to raise the course above the level of hortatory or anecdotal triviality.

The first result that one would expect from the past absence of meaningful legal ethics courses in law schools is that graduates would not know the ethical obligations of the lawyer to his client and to the court. This ignorance could be removed under tutelage by older members of law firms, or by continuing legal education programs organized by bar associations. The Joint Committee on Continuing Legal Education of the American Law Institute and the American Bar Association became concerned about legal ethics in the late 1950's and organized courses for practicing lawyers that stressed ethical responsibilities as well as legal skills. Course materials were prepared, usually by law teachers, on the practice of criminal law, conducting international transactions, planning small estates, and trying a civil action. Additionally the Joint Committee undertook to publish regularly in its periodical, *The Practical Lawyer*, articles with significant ethical responsibility content.

To the extent that the present concern about the state of legal ethics is caused by ignorance, perhaps Judge Frankel's challenge to law teachers could be satisfactorily met by pointing to recent law school and professional association actions of providing more and better teaching materials and improving or introducing courses on the ethical responsibility of lawyers.

DELIBERATE NONCOMPLIANCE WITH ETHICAL OBLIGATIONS

Perhaps the present concern about legal ethics is occasioned by actions that are the product not of ignorance but of intentional noncompliance with ethical obligations. At this point it is pertinent to question the efficacy of a law school course in legal ethics. Men and women enter law school after graduation from college. Is it not prudent to expect that their disposition to comply or not comply with community-imposed obligations is firmly established and unlikely to be altered by a course specifically directed to the ethical obligations of the lawyer? I think the answer is, Yes. But the suppositional matrix of the question is concern about the occasional bad apple. I sense that the suppositional matrix of Judge Frankel's remarks, and of many other current expressions of concern about the state of ethics, is a more widespread deliberate dereliction of ethical duty.

If the problem is widespread deliberate noncompliance with the lawyer's ethical obligations, two possible causes—which may be operating jointly—suggest themselves. One is that lawyers are participating in a general trend in the United States toward rejection of community-imposed obligations. The other possible cause is that a set of conditions conducive to deterioration of legal practices have come into existence in one or more places.

Gray Dorsey

A POSSIBLE GENERAL TREND TOWARDS
REJECTION OF COMMUNITY-IMPOSED OBLIGATIONS

In the past two decades we have experienced in the United States a number of movements in which a presumed good result was sought to be achieved, at least in part, by urging persons to act in accordance with their own moral judgment instead of complying with obligations established by the ordered functioning of community institutions, such as the state, the family, the church. Instances are the civil rights movement, the opposition to the Vietnam war, the women's liberation movement, the movement for more open and free expression of sexuality.

The restraints necessary to civilized life are maintained by sets of inhibitions, which can be destroyed by creating a social climate that tolerates noncompliance. This point was made with respect to controlling aggressive actions by the ethologist Konrad Lorenz in his recent dialogue with Richard I. Evans.[2]

Overriding inhibitions, as we all know, becomes progressively easier. An inhibition is most effective when it does not present itself to our consciousness; when the action that is its subject is simply unthinkable. When we give full and concerned consideration to whether a community-imposed obligation or a desired moral good should control our actions we have accepted the idea that inhibitions can be rejected. A single instance of joining a civil disobedience movement leaves us with our inhibitions nearly intact. We can put that instance out of mind as an exceptional response to the demand of high and compelling good. Doubtless this assessment of the end sought will reasonably appear to us as objectively correct because of the number and evident moral stature of other persons who are calling for noncompliance with community-imposed obligations in the name of higher justice and greater moral sensitivity. When one movement after another, some of whose assumed moral imperatives may not be quite so obviously good, demand repeated rejection of inhibitions, the test rather quickly changes from objective high and compelling good to personal conviction of sufficient moral worth to warrant noncompliance with community-imposed obligations. With time almost any end that is personally advantageous or satisfying can meet that test.

By the suggested chain of events a series of civil disobedience movements can seriously erode the set of inhibitions that are largely responsible for voluntary compliance by the great majority of persons with community-imposed legal and moral obligations.[3] The erosion of inhibitions results in a general trend towards noncompliance with community-imposed obligations. If there is such a trend in the United States it would doubtless proceed at different paces in different peer groups, but we could not expect lawyers to remain immune.

If such a general trend exists it is, of course, far beyond the scope of a law school legal ethics course. One might reasonably expect, however, that law teachers and lawyers would be the first to warn against seeking presumed good by means that threaten to create anarchy, thus making it impossible to achieve any good whatever.

CONDITIONS AFFECTING THE STATE OF LEGAL ETHICS

Judge Frankel says that in the present state of legal ethics lying, concealing and distorting are accepted practices. I do not understand him to be saying that these practices occur occasionally and aberrationally and the impossibility of completely eliminating them is generally acknowledged. I believe he is saying that these practices are so prevalent as to taint the whole legal process and they are generally accepted as a necessary, if not desirable, part of the practice of law.

In any set of organized human activities there will always be some persons who succumb to the venal urge to gain by cheating. When the activities have to do with establishing propositions of fact and law that will control the distribution of money, status, and other values, cheating will take the form of lying, concealing and distorting. When these practices occur with relative infrequency, and are treated as reprehensible and punishable breaches of professional obligation, they are serious for the persons immediately affected but they do not taint the whole legal process.

It is reasonable to expect that practices motivated by venality will increase with greater temptation and less chance of exposure and punishment. Conditions in the practice of law that are conducive to such an increase are: too few judges; large sums of money at stake; an avalanche of cases that exerts pressure to settle without going into rights and wrongs, either as to the substantive claim or as to lawyers' practices; the weakness of peer and leadership group influences in a large city. These conditions exist to some extent in any large city. When they all exist to a high degree it would not be surprising if unethical practices became so widespread that even those who would prefer to resist the venal urge were forced to adopt the same practices in order not to put their clients at a serious disadvantage. Perhaps it is such a situation in New York City to which Judge Frankel refers. If so the remedy lies not in rethinking legal ethics but in rethinking the size of cities.

QUESTIONING THE ADVERSARY SYSTEM

Is the Adversary System Incompatible with Honest and Fair Dealing?

Judge Frankel indicates by a rhetorical question and pejorative language that he believes that the adversary system is incompatible with honest and fair dealing. He asks, "How *do* you train or encourage a student to fight with all his skill for the vindication of a crooked client and at the same time cherish honest and fair dealing as prime values?" He says that lying about what a client would be prepared to accept is one of the "time-honored techniques" of legal negotiation; that "settled axioms" of law practice include the propositions that a lawyer must "seek victory for his crooked client over the wronged opponent" and must "use the tricks of cross-examination to make the truthful witness on the other side look like a liar"; and that it is a "bedrock principle" of the adversary system that "the lawyer is to be the client's loyal champion, not only preserving his confidences, but seeking at almost any cost to crown his efforts with success, confounding the innocent, and thwarting deep interests of a wider public."

Unfortunately Judge Frankel's references to the adversary system are almost entirely accusatory. He does not explain how the system operates, so that the layman can reach informed opinions as to whether the charges are factual or hyperbolic and whether unethical practices are abuses of the adversary system or an expression of it.

There is hyperbole. The most impeccably ethical lawyer could in good conscience fight with all his skill to vindicate a "crooked client" who had not in fact committed the particular crime of which he is presently charged. I find surprising the implication that in negotiating a settlement the lawyer will be guilty of lying unless at the first opportunity he discloses the lowest amount his client will accept. Surely it is true that the client will accept more if the other party is willing to pay it. It is my understanding that any lawyer who knows his way around in the courtroom will avoid like the plague any suggestion or insinuation that an opposing witness is lying unless he is absolutely sure he can prove it beyond the shadow of a doubt, because to put the accusation in the jury's mind and fail to sustain it invites a crushingly adverse reaction. Further, the particular case of using the tricks of cross-examination to try to discredit an opposing witness whom the defense attorney knows to be truthful is certainly not a "settled axiom" of law practice. The suggestion by Monroe Freedman that this is an ethically justifiable action has stirred up a storm of protest.[4]

More serious than the hyperbole, however, is Judge Frankel's charge that the adversary system is incompatible with honest and fair dealing. This implies that a high level of unethical practices, sufficient to taint the whole legal process, will result *of necessity* from the adversary system; that it is impossible under any conditions for unethical practices to be kept at an endurable minimum. Allow me to discuss briefly some aspects of the adversary system that Judge Frankel did not mention in order to indicate devices within that system which are calculated to keep unethical practices in check.

Under the adversary system each lawyer presents the best case that can be made for findings of fact and conclusions of law that will result in a judgment benefitting the interests of his client. The zeal, and rewards, of advocacy may tempt a lawyer to conceal, distort, and lie or condone lying by his client or witnesses, but he is not dependent solely upon his conscience or what he remembers from a law school legal ethics course to suggest to him reasons why he should not engage in these practices. He is under the supervision of the court, and particularly in the case of the federal bench, where Judge Frankel sits, the judge has very considerable power to root out and punish lying, concealment and distortion, as Judge John J. Sirica amply (some would say abusively) demonstrated in the Watergate investigations and trials. Further, the lawyer's actions are constantly subject to the scrutiny of the opposing lawyer, who can be expected to be astute to detect and expose such practices.

Regardless of how hard he may press, the advocate can not control the ultimate decisions of fact and law, because he does not make them. He can only influence those decisions by persuading the jury and the judge, who respectively decide what the facts are and what rule of law is controlling. Therefore the consequences of discovered lying, concealing, and distorting include the very real, and severe, possibility of adverse decisions by judge or jury on all matters in issue because the lawyer has shown himself unworthy of trust and confidence in one instance.

I think it reasonable to believe that at some times and places and under some conditions the adversary system's safeguards against unethical practices can work well enough to keep those practices at an endurable minimum. I think I have observed instances when this has occurred and I think most other lawyers could say the same. When unethical practices are kept at a minimum the practice of law in accordance with the adversary system, and specifically vigorous advocacy, is not incompatible with honest and fair dealing. The system-tainting level of unethical practices does not arise *of necessity* from the adversary system.

REDUCING PARTISAN CONTROL
OF THE JUDICIAL PROCESS

Even if the adversary system is not incompatible with honest and fair dealing it might, nevertheless, be less desirable than some alternative system. We should consider, therefore, Judge Frankel's suggested modifications. He believes that a "more fitting scheme of values—giving a higher place than we have to truth, fair dealing, and wide community interests" would entail serious revisions, of which he says:

> Specifically, in ways I am not prepared to forecast in detail, I think we
> shall want to restrict the authority we now leave with partisan contestants

to define the issues, investigate the evidence, and present only what they want to as the essential method of resolving legal disputes in court. For similar ends, we need to rethink and recast the attorney-client relationship, modifying the lawyer's role as hired gun, adding to the lawyer's obligations as an officer in a learned and public profession.

I accept Judge Frankel's values of truth, fair dealing, and wide community interests and propose to make some comparisons between alternative systems with respect to their respective capacities to serve these values. In this section I will compare the adversary system with a system in which partisan control of the judicial process is restricted. In the next section I will compare the adversary system with a system in which the role of advocate is substantially weakened.

The civil law countries of Europe have an inquisitorial system instead of an adversary system. Perhaps the most pertinent experience is that of the French administrative courts, which have jurisdiction over all questions concerning the relationships between persons and any department of government. The Conseil d'État was formed in 1799. It has administrative sections and a judicial section. The administrative sections perform consultative functions, advising on draft bills and proposed regulations, and proposing legislative and administrative reforms on their own initiative. The judicial section of the Conseil d'État hears, either as a trial court or on appeal, every case brought against the government.

Let us assume that a case is filed with the Conseil asking for annulment of an action by a government department. It will be assigned to a subsection of the judicial section and a member of the subsection will be appointed as reporter for the case. The reporter is responsible for preparing the case for decision in accordance with guidelines established by the subsection. He examines the petition, the answer, and the files of the government department whose action is sought to be annulled. The reporter determines what facts are necessary in order to form an opinion on the issues raised in the petition and answer and then proceeds to gather those facts. He may do this by telephone, letter, or personal interview. Neither the petitioner nor the government department complained against has the right to be represented by an advocate who would gather and present evidence considered important for the protection of the interests of his client. Nor does either party have the right to have an advocate present during the gathering of information to see that it is fairly and impartially done. The reporter can make an entirely *ex parte* investigation. Neither party has the right to call an expert witness. If the reporter decides that expert testimony is needed he will call upon one of the persons on a permanent list maintained by the Conseil of experts in all professional fields.

When the reporter has completed his investigation he submits a report together with recommendations for a decision to his subsection, and forwards the record to a government commissioner, who is also a member of the judicial section of the Conseil d'État. The subsection debates the recommendations of the reporter. The commissioner makes a second independent investigation of the whole case. Again, advocates for the parties are excluded from any significant role. The commissioner prepares conclusions on how the case should be decided, and reasons in support of the conclusions.

At this point the subsection of the Conseil to which the case was assigned and another subsection convene for a hearing on the case; but it is not advocates for the parties that are heard. They merely make formal statements referring the court to their written pleadings. It is the government commissioner who is heard. He presents his conclusions and his supporting reasons. Advocates for the parties have no opportunity to challenge findings of fact—to attempt to show that a witness is lying or has a bad memory—or to argue that inferences from the facts other than those drawn by the reporter or commissioner are equally, or more, persuasive.

At the close of the hearing the court, consisting of the two subsections of the Conseil (one of whom has already heard and debated the recommendations of the reporter before the hearing) begins its deliberations. A decision of the whole body is rendered, with no opinion by the court explaining and supporting the decision, and no dissenting or concurring opinions. The only published analysis of the case is the commissioner's conclusions, which are not binding on the court. This is the end of the matter. There is no appeal from a decision by the judicial section of the Conseil d'État.[5]

Before comparing the French inquisitorial system with the American adversary system with respect to truth and the other values, I must discuss briefly the meaning of "truth" in relation to a legal system. I must be brief. Therefore, I will state some propositions that I think wholly justifiable, but which I will not here attempt to justify, and I will assume those propositions as the basis of further remarks.

Any mature legal system seeks to implement, by authoritative official means, values generally accepted as valid for directing and limiting social organization and action and for requiring, permitting and limiting the actions of persons. For present purposes three levels of truth can usefully be distinguished. One lies above and two lie below the values that a legal system seeks to implement. I shall call them philosophical truth, instrumental truth, and factual truth.

By philosophical truth I mean propositions resulting from attempts to formulate accumulated human experience in general terms. Examples are: The essential nature of human beings is rationality; Universal Spirit objectifies itself in the physical world and in history; It is not the consciousness of men that determines their existence, but their social existence that determines their consciousness.

Legal systems do not seek philosophical truth, although it can profoundly affect the nature of a legal system. Philosophical truths that are so generally and pervasively believed by a people that they constitute the reality in which they live, generate and limit the opportunities open to, and the problems faced by, a people and therefore shape the choices open to them. Within such a context people organize the auxiliary and complementary actions of society in accordance with generally accepted, and therefore shared, values.

Values are generally accepted partly because they are consistent with prevailing philosophical truths, but also partly because of the pleasures and satisfactions which they are expected to yield. I do not refer to values as a level of truth because their validity as ends of organized human activities, including legal activities, rests not upon their being true, but upon their being generally consented to—accepted, shared. Examples of values are: The equal competence under law of all persons in the making of important decisions; The merging of the subjective will of the individual into the objective will of the state; Conforming production relations and corresponding parts of the legal system to objectively known real conditions of production, such as the current stage of technology.

By instrumental truth I mean the implications of shared values for the actions and restraints of individuals and groups. The legal system seeks instrumental truth. The task involves determining broad goals and principles and moving objectively from them to the determination of the controlling rule in each concrete situation. The pursuit of instrumental truth occurs in the legislative process, in the formulation of executive policies and directives, and in judicial interpretation of provisions in constitutions, statutes and prior judicial opinions. Examples of instrumental truth at the level of general principles are: All persons shall be secure in their persons, houses, papers, and effects, against unreasonable searches and seizures; The will of the people, expressed by their leader, is the supreme law of the land; No private individual has the right to own land or machinery used for production.

By factual truth I mean accurate information about actions, events, statements, states of mind, and conditions. The legal system seeks this kind of truth, as the basis for legislative or executive decision making or action, and as the basis for judicial resolution of disputes. Examples are: Doe struck Roe on the head with a blunt object; The production of Hertzl Steel Works increased 31 percent in 1974; The weather was unfavorable to grain production in the Soviet Union in 1974 and 1975.

In the judicial process of dispute settlement, the pursuit of instrumental truth has as its object the controlling rule of law. The pursuit of factual truth has as its object an accurate account of pertinent actions, etc. In comparing the pluses and minuses of the inquisitorial and the adversary system with respect to the pursuit of truth, it is quite common to focus on the pursuit of factual truth to the exclusion of the pursuit of instrumental truth. This focus of attention arises quite naturally from the fact that it is partisan participation in the fact finding process that gives rise to the obvious ethical problems.

The argument is appealing that impartial investigators with professional training and public responsibility will come up with a more accurate and complete picture of the pertinent facts than will result from opposing presentations of evidence to the jury by advocates who may be tempted, in their client's interest, to conceal or distort some facts, and cast doubt on others. Why not avoid the unfair dealing to which advocates might succumb and serve the community interest in having disputes settled on the basis of the true facts by adopting the inquisitorial system?

Unfortunately the matter is not so simple. It is unrealistic to consider the pursuit of factual truth apart from the pursuit of instrumental truth. With respect to factual truth the significant issue is, "*How* shall the truth be sought?" e.g., by partisan gathering and presenting of evidence or by impartial professional investigators. But with respect to instrumental truth the significant issue is, "What truth shall be sought?" It often occurs that with respect to the particular events or transactions giving rise to the dispute, two of the values generally accepted in the community generate implications of principles and rules that are appropriate for decision of the dispute, but different, perhaps contrary, settlements of the dispute would result depending upon which value is held to be dominant (in this case) and which set of principles and rules, therefore, are held to be controlling. The choice has a crucial effect upon the pursuit of factual truth, because the facts that will be pertinent are those needed to prove or disprove the issues and the issues are framed in accordance with the principles and rules of law that are held to be controlling. I will give an example.

Assume that the following case has come to the French Conseil d'État on an application for annulment of the action of the Ministry of Export. A French law requires purchase in advance of export licenses. Purportedly for the purpose of enabling Export Ministry economists to accurately forecast levels of export, the Export Ministry by administrative regulation requires a performance bond in the amount of 30 percent of the value of the goods covered by the license. ALORS, Inc., purchased a license to export 20,000 bottles of wine within the next 60 days, and was required to post a bond in an amount equivalent to $17,000. The market price for wine declined in Canada, where ALORS had planned to ship, and it only exported 8,000 bottles during the period of the license. The Bond Committee of the Ministry declared the bond forfeit, the Export Ministry Administrative Agency affirmed the forfeiture, and ALORS has asked the Conseil d'État to annul the action of forfeiture.

The competing values are: Sufficient stability in exports to enable national economic plans to be effective; and just treatment of individuals by the government. The competing sets of principles and rules are those concerning: Organization and operation of the Export Ministry, especially its rule making and enforcing authority; and Rights of natural and legal persons (corporations, like ALORS) against arbitrary exercises of governmental power.

When ALORS, Inc., through its attorney, asks the Conseil d'État to annul the forfeiture of the bond it will assert that the forfeiture is unjust because the amount was out of all proportion to the purpose sought to be achieved and therefore the forfeiture amounted to a penalty for a failure to perform that was caused by events beyond the control of ALORS. ALORS will also claim that the forfeiture was not done in accordance with the established procedures of the Export Ministry.

Now let us assume that the same events occurred in the United States and the American company, THEN, Inc., is filing an action in the appropriate United States District Court to have the Export Bureau enjoined from enforcing the bond forfeiture. THEN will allege that the forfeiture violates the constitutional protection against taking property except for a valid public purpose because the amount of the bond is out of all proportion to the governmental purpose sought, and it will also allege that the forfeiture is invalid because the actions of the Export Bureau were not in accordance with procedural due process.

In the United States District Court case, counsel for THEN will gather and introduce evidence tending to show that the forfeiture was arbitrary and therefore in violation of the constitution, and it will also gather and introduce evidence tending to show that the Export Bureau did not meet procedural due process for administrative actions. Counsel for the Export Bureau will gather and introduce countering evidence on both issues, the judge will instruct the jury on the controlling rules of law on both issues, and the jury will bring in verdicts on both issues. If the jury finds that the forfeiture was arbitrary the court will require the Export Bureau to return the forfeited amount even if its procedure was entirely fair.

In the Conseil d'État case, counsel for ALORS will not be permitted to gather and introduce evidence tending to show that the forfeiture was arbitrary and unjust, and will not be permitted to gather and introduce evidence tending to show that the proper administrative procedures were not followed. The difference between the two systems would not be as important as it is, however, if the reporter and the commissioner would investigate the facts and analyze the law and make recommendations upon the issue of the fundamental injustice (unconstitutionality) of the forfeiture as well as the administrative regularity with which it was done. But they will not do so.

It would be misleading to leave the impression that the question of fundamental justice to persons affected by French governmental actions is not considered in the French legal system. It is. But persons adversely affected do not have the right to raise it and have it answered in judicial proceedings by application of principles and rules to the facts as found by the jury. That is the method of the American adversary system. The method of the inquisitorial system of French administrative law is to have issues of fundamental justice decided by the most able of professionally trained administrators.

The National School of Administration, admission to which is by competitive examination, trains administrators for all government departments. Members of the Conseil d'État are recruited from the highest ranking graduates of the National School. It can be assumed that the professors of the National School are the most able professional administrators in France. It is they who teach the proper procedure in every situation, and it is their obligation to consider the rights of persons who will be affected by governmental actions and to specify administrative actions that will accord the proper deference to those rights.[6]

When a claim is made that governmental action violated a person's basic rights, the Conseil has jurisdiction only to inquire into whether the governmental department acted in the ways approved by the National School. The claim of violation of basic rights becomes only one type of allegation of improper procedure because all approved procedures are just, by definition. Thus there is no need for judicial review of constitutionality, and the members of the Conseil are not competent. Only the professors of the National School of Administration can make that determination and they are not required to hear the arguments of persons adversely affected by governmental actions. They may reconsider a principle or rule in the light of its effects as seen in cases coming before the Conseil, but adversely affected persons cannot require them to do so. Judicial review for the purpose of protecting individuals against governmental actions does not exist in France.[7]

Nothing I have said gives much basis to compare the French inquisitorial system with the American adversary system with respect to fair dealing. Maintaining the professional integrity of the French system against unethical practices would require safeguards against corruption of professional bureaucrats instead of against cheating by interested advocates. I do not think either is demonstrably easier to accomplish than the other.

With respect to truth, it is not a matter of seeking truth; nor of seeking truth by partisan advocates versus seeking truth by impartial investigators. The most important consideration is whether the individual person is entitled to raise and have answered in court the question of the justice or injustice of governmental action adversely affecting him, or whether this decision will be made in advance and in the abstract by an elite group of professional bureaucrats.

The inquisitorial system of French administrative law shows the direction we would be moving if, as Judge Frankel suggests, we restrict the authority of partisan contestants to define the issues and gather and present the evidence. Whether moving in this direction would serve wide community interests depends upon whether Americans want to change from an individualistic to a paternalistic society. My preference is against Judge Frankel's proposal.

WEAKENING THE
ROLE OF ADVOCATE

There is no doubt that the adversary system does result in some persons being acquitted who in fact are guilty of the crimes of which they are accused. Further, there is no doubt that the acquittal of these persons would not occur but for the actions of their attorneys. Would truth and the other values be served by weakening the role of advocate so that some of the actions resulting in acquittals would not be permitted? In order to answer that question some distinctions must be made and the effect of weakening the role of advocate must be examined.

There is no controversy when the lawyer's action is itself a crime, such as bribing a juror or suborning the perjury of a witness. These actions clearly are not "within the bounds of the law," which is the limiting phrase to the admonition of Canon 7 of the Code of Professional Responsibility that "A lawyer should represent a client zealously. . . ."

The advocate is obligated to serve his client's interest and, as an officer of the court, he is also obligated to serve the public interest by upholding the law. The troublesome conflicts between these two obligations arise in the area where acquittal of the client is sought by actions that obstruct or vitiate the pursuit of the factual truth about guilt or innocence. The line between legitimate and improper advocacy must be drawn at a place that represents a balance, acceptable to the community, of implementation of the competing values of effective law enforcement and providing vigorous and competent advocacy for the accused.

There will always be differences among reasonable persons about whether some actions are within or outside legitimate advocacy. Is it proper for a lawyer to seek acquittal of a client who, as a part of the privileged attorney-client communication, has admitted his guilt? Or should the lawyer seek only to mitigate the sentence? Is it proper to put a client on the witness stand when the lawyer knows, by privileged communication, that the client intends to commit perjury? Is it proper to use the forensic traps of cross-examination to try to discredit a prosecution witness whose testimony the defense lawyer knows to be accurate and truthful? Because the answers to these and other similar questions depend upon practical judgment about the proper balance between implementation of competing values in complex situations, no two of which are exactly alike, we cannot expect to achieve advance agreement on a set of specific directives covering all ethical problems of the defense attorney.

We have always had the problem of hard choices between competing goods, but we are now experiencing an unprecedented questioning of the role of the advocate. What has changed? I suggest that the most significant change is in the perceived purpose of the judicial system. When the purpose of the judicial system is viewed as law enforcement within the accepted social matrix of an individualistic society, excesses of advocacy are viewed as not really serious injuries to the public interest. Specifically in the criminal law area we are all familiar with the aphorism, "Better that a hundred guilty persons should be acquitted than that one innocent person should be convicted."

The current critics of the role of the advocate, I suggest, have in mind for the judicial system a larger purpose than law enforcement. What that purpose is can be inferred from Judge Frankel's reference to Mr. St. Clair, who was President Nixon's attorney in the Watergate proceedings. The judicial system is sought to be used to purge the nation of corruption in high places. Any obstructions to the attainment of such a noble purpose must be swept aside. Those who hold the authority and power of the United States government are not to have the toleration of excessive advocacy that is accorded the ordinary murderer, and perhaps should not be entitled even to vigorous advocacy. The focus of attention is shifted from the guilt or innocence of the accused persons to the greater cause of preventing the corruption of governmental processes. Before such a public interest the rights of the individual pale into insignificance. Hence the call for modifying the role of the advocate, who is seen not only as shielding the malefactors but also as frustrating the larger purpose of protecting the integrity of democratic government.

The bending of the judicial system to the pursuit of a moral or ideological crusade always clothes itself in the language of seeking truth and serving the public interest. But it should be recognized that what is sought to be accomplished is not preservation and strengthening of the integrity of the pursuit of instrumental and factual truth so that the legal system can better fulfill its function of enforcing the law. On the contrary, the integrity of the legal system is sought to be weakened. Safeguards of the rights of individuals become "technicalities" to be thrust aside so that the legal system can be the instrument to accomplish a higher moral good.

Weakening the role of advocate under the banner of truth and the public interest has a dark history indeed. Defense lawyers of the Soviet Union were prepared for their non-obstructive roles in the sham trials under Stalin by the teaching of Soviet jurists that the defense lawyer must help the court to find the truth. Vyshinsky wrote that it is the duty of the defense lawyer to help the court "to find the real essence of the case, the real character of the accused, the real solution of the given case."[8] Golyakov said that "numberless examples of bourgeois justice prove that the role of counsel in court is often reduced to a shameless exculpation of the client in order to avert a more or less heavy punishment for him. To this purpose counsel hides the truth, strives to limit the questioning of persons whose testimony is detrimental to his client, thoroughly challenges jurors who are most competent in the case." In contrast to this advocacy of private interests, Golyakov said the work of Soviet defense lawyers "rises to a genuine, real service to society and the state and in practical activity becomes one with the activity of the entire Soviet people in the fight for the success and prosperity of the Socialist fatherland...."[9] Rasulov proclaimed that "The Soviet defense counsel must serve the great humanitarian purpose of the defense of the law of the socialist society, of truth and justice."[10] Specific modifications in the role of advocate, in order to carry out the principle that defense counsel must serve objective truth instead of his client's private interests were: Defense counsel was not to seek acquittal for the client unless he honestly believed him to be not guilty; Defense counsel must reveal inculpating evidence to the court even if received in confidence from the accused; Defense counsel must present a true characterization of the accused and a true account of the crime even if these were more damaging than those given by the prosecutor.[11]

These modifications in the role of the advocate were part of the changes instituted in order to make the judicial system an effective repressive instrument in the struggle to force the people of the Soviet Union into a structure of society that, according to the infallible science of dialectical materialism would lead to a utopia in which no person would exploit another.[12] In the post-Stalin effort to establish "Socialist legality" it was admitted by Deputy Minister of Justice N. S. Prusakov that in the Stalin period "defense counsel were not seldom subject to disciplinary prosecution because they defended in principle the rights and lawful interests of citizens."[13]

Today, the advocate in the Soviet judicial system is not permitted to serve his client's interests as fully as in the United States, or Western Europe—or for that matter, as in Czarist Russia[14]—but defense counsel is no longer viewed as an aid to the court in finding the truth, and is not expected to reveal inculpatory information received in confidence from the accused. It is now recognized, except in political trials, that the defense attorney serves public and state interests by presenting to the court all possible exculpating and mitigating facts and suggesting all possible inferences favorable to his client. It is left to the prosecutor to bring forward inculpating facts and inferences.[15] Thus we have in the Soviet experience the remarkable fact of movement back towards recognition of the value of advocacy of private interests as a corrective to the shameful role of the Soviet judicial system in the period of Stalin, when it gave the facade of justice to the extermination of millions of persons in the struggle to impose a new order of society.

Truth, fair dealing, and wide community interests would be served by eliminating the excesses of advocacy in pursuit of the interests of accused individuals. But, so long as the purpose of the legal system is understood as being law enforcement, excesses of advocacy have been viewed as a tolerable price to pay to be sure the innocent are not convicted. The instant call for weakening the role of advocate is not calculated to strengthen the integrity of the legal system to achieve its purpose of law enforcement. It is calculated to weaken the integrity of the legal system so that it can be used as an instrument to purge the nation of corruption in high places. The dark history of the weakening of the role of advocate in the Soviet Union indicates that moving in that direction would be highly dangerous to the rights of individuals in a free society, and would not serve any version of truth, fair dealing and wide community interests consistent with such a society.

CONCLUSION

The fact that a person with the professional stature of Judge Frankel could suggest, as a cure for an unsatisfactory state of legal ethics, moving in the direction of restricting the partisan control of issues and evidence, and weakening the role of advocate, possibly without being aware of, and certainly without presenting and discussing, the serious threats to an individualistic, free society posed by such movements, indicates that the law schools need to do a better job of teaching the new and the older lawyers. But it would appear that the efforts should be directed towards legal history, comparative law, and legal and social philosophy, in addition to legal ethics.

NOTES

*Thanks for helpful suggestions are gratefully extended to colleagues on my own faculty, Dean Edward T. Foote, Robert G. Dixon, Jr. and Patrick J. Kelley; to E. Ernest Goldstein, Coudert Frères, Paris, and to Presiding Judge Joseph J. Simeone, Missouri Court of Appeals, St. Louis.

1. Countryman & Finman, *The Lawyer in Modern Society*, Little, Brown and Company, 1966, with 1971 Supplement; Thurman, Phillips & Cheatham, *Cases and Materials on the*

Legal Profession, Foundation Press, 1970 (successor volume to a Cheatham book by the same name published 1938, 2d ed. 1955); Mathews, *Problems Illustrative of the Responsibilities of Members of the Legal Profession,* Council on Legal Education for Professional Responsibility, Inc., 2d ed. 1968, 1st ed. 1965; Pirsig, *Cases and Materials on Professional Responsibility,* West Publishing Co., 2d ed. 1970, 1965 (successor volume to two earlier books by Pirsig, going back to 1949); Freedman, *Lawyers Ethics in an Adversary System,* Bobbs-Merrill Company, 1975. The titles of Pirsig's books indicate a trend away from using "legal ethics" to denote the subject area. His books, and copyright years, are: *Cases and Materials on Legal Ethics,* 1949, *Cases and Materials on the Standards of the Legal Profession,* 1957, and, as above, *Cases and Materials on Professional Responsibility,* 1965, 2d ed. 1970. The shift in name was accompanied by a broadening of the subject area to include a study of the role of the lawyer.

    2. Evans, "A Conversation with Konrad Lorenz . . ." in *Psychology Today,* November 1974, 83-93, at 90.

    3. See Bickel, *The Morality of Consent,* Yale University Press, 1975, pp. 119-120.

    4. Johnston, Review of Freedman's *Lawyers' Ethics In An Adversary System,* in *The New York Times Book Review,* Sept. 28, 1975, pp. 5-6.

    5. Stein & Hay, *Law and Institutions in the Atlantic Area,* 1967, pp. 118-122.

    6. See Hamson, Remarks at University of Michigan, quoted in Stein & Hay, *Law and Institutions in the Atlantic Area,* 1967, p. 123.

    7. In the French Republics prior to World War II, judicial review was out of the question because the full authority of the monarch was transferred to the legislature. In the 1958 Constitution of the Fifth Republic, which limits legislative power to enumerated subjects, judicial review is adopted for the purpose of curbing legislative incursions on executive powers but not for the purpose of protecting individuals against unjust governmental actions. Dietze, "Judicial Review in Europe," 55 Mich. L. Rev. 539, 550-552, 558-560 (1957); Waline, "The Constitutional Council of the [Fifth] French Republic," 12 Am. J. Comp. L. 483 (1963).

    8. Kucherov, *The Organs of Soviet Administration of Justice: Their History and Operation,* 1970, p. 522.

    9. *Ibid.,* pp. 525-26.

    10. *Ibid.,* p. 527.

    11. *Ibid.,* pp. 506-20.

    12. "For the complete eradication of the harmful consequences of the Cult of the Individual in Soviet Jurisprudence." Current Digest of the Soviet Press, Vol. 14, No. 21, June 20, 1962, pp. 5-10. The "cult of the individual" is the Soviet euphemism for Stalin's regime.

    13. Kucherov, op. cit. p. 525.

    14. *Ibid.,* pp. 523-24, 527-28.

    15. *Ibid.,* pp. 533, 569-70, 558 et seq

Academic Freedom and
Professional Responsibilities

Sidney Hook
Emeritus New York University
Senior Research Fellow,
Hoover Institution, Stanford

Many myths about academic freedom have grown up in recent years. Before the nineteen thirties it was the rare university, if any, which openly committed itself to the principles of academic freedom, despite the 1915 Declaration of Principles of the American Association of University Professors, and despite the findings of its Committee A on Academic Freedom. Beginning with the nineteen forties more and more universities accepted as their own the AAUP declaration of principles of 1940 and subsequent explications of their meaning. Today it is the rare university which has not officially accepted those principles of academic freedom.

As is often the case when principles are almost universally endorsed, there is much ambiguity in the way they are interpreted. Sometimes the verbal agreement functions as a method of reconciling or concealing differences. With respect to practice, however, the greatest threats to academic freedom on American campuses in the last decade have come not from administrative or governmental authority but from militant minorities among students and faculty bodies. The most vehement groups have not hesitated on occasion to proclaim that "racists" and "fascists," defined very vaguely in terms of doctrines badly understood and often misstated, are not entitled to academic freedom in their teaching and research. On occasion meetings and classrooms have been forcibly disrupted and speakers and teachers threatened with physical harm—something almost unprecedented on American campuses. Despite temporary lulls in political activism among students and faculties, it is safe to predict that we will witness a recurrence of the phenomenon of intolerance and bigotry by ideological fanatics. A clearer understanding of the meaning of academic freedom may help mitigate the situation when political passions flare up again. It may suggest ways of coping with excesses firmly and justly.

One of the most widespread myths about academic freedom is that it is a human right or at least entailed by the rights enumerated in "the Bill of Rights" of the Amendments to the American Constitution. This is a gross mistake. However human rights or civil rights be defined, they belong to individuals in virtue of their participation in the human community or as citizens of the democratic commonwealth. They do not have to be earned. Everyone has a human right to a fair trial or to freedom of speech. But not everyone has a right to academic freedom. That must be *earned*. It is only the person who is professionally qualified in some relevant sense who is eligible for academic freedom.

Another myth about academic freedom is that it is bound up necessarily with political freedom or democracy. This is both historically and analytically false, although a plausible case can be made for the contention that in a properly functioning democracy the likelihood is that academic freedom will flourish more widely than elsewhere. There was greater recognition of the principle of academic freedom in the universities of imperial Germany during the last century than in the universities of the much more politically democratic Great Britain. Although sometimes breached, even the Prussian Constitution of 1850 expressly declared that "Science and its teaching shall be free." (The German word "Wissenschaft" embraced not only the sciences but the entire domain of scholarship.)

Nor is academic freedom synonymous with continuous or permanent tenure, although without provisions for the achievement of tenure, academic freedom is easily jeopardized. Strictly speaking, of course, tenure can never be absolute. What it means is that after tenure has been gained, it is automatically renewed and cannot be lost except after due process. The rules of academic tenure cannot be identified with the principles of academic freedom if only because we believe that even those who are untenured or who have not yet won tenure are also entitled to academic freedom. Theoretically it is possible for an elite university that perpetually seeks to improve its faculty on the same principle that leads a museum always to improve its holdings by sale, purchase, and exchange, to refuse to award tenure to anyone and yet scrupulously respect the academic freedom of its staff. Such a university is not likely, however, to recruit an excellent faculty under such conditions, particularly if other intellectually respectable institutions offer tenure. For no matter how good one is there is always the possibility that someone better may turn up tomorrow.

Finally, many professors are loath to recognize that the right to academic freedom is a special right that carries with it a "privilege" most citizens do not enjoy. Most citizens, even in the freest political community, cannot escape the sanctions of their customers and clients if the latter find their ideas and opinions or personality and manner obnoxious. No matter how outrageous one's opinions are in a community that abides by the Bill of Rights, one will not incur any *legal* punishment whatsoever. One will not (and should not) be deprived of freedom or suffer any loss of legal rights for any heretical view on any subject matter. But in a free society, one will be unable to escape the moral judgment of citizens which inevitably expresses itself in a refusal to traffic or trade or consort with the person expressing the position or opinion deemed offensive. The man who proclaims that the *Protocols of Zion* are authentic and justifies Hitler's racist policies, or who urges the wisdom of the South African policy of Apartheid, or who contends that the Kremlin's policy of sentencing dissidents to insane asylums is perfectly justified, enjoys the legal right to defend such barbarous practices, but I have the moral right not to accept him as a friend, neighbor, partner, patron or tradesman. The result may be that in a free society, even where there is no governmental or official prosecution or discrimination of any kind, the heretic or rebel or dissenter may incur severe economic sanctions sometimes strong enough to deprive him of any possibility of practicing his vocation or remaining in business. Legally I am free to denounce my neighbors on racist or religious or political grounds, with or without rhyme or reason. They are free legally to take their trade elsewhere, to boycott me, not to give me the time of day even if this spells economic and social disaster. That is the price I pay for my freedom, and anyone who exercises his freedom of speech must be prepared to pay that price and not to whine if the fallout of public reaction adversely affects him or her.

Those who enjoy academic freedom to pursue and proclaim the truth as they see it do not and should not pay that price for their freedom. They are the beneficiaries of a privilege, economic security, that the overwhelming majority of their fellow citizens do not possess and do not dream of demanding. Those who do not possess this privilege sometimes ask: Why should it be accorded to teachers and scholars?

Before answering this question let us make sure that we understand the momentous character of the privilege we extend—and rightfully extend—to those who are protected by academic freedom.

The following hypothetical situation differs only in detail from others that are historically well confirmed. I share the platform with a grocer, a pharmacist, a lawyer, a physician in private practice, and a realtor. All of us defend variations of the same position in favor of abortion of the embryo at any time and for any reason on demand by potential mothers, and in favor of voluntary euthanasia for adults at any time at their request. Widespread publicity is given to the event and our views are accurately reported. Within a few weeks the grocer and pharmacist observe that they have lost a great many of their customers. Within a few months the lawyer and physician find their offices empty. The realtor is worried sick lest the name of the realty company where he is employed be made known, for if the members of the community boycott that company in which he is a salesperson, the manager will discharge him if business falls off. I, however, who enjoy academic freedom and tenure at the community college have nothing to fear. The faculty and administration must protect me in my post against any and all demands of enraged parents whose sons and daughters I teach, even if the faculty and administration on the whole either abominate my views or my provocative way of expressing them. I can thumb my nose at the community with complete immunity.

Can anyone deny that I enjoy a greater freedom than the other members of the platform panel, and indeed, most other professionals as well as most other citizens who do not have tenured jobs?

The reason why I and other teachers are entitled to academic freedom, and to immunity from penalties and sanctions by the taxpayer who directly and indirectly subsidizes the institutions, is not that we are *personally* privileged but because we perform a *public* function of great value. The greatest obstacle to the development of academic freedom in the United States has been the failure of the universities to make the community cognizant of the fact that everyone, so to speak, who has a regard for the public good has a vested interest in the establishment and defense of academic freedom. In other words, it is not the case that academic freedom is a vested interest of the professors alone. The advance of scholarship and research, the effectiveness of teaching, and the ensuing benefits that are shared by all, depend upon untrammeled inquiry. There are no watertight departments among the intellectual disciplines. The practice of freedom or repression in any field may ultimately have effects on every other field. The nature of free, rational inquiry is self-corrective. Error, therefore, *honest* error, plays a role, for in the elimination of error we approach the truth more closely.

We therefore need not be unduly apologetic about the fact that as professors we require a freedom greater than that enjoyed by most of our fellow-citizens, and one that needs legal protection against pressures for conformity from without and within the academy. A survey of the history of thought will reinforce the wisdom of this policy, even if it be acknowledged that at any given time the overwhelming number of professors do not find themselves ideologically at war with their societies, and less than ten per cent are engaged in original research. For sometimes the accepted truth is intolerant of the truth struggling to be born. Where academic freedom functions as the common law of the mind we can keep an open yet critical house for heresies regardless of their intellectual outcomes.

Nonetheless the fact that academic freedom gives a shield of special protection to teachers and scholars, not shared by most of their fellow citizens, imposes special obligations and duties upon them. Until recently the emphasis has been primarily upon the right to academic freedom because of encroachments on that freedom by administration and government. There was always a need to make explicit the responsibilities of faculties to their students, to their subject matter, to their colleagues and to the rationale of intellectual inquiry in the pursuit of objective truth. These responsibilities were taken for granted as well understood. But with the increasing politicalization of university campuses and of their curriculum of studies, it has become clear that the presuppositions of membership in the republic of arts, letters, and sciences were not always well understood.

The American Association for University Professors, in a document entitled "Freedom and Responsibility," found it necessary to declare that:

> The expression of dissent and the attempt to produce change . . . may not be carried out in ways which injure individuals or damage institutional faculties or disrupt the classes of one's teachers or colleagues. Speakers on campus must not only be protected from violence, but given an opportunity to be heard. Those who seek to call attention to grievances must not do so in ways that significantly impede the functions of the institution.

The declaration of the AAUP would never have been issued unless the accumulation of incidents to which it refers had not reached considerable proportions. Even the relations between faculty and students were apparently not properly understood by political activists among the faculty. "The student," warns the AAUP, "should not be forced by the authority inherent in the instructional role to make particular personal choices as to political action or his own part in society. Evaluation of students and the award of credit must be based on academic performance professionally judged and not on matters irrelevant to that performance, whether personality, race, religion, degree of political activism, or personal beliefs."

It would not be difficult to compile a case book of studies in which these irresponsible violations of the freedom to teach and learn have occurred. There is no hesitation in repudiating the notion that "anything goes" or "all is permissible" in the classroom. "Thus, it is improper for an instructor persistently to intrude material which has no relation to his subject. . . ."

That the AAUP should have considered issuing this Declaration is of enormous importance in its bearing upon the question of academic responsibility. The practices it condemns, as well as many others, surely establish a *prima-facie* case of professional unfitness. By no stretch of reasonableness can such practices be assimilated to the procedures of legitimate intellectual inquiry. Such teachers, far from being entitled to the special privilege of the profession, are entitled to no protection at all when their behavior comes to light.

The chief responsibility for seeing that there is adherence to the norms essential to the academic life rests on the faculty. There is no need to bring in the State. Every faculty should draw up a set of guidelines which expresses both its commitment to academic freedom and the duties and obligations of the teaching and administrative staff. Such a code of professional ethics would, so to speak, be equivalent to the Hippocratic oath of the medical guild. It would spell out the details of due process and possible sanctions in the event that faculty members are charged with violating the academic freedom of their colleagues, their students, and of guests of the university in the performance of their academic function.

The rub is that some universities which have adopted such codes of professional conduct have been loath to institute proceedings against faculty members who have been charged with inciting students to violence. In one case in which such action was taken, the long, drawn-out procedure consumed so much time, energy, and expense that some members of the faculty have expressed doubt whether the game was worth the candle, especially where student militants solidarize themselves with the defendants, and throw the campus into tumult and uproar by demonstrations that disrupt judicial procedure and generate an atmosphere in which freedom to teach and learn is abridged.

Unless faculties undertake to regulate themselves when any of their members violate the codes of acceptable academic behavior that have been established by the consensus of the faculties themselves, there is a grave danger that outside non-academic agencies will step in to undertake the regulation. When proceedings are brought against a faculty member they can be scrupulously fair without being protracted for months on end or patterned literally on strict judicial principles that operate in a court room, particularly with respect to the admissibility of relevant evidence. Those who are found guilty by faculty bodies always have recourse to the courts. The codes that have been adopted by American universities are far and away superior to practices followed or advocated even in democratic countries like England. The late R. H. S. Crossman, a left wing Laborite notable for his mordant criticism of the United States, commenting on the declaration of support by a group of faculty members in behalf of a faculty member who urged students to resort to violence, said that if he had been Minister of Education, he would have informed all the signatories that he considered their statement tantamount to a letter of resignation from the academy. He was prepared to act even without granting these supporters of violence a hearing! A hearing with all necessary safeguards for the right of the accused is always in order. But it need not be turned into a farce or existential theatre by opening it to the general public.

Ultimately the preservation of academic freedom against those of its enemies within the academic family who are prepared to encourage and incite violence on campuses is in the hands of the faculties. When the detailed history of the academic violence of the years from 1964 to 1975 comes to be written, the evidence will show that the chief responsibility for the violent sit-ins, the disruptions of classes and meetings, the burning of books and libraries, the assaults against persons, the bombings and vandalisms rests with the faculties themselves. Usually the failure to take proper disciplinary action at the first outbreak of violence encouraged more extreme behavior by those responsible or their sympathizers to a point where the ultimate intervention by non-academic authority was experienced by students as an unjustified intrusion into the life of the campus even when the process of education ground to a halt, and in some cases led to the destruction of laboratories, offices and libraries.

At the present time American universities have not suffered the ideological ravages by extremist groups that have devastated some of the great universities of Western Europe. But there are tendencies and representatives of the same movements that have transformed academic life in these centers present and active on the American scene. In the struggle to preserve academic freedom the existence and implementation of codes of professional responsibility, enforced by the faculties themselves, may be the first line of defense.

The Ethics of
the Art of Teaching

Lee Nisbet

Executive Editor, The Humanist

Teaching is an art form. The educator is an artist and, as artist, aims at creating an experience of enduring meaning. Varieties of techniques are developed to generate this extraordinary experience. Success is measured in the degree that students and educator *have* this experience.

Sharing in, or participating in the development and enhancement of knowledge is one of the richest of aesthetic moments. The rare teacher who understands and creates the conditions for such moments becomes a seminal image in student memories. Students who participate in a magic moment of learning become and remain a source of delight and pride for the artist—they become, with reverence, *his* or *her* students. But, if education does have an aesthetic dimension, what is it and what is its connection with the ethical constituents of teaching and learning?

The answer is found when learning is conceived of as a shared experience given form by a most special aim or end. The point at which the tensions of struggling individual selves, the distinctions of rank and function flower into a unity of shared meanings that enhance the experience of teacher and student constitutes the end, the target, the bull's eye of the academic process. An understanding of *what* shared meanings enhance our lives indicates *how* they are to be shared, that is, what the ethics of teaching are.

Teacher and learner strive to know how the social, biological, and physical processes that constitute existence can be unified in ways that render our lives more wondrous, more humane, more gratifying—that is, more wise. This communal process, the communal development of wisdom itself, becomes the criterion, the aesthetic measure of the *quality* of teaching and learning. To repeat, the aesthetic objective—the sharing of meanings in ways that promote mutual growth—serves as the criterion to evaluate the *worth* of the means employed to teach. Are the means employed conducive to developing habits that constitute intelligence and confidence in judgment? Do the means render one more sensitive to the beauty of learning from and teaching others? Do we gain a growing appreciation of what actions establish connections with the social, biological, and physical world that sustain becoming?

The "ethics of teaching" is quite clearly, then, the effort to understand and implement those actions that stimulate individual growth through cooperative effort. Teaching is the value-laden moral enterprise par excellence. What does the teacher teach if he or she behaves like a tyrant, cruelly puts down "inadequate" answers, demands adherence to a "party line," or encourages destructive, vindictive competition? In such a situation the students become victims to be used and abused. Given the criterion of enhancement of intellectual and social capacities through conjoint efforts, such behavior is clearly unethical, because it destroys the students' and teacher's opportunities to become more than they are.

As noted, teaching so defined is not a science; it is an art, for it aims at producing shared *qualities* of action. Teaching defined as an art has an objective, and hence contains an intrinsic criterion of value, an intrinsic ethic. The implications of this conception of the ethics of teaching are far reaching. The educator, the teacher, the artist is the moral philosopher—one who seeks to criticize reflectively and thereby *transform values*. To argue that such a function lies outside the proper domain of the educator is to suggest that the most important of human actions—the exercise of informed choice—is not a proper object of inquiry. If a major purpose of education is to promote intelligent, informed, independent judgment, placing taboos on the study of various techniques of evaluating preferences is palpably *unethical*. Is prejudicial "judgment" in matters racial, political, interpersonal, religious, moral, as worthy a mode of decision-making as inquiry into the conditions and consequences of acting on a preference? Education is so value-laden that the question is rhetorical. The educator is decidedly not a value legislator, but it is clearly his or her *duty* to instruct in the art of rendering informed judgments.

Commonsensically, education is only meaningful and worthwhile if it makes a positive difference in conduct. The educator as artist and moral philosopher will necessarily find him or herself engaged in a *Kul-*

turkampf of the greatest importance. As John Dewey succinctly observed, "A culture which permits science to destroy traditional values but which distrusts its power to create new ones is a culture which is destroying itself." The objectives of the educator's task therefore require commitment to engage in the struggle to create the cultural conditions for personal maturity—maturity of judgment. In an era characterized by apathy, mindlessness, and small thinking the task is formidable. Timid accommodation to the authorities that be, retreat into the ivory tower, the fetishism of introspection or mindless revolt are behaviors not worthy of educators, artists. Nietzsche said it well.

> If a man is praised today for living "wisely" or "as a philosopher," it hardly means more than "prudently and apart." Wisdom—seems to the rabble, a kind of escape, a means and trick for getting well out of a wicked game. But the genuine philosopher—as it seems to *us* my friends?—lives "unphilosophically" and "unwisely," above all, *imprudently*, and feels the burden and the duty of a hundred attempts and temptations of life—he risks *himself* constantly, he plays the wicked game. *(Beyond Good and Evil)*

Those committed to democracy, inquiry, and tolerance find themselves in a wicked game indeed. The game of education has to be played hard and smart, for the stakes—freedom—are very high.

The Ethics
of Research

The Scope and Promise of Science

Eugene Wigner
Rockefeller University

The mode of human life has undergone enormous changes from the past to the present. Most of these changes resulted from an increase in human knowledge and understanding, from one or another kind of "invention." Tools have been invented, languages, weapons, and many other things including a new method of creating or controlling progeny. Each of these inventions has introduced enormous changes in the mode of life of man. I believe we are at the threshold of a similar change. Science has done something wonderful for mankind, something really miraculous. It has made a carefree life physically possible. By "carefree life" I mean that everybody can be assured of food, clothing and shelter—literally everybody. This, of course, was not possible before. It is an accomplishment of modern science and technology. It is not yet an accomplished fact all over the Earth but, physically, it is possible.

The question naturally arises whether the new situation we face also had some unfavorable consequences as, I am sure, all the earlier changes had. The unfavorable consequence most apparent to me is that we have to find new purposes of life. The mere maintenance of life for ourselves and our beloved ones is no longer a purpose requiring a true effort. Yet man needs a purpose. I like to quote a Hungarian poet: "The world won't last forever, But while it lives and while it lasts, It builds or rents, but never rests." The question is, therefore, at least in part: how can science contribute further to human happiness now that, what appeared in the past to most people as its main purpose has been accomplished?

Two ways for such a contribution present themselves most naturally. The first is to explore more thoroughly the emotional life of man. When the question of the cause and condition of human happiness is raised, one receives no real answer. It would be good to know more about this question, and I suspect writers and poets now know more about it than scientists.

The other way that science could contribute more to man's spiritual welfare is by extending the pleasure science has furnished scientists to a larger number of people. When I was a high school student we had a club which had a meeting every other week. At each of these, one of us gave a talk on some subject of his choosing, and we had a discussion afterwards. The talk did not cover a new subject or a new discovery. It gave us pleasure anyway, listening to a friend and engaging in a discussion afterwards. It not only gave us pleasure but also strengthened our friendships, and the coherence of our group. I believe that the creation of such clubs, and of other ways to interest people in science, could give pleasure to many people. It might also divert some from the rampant quest for power. It may also lead to important scientific results. Einstein's example shows that one does not have to be a full-time scientist to make an important discovery. He created the special theory of relativity during his employment in the Swiss patent office. I realize, of course, that not all of us have the abilities of Einstein, but I am convinced that a closer relationship with science can give pleasure to many more people than derive pleasure from science now, as it gave pleasure to us in our high school club. When I speak of science, I do not mean only mathematics and physics. There is history, geography, botany and several other subjects.

More in the foreground, probably, is the question of the extent to which society should regulate, and the extent to which it should support, science. As to support, I believe its magnitude should be left more clearly to society at large. The voter should have an opportunity to indicate what fraction of the gross national product should be devoted to science; also, how much should be spent to find a better way to produce energy, or to keep the environment free of pollution. I think a more direct influence of the populace on the magnitude of the support of science would bring science, and the understanding of its benefits, closer to the common man.

As to the next question, the question of the regulation of science, my views are probably those of the majority of our colleagues. The subject matter of science should not be regulated. Everyone should be free to pursue his cognitive interests. The regulation of the subject matter of science was attempted in the case of Galileo. It led to very unhappy results. I find it very disturbing that some who abhor the impediments put in Galileo's way now want to forbid some areas of investigation. I think it is arrogant for a group, particularly a self-chosen group, to attempt to regulate or censor the scientific, that is, the cognitive, endeavors of others. How the informations gained by science should be made available to the public is, on the other hand, a very difficult question. To cope with it properly requires a dissemination of the information, and this is difficult to achieve to the appropriate extent. I, for instance, am unable to find out how radio time is distributed—a question, the answer to which all of us should have access.

As to the use of scientific results, I agree with those who say that the use—in contrast to the discovery or "creation"—of scientific results is a responsibility of all people. If the people of this country had voted against the use of nuclear weapons, after having access to both opinions for some time, the weapons should not have been used. This is, I believe, the responsibility of the common man: not in limiting the subject of research (as long as this leads only to cognitive results that do not harm anybody), but by limiting the application of the knowledge. In particular, I am deeply disturbed when I hear passionate arguments that weapons research should not be undertaken. My conviction that this should not be controlled by a self-appointed group was much strengthened when one of the participants of the other side boasted at a Pugwash meeting that the first hydrogen bomb explosion was triggered by them, not by the United States. If there were perfect peace in the world, weapons research would not be needed. As long as our country and freedom must be defended, I stand up for such defense and for research in the weapons of defense, even if this makes me unpopular.

The Ethics of Research:
A Case History and Its Lessons

John L. Horn
University of Denver

Our history is a record of an arduous, often faltering, struggle to expand human freedoms—freedom from the wants and deprivations imposed by Nature and freedom from the subjugation of one people by another. This record is strewn with examples of restrictions of reasonable freedoms being imposed by people of one persuasion for reasons that are said to be well founded. At their base most such restrictions are limits on freedom of inquiry. In the objective light of historical perspective, restrictions on freedom of inquiry are usually found to be, in effect, power politics exercised in loyalty to one set of beliefs to the detriment of other beliefs that may hold equal, or greater, promise for improvement of the human condition. In the modern period, in such places as the U.S., beliefs that constitute a prevailing dogma in this sense are those specifying that the rights of an individual are inviolate above all else. Nothing can be done that could possibly jeopardize a particular individual even if other individuals, considered collectively, are put in jeopardy or are not advanced by failure to do something promising. Always powerful in the U.S., this dogma has gained exceptional strength since the 1960's. Today, the belief is the raison d'etre for a monstrous collection of codifications and forms, committees and agencies, one on top of the other, duplicating and communicating, each in its way intended to ensure what are called the rights of individuals. What follows is a tale about a research proposal that fell into a tiny part of this maelstrom of bureaucratic activity.

The story begins with a request for money the writer submitted in 1974 to the Small Grants Section (SGS) of the National Institute of Mental Health (NIMH). The proposal grew out of efforts by the applicant and Raymond B. Cattell to construct tests that would be more nearly culture-fair than existing tests and yet would measure important aspects of intelligence. Some 25 distinct tests had been constructed. They had been tried out in small pilot samples, but they had never been studied in any systematic way.

In 1968 Professor Cattell suggested to Harry E. Anderson, Jr. that our experimental tests might be of use in a large study of academic achievement which Anderson was then conducting. The tests might help, Cattell suggested, to describe academic achievement in terms of abilities not taught very much in school. Anderson apparently saw some possibilities in this regard, for he used the tests in a part of his study conducted in 1968-69. In all, some 624 middle-class urban white children and 209 lower-class rural black children took the tests.

Roughly four years after the tests had been given, and after Anderson had used the results for the purposes of his study, the applicant arranged to obtain the item data of the tests — i.e., a score to indicate correct or incorrect for each item of every test. A limited amount of other data was also obtained. This included ethnic group, age, grade point average in different school semesters, and questionnaire measures of personality traits. No names were obtained, nor any other information that would allow for direct identification of subjects. Some preliminary analyses were done with the data to establish that there was satisfactory item variance and that the subsamples were comparable in terms of age and year in school.

Such a sample of data is in some respects ideal for studying whether or not items and tests can measure in much the same way in groups from quite diverse subcultural communities. In particular the sample is appropriate for studying possibilities of constructing culture-fair tests. That, in essence, is what was proposed in the research application. A number of itemetric and statistical analyses were to be conducted to help determine whether a test could be constructed to measure important intellectual abilities for which there is a minimum of difference between children from upper and lower social, economic and educational classes.

In sum, then, the research proposal was to do analyses on data that had been gathered some five years previously by another investigator. Because the data had already been gathered, the cost of doing the research was considerably less than the cost for a comparable study in which the data had yet to be gathered.

The SGS Review Committee that evaluated the proposal judged it to be quite adequate on scientific and technical grounds. Considering only these matters the proposal could have been approved and ranked for funding at a level that, at that time, probably would have resulted in funding. The proposal was rejected, however, for reasons pertaining to the ethics of research.

The letter of rejection is not precisely clear on this point, but the following excerpts from that letter indicate the nature of the reasoning said to justify the final decision:

1. The reviewers were seriously concerned about the potential risks both to the subjects themselves in this study and to the classes of persons represented by the subjects. In regards to the former, no information was given in the proposal that the children's parents gave consent to have their children's test performance used for research purposes of this kind. . . .

2. Even more seriously, the reviewers felt that this study was liable to potential social and political misuse. They were well aware that you had intentionally confounded race and class in an attempt to prevent invidious comparisons between groups, but given today's climate, the reviewers were not sure that any precautions could be successful in that respect. Even you, while generally careful throughout the application, do in a few spots refer to the groups as the minority group and majority group children, and, in one place, to black and white children. The reviewers felt that others would be likely to be less careful than you in pointing out the many ways in which these two samples differed. . . .

(Stephanie B. Stolz, Chief, Small Grants Section, March 26, 1974)

Thus it seems that the proposal was judged adversely, if not rejected, because it was believed that the subjects would be (or would have been) put at risk, that somehow this risk could be eliminated or reduced by presenting evidence that the parents approved (presumably the referent here was the original testing, but there is some suggestion also that the reference is to the analyses of the proposal) and that the applicant had not provided proof of parental consent.[1] In a letter that contains a number of inaccurate characterizations of the proposed study, and was intended to explain the rejection decision to Congressional inquirers, this last reason for the decision was stated rather forcefully.

It was the judgment of the Mental Health Small Grant Committee that information was lacking on whether the parents had given consent. The reviewers felt that this was critically important information in a study of this topic.

This letter went out on November 5, 1974 over the signature of Thomas F. A. Plaut, Acting Director of N.I.M.H., addressed to U.S. Representative Edward Madigan, and again on January 2, 1975 over the signature of Bertram S. Brown, Director of N.I.M.H., addressed to U.S. Senator Adlai Stevenson.

One issue adumbrated by these remarks came to be known as that of "secondary analyses." Is it ethical for a researcher to analyze data that were obtained by another investigator, at another time, by procedures that are now judged to be unethical? The issue is interesting in this case partly because the data already were in hand at the time the proposal was submitted. It is interesting also because N.I.M.H. directives suggesting that parental consent should be obtained for gathering research data of this kind had not been in effect at the time the testing was done.

Also at issue here are questions pertaining to risks to research subjects and informed consent. Apparently the reviewers of this proposal believed that something undesirable would happen, or had already happened, to the subjects of this research. Apparently they also believed that it was unethical to conduct research of this kind without obtaining the consent of one who presumably knew about, or could understand an explanation of, the possible ways in which the children would be harmed by the research.

But it seems that the major reason for rejection was a belief that the results from the study might be used or misused (mainly by people other than the applicant) to the detriment of a class of people believed to be represented in the sampling. Apparently the belief was that the harm that could be done by the study was not so much to the subjects, as such, as it was to a class of subjects. It is implied more than it is stated explicitly, but it seems that the class of people it is believed would be harmed is that represented by the black children. This came to be known as the "class risk" principle, and will be so identified here. The issue is interesting here partly because the research was directed at minimizing test differences between the black and the white children. But it seems that the reviewers reasoned that nevertheless there would be differences and these would reflect unfavorably on the black group. Thus apparently the reviewers assumed that the results of the study could be well predicted before the study was done and that an undesirable impact of the results could also be anticipated.

These reasons for rejection were stated again in a letter sent on August 9, 1974 by Katherine Duncan of the Institutional Relations Branch (IRB) of the Division of Research Grants of the National Institutes of Health (NIH). This agency has the authority to cut off NIH funds to a university as a whole. The letter was addressed to the Dean of the Graduate College and Chairman of the Human Rights Review Committee of the applicant's university. Again there are some inaccurate characterizations of the proposal in this letter, but these are not essential to an understanding of the reasons cited for rejection of the proposal. The policing functions of the IRB, as well as reasons for rejection of the proposal, are indicated in Duncan's letter:

One of the chief responsibilities of this office is the negotiation and administration of institutional assurances for the protection of human subjects in work supported by the Department of Health, Education, and Welfare.

Following Council meetings last March, an application from the University of Denver was called to our attention. (There followed the name of the applicant's proposal.) . . .

Our office is interested in conveying to the committee responsible for the review of all such applications (i.e., the Denver University Human Rights Review Committee) the concerns expressed by the reviewers regarding human subjects.

In general they were concerned about the investigator's apparent failure to consider the probable social consequences of the study. (There then followed the statement numbered 2 above from Stolz's letter of rejection.)

This letter thus not only reiterates the class risk issue but also rather clearly points to the general question about whether or not, or to what extent, an investigator is ethically obligated to anticipate probable social consequences of his research. This will be referred to as the anticipation of social consequences issue.

Duncan's letter ended with the following assurances.

This letter is only for purposes of conveying concerns expressed by the reviewers and is not intended to direct either the institution's or the investigator's research aims.

This disclaimer, coupled with the previous parts of the letter, raises an issue having to do with a distinction between informing and threat. One understanding of letters such as Duncan's is that they simply call attention to a problem in the treatment of subjects and thus provide feedback, indicating bases for decision, to local review committees. Another understanding is that such letters constitute threats to the institution and/or to the investigator. Funds to an institution have been cut off for what are regarded as failures to conform with directives from Federal agencies (e g , in affirmative action cases), and thus it is not unreasonable to suppose that letters such as Duncan's are reminders of this possibility. Also, of course, the letter is a criticism of a faculty member directed to an administrator of his university. There is nothing in Duncan's letter to discourage a Dean from placing it in the employee's file and treating it as relevant evidence for considerations relating to promotion and tenure. Thus it is not unlikely that an applicant would feel that such a letter was a threat to his freedom of inquiry—i.e., freedom to pursue a line of research he thought was important enough to justify a request for support funds.

Other ethical issues are raised by this research proposal, its review, and subsequent developments, but the above are sufficient to provide a basis for subsequent discussion. By way of summary they can be briefly listed as the issues of:

Secondary analysis
Risks to research subjects
Informed consent
Anticipation of social consequences
Information-threat

It should be added here, also, that a major issue pertains to whose ethics are being, or should be, under scrutiny—those of the researcher or those of the evaluator of the researcher.

The applicant's reaction to the letter of rejection (i.e., Stolz's letter) was very mild. He had anticipated most of the objections raised in this letter and thought that probably the decision meant only that the review committee had not read his statements on the questions at issue. Concerning the class risk issue, for example, he had written in Form MH-441 that:

It is possible that there will be differences in the subsample means for tests or for factors developed from the tests. In this respect, it should be noted that a principal objective of the study is to develop measures for which these differences are kept at a minimum. Judging from previous results, however, a likely outcome . . . is that the minority-group means will be lower than the means for the majority group. It is carefully pointed out in the proposal that it is logically incorrect to infer inherent racial or immutable ethnic differences from such results.

In previous publications (e.g., Horn, Bressler, Jensen & Scriven, 1972) the investigator has been forthright in pointing to this logical difficulty in other data upon which claims for racial differences have been based. Hence it is reasonable to expect that the investigator will be sensitive to the need to, and careful to, ensure that results are not misinterpreted. Nevertheless, it must be recognized that some who read or hear about the results from this study (if, indeed, they do indicate differences between the subsamples) may try to use the results to make invidious comparisons between populations which they (the users) believe to be represented by the sampling. There is no way to ensure against this unfortunate use of the results short of preventing the analyses or suppressing publication or distorting the results. An important fact to notice in this respect, however, is that any such use of results will not have the sanction of the scientist who reported the results. This is important because it denies the stamp of authority to the user who would present a racist argument. This both reduces the probability that the results will be used in this inappropriate way and makes such use less potent if it does occur.

Concerning risks to the individual subjects, as such, he pointed out that:

The data to be analysed were gathered in 1969 by another investigator. . . . It would seem that any risk to the individuals . . . would have occurred prior to now, and thus no further risk of this kind will be occasioned by the study here proposed. . . . The data-gathering procedures used at the time were those generally in use. Today, such procedures might be questioned on ethical grounds, but it is academic to consider this question in respect to the proposed study. The only questions now to be considered are those pertaining to analyses and reporting of data presently available. No names are available. Hence, it is impossible to use the results of any particular subject in a way that would harm (or help) that individual. . . .

In summing up the overall risks and benefits of the study he had reasoned that:

The results can be of considerable benefit to society, particularly in the long run—i.e., recognizing that this study can help to lay the foundation for other studies. There is no doubt that it is desirable to obtain better means for understanding the capabilities of children. When used wisely, diagnostic instruments can be of very notable value in facilitating a child's development. There is little doubt but that the need for such improved understanding of a child's capabilities is most pronounced in efforts to help children who exist under deprived conditions.

The risks to the individuals of the subsamples are minimal and, in any case, have been realized.

The risk to a class, or to classes, of individuals cannot be established with any accuracy, but the probability of such risk cannot be regarded as zero. . . .

While the risks thus appear to be academic and perhaps remote, the potential benefits seem to be real and present. The possibilities for helping minority-group persons, as well as majority-group persons, are genuine and the benefit could be considerable.

The data have been gathered. The cost (in subject time and effort, as well as in public support of research) of doing analyses on data already gathered is many times smaller than the cost of gathering new data.

... it seems that most of the arguments from ethical considerations are on the side of encouraging the study rather than discouraging it.

As noted before, in her letter of rejection Stolz had stated that the form containing the above statements had not been returned "by the time of the initial review group's meeting. Thus, the reviewers simply lacked information." It seemed possible, therefore, that the proposal rejection mainly reflected a fact that the review committee had lacked information on some points and had reasoned that the safest course of action was simply to reject. Considering the question of whose ethics are at issue, it is interesting that apparently neither the review committee nor the officials of SGS thought to delay decision on the proposal until the form MH-441 could be found or the applicant could be phoned to obtain the information that was deemed to be lacking. Interesting also in this respect is the fact that the MH-441 form was in hand at the time the letter of rejection was written.

Be these matters as they are, the applicant's initial response to Stolz's letter of rejection was simply to let the matter pass. It wasn't until Duncan's letter (from the Institutional Relations Branch) arrived with the University Dean that the applicant became really concerned and the enormity of possible threats to freedom of inquiry began to emerge. Given the applicant's rather careful efforts to deal with the class risk issue, one can well understand his reaction to Duncan's reference to ". . . the investigator's apparent failure to consider the probable (N.B. not possible, but probable) social consequences of the study." And other elements of unfairness also contributed to a reaction of anger at this time. This emotion "charged" the applicant's motivation to look again at the basis for rejection of his proposal. The resulting reconsideration suggested that the rejection might possibly mean that granting agencies, or individuals with influence in such agencies, were attempting to force research institutions and individual researchers to abstain from certain kinds of controversial research — in particular, research concerned with racial or ethnic differences. Arthur Jensen's work on this topic was still very much in the news and it seems possible that any research that had a semblance of relationship to the Jensen hypothesis[2] was being branded, almost reflexly, as taboo. Also, although the applicant was a tenured professor and did not feel that Duncan's letter to his Dean was personally threatening, it seemed possible that such letters could be construed as threatening to the individual researcher and thus could represent a governmental threat to academic freedom and unwarranted interference in the affairs of the academy.

With these as the principal concerns, the applicant wrote first to Duncan to ask for clarification of her letter and then to a few well known and highly respected colleagues to lay out the case and ask if the applicant was over-reacting to an unfavorable outcome of his request for research support. The colleagues he contacted were:

Raymond B. Cattell, a mentor and co-worker, and a person who had recently written an important book on ethics and science (Cattell, 1972),

Stuart W. Cook, Chairman of an American Psychological Association (APA) Committee on Ethics, a committee that had just completed an extensive write-up of a code of ethics for the profession,

Lloyd G. Humphreys, a mentor, and a person noted for his good judgment and forthright stands on controversial issues within the profession (psychology) and the academy, and

Kenneth Purcell, Chairman of the applicant's department, and a person who had been active in various facets of APA affairs.

No reply came from Duncan's office,[3] but all of the colleagues replied. Without exception, they were critical of the positions taken by the SGS review committee and by the NIMH and NIH officials who had considered the case. This was the dominant reaction, also, of colleagues with whom the applicant very informally discussed the case.

The four colleagues who were contacted considered the general issues listed above as well as some of the particular aspects of the proposal and its treatment.

In dealing with the specifics of the proposal, as such, Stuart Cook considered questions about DHEW authority for the actions that were taken, as well as the ethical principles on which these actions were supposedly based. He wrote:

The statistical analyses you proposed to do—i.e., your research proposal—did not put the individual human subjects at risk and, hence, informed consent was not required. . . .

If the HEW action implies that the data cannot be used in later analyses because informed consent was not obtained five years earlier by the original investigator, this represents a highly questionable and, in my view, entirely unwarranted extrapolation of the informed consent principle.

. . . the potential misrepresentation of your results by others is not legitimate grounds for withholding support to an otherwise meritorious research project, and the HEW guidelines for protection of human subjects provide no authority for such action. . . . a reading of the HEW guidelines will make it clear that the Small Grants review panel had no authority to raise this issue in reviewing your application.

The letter to your university Committee on Human Rights Review was an even more serious error. The HEW guidelines establish the authority of the Institutional Relation Branch to cut off funds to an entire organization. In view of this, the letter from Dr. Duncan, despite the disclaimer in the last paragraph, could only be interpreted by your Committee as saying that the University's eligibility for future funds was threatened if they approved future research in which bad social consequences might follow from distortions by others of an investigator's results. This would have been appalling under any circumstances; the fact that HEW has no authority either in law or administrative regulations, to attempt to control research on these grounds makes it doubly so.

To summarize, it is my opinion that you have taken a responsible and ethical position with regard to human subjects and the representatives of HEW have taken an unthoughtful and unauthorized action in relation to your study proposal.

Each of the colleagues expressed concern about any policy that required an investigator to anticipate his results and the social consequences of his study, and to curtail his investigation on this basis. They were particularly concerned about the application of such a policy in the case in question. In a letter to Louis Wienckowski, Kenneth Purcell expressed this concern as follows.

. . . When we begin to criticize research proposals, not just for unnecessary and unwarranted risk to the subjects in an experiment (a wholly legitimate basis for criticism), but also for inadequate consideration and forecasting of probable social consequences involving groups of people not even in the experiment, we are indeed opening up a Pandora's box of censorship possibilities.

It is one thing for a group of molecular biologists to suggest a voluntary embargo on certain types of experimentation quite narrowly focused on specific health hazards potentially raised by genetically altered bacteria. It is quite another thing for a funding agency to refer vaguely to "social consequences" and "today's climate." I would hope that we have more faith in our people and in the public scientific process than to adopt the attitude which says "There are things which ought not to be investigated because we may not be able to live with the information we get."

Cattell put his position on this matter in terms of an example.

Let me quote a few pages from what a contemporary citizen's diary might look like if the present policy of Washington had existed at the time of Michael Faraday.

"We all know that Michael Faraday's application for a government grant in 1821 to pursue the study of electro-magnetism was turned down because of the investigator's apparent failure to consider the probable social consequences of the study. Obviously he had not foreseen the invention of the dynamo would enable submarines to prowl the ocean and drown thousands of innocent people, or that the magneto would be indispensable in airplanes to bomb cities into total destruction. Writing tonight by my feeble candle in this freezing house, I, nevertheless, feel grateful that 'given today's climate of opinion,' the government grants committee promptly stopped his research. . . ."

The issues of class risk often merge in the present example with those pertaining to whether a researcher can or should anticipate the social consequences of his study and not do the study if the estimation indicates unfavorable outcome. Thus, issues in regard to possible misuse by others are merged with issues dealing with possible social consequences and class risk. Yet these three sets of issues are logically distinct. For example, it is logically possible that a course of action may be associated with considerable, and highly probable, risk to a particular class of people, and for the social consequences of this risk to be still judged favorable and for the actions to be judged ethical. The drafting of young men to fight to their death in a war against Nazi Germany may be taken as a case in point. Informed consent was not obtained in this "experiment," presumably because many of the subjects would not participate and it would be unfair to take only volunteers. In other cases the consent of the individuals of the class at risk cannot be sought because the social benefit of the activity would thereby be lost.

The building of the atomic bomb to use against the Japanese illustrates an extreme of this possibility. Informed consent was not obtained from the Japanese partly because to seek such consent may have given the Japanese additional encouragement to build their own bomb, which, had they built a bomb, would have rendered our bomb less effective as a means for bringing the war to a successful (ethically sound) conclusion. The building of the bomb is also an example of a case where the scientist might be called upon to anticipate uses to which he would not put his results but which others might. It is clear that the social consequences of research might be adverse even when no particular class of people was put at any greater risk than another class. But in the case here under consideration the social consequences that the investigator was required to anticipate were uses of his results by others to bring about harm to a class of people, and so the three sets of issues tend to merge.

In some of his comments on these matters Humphreys reasoned that:

The question as to whether the groups to which a subject belongs is put at risk by the research is a judgmental matter, and therefore a question that cannot be answered automatically. Nevertheless, it is a question that can be answered more rationally than was done by the study section responsible for the decision on John Horn's research application. The judgment should be made on the dimensions of purpose and competence of the investigator. Given competence, purpose is the important variable. If the motives are forensic rather than scientific, the grant should not be funded. On the other hand, the possibility or even the probability that someone other than the investigator might misrepresent the research findings is completely unacceptable in a democratic society.

Cook cited two discussions in the APA Ethical Principles (the code of ethics prepared by his committee) as dealing with general issues in this regard.

One discussion occurs on page 97; it deals with the research subject's concern not to contribute to the compilation of derogatory information about a social group to which he belongs. It is not truly relevant to your analyses of test results from black and from white subjects since you are explicit about the irrelevance of your analyses to the matter of racial differences in intelligence. However, since I suspect that this was the thinking of the Small Grants review panel, and, subsequently, of the Institutional Relations Branch, let me review this point, nevertheless.

To take a clear case, suppose an investigator was using tests of "crystallized intelligence" to study genetically-based racial differences in learning potential; assume that he was convinced that such tests were legitimate for such purpose while the children (or their advisors) did not agree. The discussion suggests that consent based on knowledge of the purpose of the research should be obtained. However, it says, also, that in some such value conflicts society's need for knowledge should prevail. . . .

A second facet of the potential-misuse issue is discussed on page 102. This discussion urges the investigator to consider the danger of ill-intentioned distortion of his research results . . . he should feel responsible to anticipate and prevent misinterpretations of his work and to combat distortions of it if and when they occur. I feel you have given ample evidence of being sensitive to this problem and have gone through exactly the kind of value analysis suggested in the "Ethical Principles" discussion.

Underlying these various considerations of the ethics of research in this case are the subtle forces adumbrated with the expression "given today's climate" in Stolz's letter of rejection. The expression apparently refers to a belief that whereas it might be reasonable at some point in history to have research that might indicate racial or ethnic differences in a valued attribute, such research at the present time will produce undesirable social consequences of sufficient magnitude to render it unethical to do the research. But it is questionable whether research results indicating that one racial or ethnic group is different from another have any substantial effect on prevailing opinion (some people are persuaded that others are inferior without recourse to data of any kind, much less research data), or if they do, that this effect is detrimental at all, or systematically detrimental to any particular class of individuals. The belief that such results will be detrimental to anyone is thus an opinion held by some people but not by others. The belief is akin in this respect to a belief about the efficacy of Keynesian economics. It is by no means an ethical precept or principle. When viewed in this light the decision about the proposal in question can be seen to be political rather than ethical. That is, it represents the fact that exponents of one opinion on which there is controversy were "in power" and thus able to enforce the provisions of that opinion, much as the Democrats in power in the 1930s were able to enforce the provisions of Keynesian economics (the New Deal).

This aspect of the problem was confronted head-on in some of Cattell's comments. He wrote:

The attempt to discourage research in scientifically important and legitimate direction on the ground that some lobby or minority political group will strongly object is not to be tolerated by dedicated scientists in a mature culture. . . . The authority which forced Copernicus to postpone publication until his deathbed, and the Inquisition which threatened Galileo with torture, began with equally gentle statements about not being "sure that any precautions would be successful in preventing others from" misinterpreting religious—or in this case political—implications. . . . Admittedly, these exponents of the view that science must shape its findings to religious and political "climates" are at present small, but they are undoubtedly here. . . . And already, if they infiltrate committees, they can evidently cut off research grants of a scientist of outstanding potency in contributing to his science.

Humphreys also developed some of the political aspects of the matter in a letter sent for publication in *Science*. He wrote:

. . . the borrowed data were highly suitable for Dr. Horn's research purposes and were less expensive by a factor of more than 100 to 1 than the alternative of obtaining new data. . . . He pointed out quite explicitly the many other differences between the two groups, but these differences in toto were directly relevant to his research purposes. . . . The letter to the University of Denver's Committee noted that Dr. Horn had been careful in this regard, but this would not prevent "others from being less careful. . . ." Apparently if others can misinterpret one's research, the research should not be undertaken. . . .

. . . The record indicates that 1984 has arrived ten years early in the Department of Health, Education, and Welfare. . . .

. . . Another term to describe 1984 is Fascism. It does not matter whether it be imposed from the left, the right, or the middle. It does not matter what the claimed motives are. Inability to do research on Jews in Hitler's Germany because someone might find something good to say about the data is fundamentally no different from inability to do research on blacks in the United States because someone might find something bad to say about the data.

Some of the reactions to this letter may also indicate the political nature of the questions at issue. *Science* refused to publish the letter on the ground that it was an over-reaction to a mere refusal to approve a grant request. A very similar letter was published in an APA newsletter titled the *Monitor* (February 1975), however, where it generated considerable response, most of which focused on Humphrey's characterization of the DHEW actions as Fascist. Michael Schwartz, for example, who was a member of the panel which reviewed the proposal, wrote a letter, also carried in the *Monitor,* in which he argued that:

. . . Humphreys' decision to describe the outcome of the concern and confusion of the Committee and that of HEW officials as "Fascism" is both unfortunate and inappropriate for several reasons.

He has confused the rather bumbling processes of bureaucracy in an essentially democratic system with the swift and murderous efficiency of bureaucracies in totalitarian systems in which appeals such as his own could not exist or most certainly would not be heard.

The use of the label is unfortunate in that it represents a thoroughly unwarranted attack upon some of his colleagues who have worked diligently to protect the integrity of scientific research and the peer review process and have done so most successfully.

To which Humphreys replied (also in the *Monitor*):

. . . I do not believe that the term [1984-Fascism] is either unfortunate or inappropriate. If 1984-type actions result from confusion, the results are nevertheless Fascistic. . . . I realize full well that a number of social scientists have recommended a moratorium on research involving minority groups. These recommendations have been mentioned regularly in letters from personnel in HEW to Dr. Horn. This suggests to me that there is a good deal of well-meaning but nonetheless 1984-type thinking in the minds of many social scientists.

I was unable to pinpoint the responsibility for their 1984-style thinking in HEW at the time I wrote the letter. I am equally uncertain today. But if I were to offer my best guess, responsibility would lie primarily with HEW attorneys. . . . (Please note that you could have rebelled against the signals you were getting from HEW.) I believe that HEW attorneys are very intent on protecting their agency from as much criticism as possible whether that criticism is justified or not. They are not primarily concerned with the support of research. Secondly, they have naive and unsupportable notions about the potential ill effects of research on human subjects.

When the basis for rejection of the proposal is regarded as largely political and the process whereby the proposal was rejected on supposed ethical grounds is said to mainly reflect bureaucratic bumbling, then questions about the ethics of review procedures are brought to the fore. Cattell brought some of these questions into focus.

John L. Horn

I think the matter should definitely be raised when these people shout about "ethical considerations" as to "whose ethics you are talking about?" The fundamental weakness of their position is that they do not have a fundamental ethical postulate from which they make their inferences, whereas we do. . . . The question runs through both psychology and medicine, and takes the practical form of "how much risk to a patient or subject should we be prepared to take in order to ensure a probability for real gain for mankind in general?"

Following up on this point, Cattell argued that the scientific community needs to be better organized in respect to the ethical positions it takes, as derived from scientific principles, a position he had developed extensively in his book of 1972 on this topic, *Beyondism: A New Morality from Science*. In his letter he put the matter thus:

[There are] organized positions by both, say, Humanists and Catholics, in a quite different way, but you have no organized position or source of pressure and values from a more modern, rational set of postulates. Most of the presently organized religions definitely take the position that you must take no risk whatever. As we know, this would have ruled out not only most medical advances, but even the discovery of America which was undertaken at great risk to certain Portuguese seamen. You will remember also that the Church opposed completely the dissection of human cadavers, and put Vesalius under the ban of stopping his experiments or going to jail. I am increasingly convinced that people who have struggled through toward what is essentially a Beyondism position should get organized in some practical way.

As noted before, the applicant was particularly incensed by Duncan's letter mainly because he believed it to represent a quite unfair handling of the case. The essence of ethicality is fairness. Thus to argue that actions stemming from HEW were unfair is to say they were unethical. In respect to this charge the applicant's reply to the Duncan letter stated in part that:

On the matter of unfairness, . . . I wonder how you could have read the relevant aspects of my proposal (and then write that you) ". . . were concerned about the investigator's apparent failure to consider the probable social consequences of the study." Such a statement seems unfair when considered in the context of my discussion on pages 17 and 18.[4] Such statements hardly indicate *failure* to consider probable social consequences. Had you read this part of my proposal when you wrote your letter?

You write, also, that . . . "no mention was made of obtaining consent from the parents to have their children's tests used for research purposes of this kind." In the proposal and in my statements in the form titled "Protection of Human Subjects" I made it quite clear that the data had (in 1969) been gathered far away (in Georgia) by another investigator (Harry Anderson) well before the time I wrote my proposal (as well as before some of the rules imposed in respect to my proposal had been enacted) . . . in fact the only identification I had for subjects was a number. Your letter implies that I could have and should have obtained the consent of parents under such conditions. Is this fair?

It is interesting in this respect also that in the various DHEW letters and guidelines and directives concerned with human rights in research there is virtually no mention of the rights of the researcher (the implicit assumption being, perhaps, that he is not human) or the class which he might represent. No provisions are made to enable the researcher to defend himself against charges that his research is unethical. There are no provisions for appeal—i.e., no way to have a rehearing of what the researcher regards as an unfavorable decision and to overthrow a decision found to be in error. In fact, in the present case, as will be shown, DHEW officials were moved to acknowledge that the rejection had been improper. But when the applicant asked if this meant that his grant was thereby approved he was told that he could resubmit his proposal and it would again go through the review process (then with a new SGS review panel).

The only chance a researcher has to defend himself against the charges that his research is unethical (which charges, as noted, are sent to officials of his university, and who knows where else?) is in his responses to the questionnaire previously referred to as form MH-441. This questionnaire is one of those of the "when did you stop beating your wife" variety. The questions ask the investigator to, in effect, furnish evidence that might prove him guilty of unethicality and then to make out his defense for any case that might be filed against him on the basis of the evidence he has presented. This quality is illustrated by some of the previously cited responses to form MH-441 in the present case. Although the reviewers apparently did not see these responses, charges of unethicality, particularly in respect to the class risk issue, might well have resulted from a reading of the researcher's development of ethical issues in respect to research of the kind he was conducting.

In short, the questionnaire requires that the defendant give evidence against himself. Both it and the entire review process involve an implicit assumption that the researcher might be guilty of unethicality and put the burden of proof on him, in advance of hearing, that he is not guilty of whatever charge might be leveled against him. When viewed in the abstract such procedures would be judged as unfair, and thus unethical (and probably illegal) by almost any standard. Yet apparently such procedures are accepted as ethical in deciding on questions of the ethicality of research.

About the same time that this situation was developing another rather similar case emerged. In this instance the proposal to SGS by an American researcher was to study curiosity in native-born English children in comparison with immigrant children from India, Pakistan, the West Indies, and Africa. The proposal was rejected partly, it seems, for reasons related to the design and theory of the study but also for reasons pertaining to the ethics of the research. Concern was expressed about the potential harm to immigrant children in England if the findings indicated that the immigrants were less curious than the native-borns. It was argued that educational authorities might use the findings to the detriment of immigrant children.

Thus again the SGS review committee invoked the arguments of class risk, as well as those suggesting that the investigator had an obligation to anticipate the results and the social consequences of the proposed research. The arguments in respect to this latter are particularly interesting in this case because the investigator's hypothesis was that the immigrant children would be more curious, rather than less curious, than the native-borns. The SGS review committee thus made a judgment about results that was the opposite of the investigator's anticipation of outcome and used this judgment as a basis for arguing that the research was unethical. The investigator presented a theoretical basis for this hypothesis of the proposal, but no such basis was presented by the SGS review committee. Again there is the question of who was arguing from the more sound ethical basis, the researcher or those evaluating the researcher's ethics?

This last-mentioned case, as well as the one previously described in some detail, attracted considerable attention, particularly within the academic-scientific community. A Committee for the Protection of Human Subjects (CPHS) at the University of California, Berkeley, under the chairmanship of Herbert Phillips, used the two cases as examples in work directed at improving the codification of principles for use in evaluation of the ethics of research. Several letters to DHEW officials, to scientific organizations, and to CPHS committees (of hospitals and other institutions, as well as universities) grew out of the work of this committee. Similarly, the CPHS committee at the University of Oregon generated letters of inquiry and concern that went out to people in government positions and to other people who might have interests or responsibilities relating to the ethics of research. Humphreys' letter to *Science* also went to Senators Charles Percy and Adlai Stevenson and Representative Edward Madigan. Stevenson and Madigan are known to have followed up on Humphreys' letter with inquiries directed at appointed officials within DHEW. The director and acting director responded to these inquiries, and these responses generated further inquiries. Copies of many of the letters from these various sources converged toward the administrators of the Small Grants Section (in particular Stolz and Wienckowski).

In general it seems safe to conclude that there was rather widespread response from the scientific community to the SGS handling of the two cases, and that this response had an impact within DHEW. In letters from NIMH and NIH there were indications that as a result of these cases there had been work on developing new policies for dealing with ethical issues. For example, in a letter dated April 10, 1975, Wienckowski and Stolz stated that considerations of the Horn case "has had a clarifying function, both for staff and for the review committee members. The staff have developed new procedures for dealing with applications on which the review committee raises ethical questions."

It seems likely that the various inquiries and protests from the scientific community may have forced DHEW to reconsider not only policy related to research ethics generally, but also decisions such as that made in respect to Horn's proposal.

At any rate, for whatever reasons, by December of 1974 it had been "discovered" that there had been no DHEW policies on class risk or anticipation of social consequences at the time proposals were rejected on the basis of such policies. In a letter dated December 9, 1974 Wienckowski wrote to Horn to explain that:

Of all the issues surrounding this application, I know you are most concerned about the Committee's comment that you had apparently failed to consider the possible social consequences of the study, and the potential for social and political misuse of the data. At the time your application was reviewed, the Mental Health Small Grant Committee and the Committee's staff thought that DHEW regulations required the peer review committees to determine whether a project might entail possible risk to the class of which the subjects were members. This, however, was a mistake by the committee. This particular risk is not, technically, a part of DHEW regulations on the protection of human subjects.

He went on to assure that:

We have recently discussed with the Small Grant Committee the issues raised by your application and the general question of risks to the class of which the subjects are members, and we have explained to them that such a risk is not included within the DHEW guidelines. The reviewers now understand the DHEW policy.

But this did not entirely decide these matters within DHEW. For one thing, Wienckowski also stated that

I am sure that you are aware, however, that this kind of risk [i.e., class risk] has been a matter of strong concern and continuing discussion among social scientists, and there is a possibility that it will be covered in some proposed rulemaking in the near future. . . .

Moreover, communications issuing from the DHEW Office for Protection from Research Risks (OPRR), D. T. Chalkley, Director, were somewhat counter to Wienckowski's assertion that class risk was not a part of the regulations. Chalkley's letter of February 20, 1975 stated that:

It appeared at one point that we might be near some internal determination that "class risks," as distinct from "individual risks" would not be a factor in recommending unfavorable actions.

It now seems agreed that we should not impose artificial restrictions on the criticisms of peer groups in this area. . . . In reviewing applications it is the position of NIMH that all types of risks, both to the individual and to the class or classes to which he belongs, may reasonably be taken into consideration.

This opinion is particularly significant because the OPRR presumably has the authority to enforce ethical policy in regards to research throughout NIH, although Stolz and Wienckowski had indicated in conversations with the author that such policy within NIMH generally and within SGS in particular could be somewhat different from that of NIH. In any case at the time of this writing it seems that in at least some parts of DHEW research review, committees are left on their own to either use or not use a class risk criterion of research ethicality. This implies that such committees are left on their own to assess the results likely to emerge from a study yet to be conducted and to judge the possible social consequences of the estimated results.

Wienckowski also commented on the information-threat issues in his letter of 9 December. On this score, too, it at first appeared that there had been a reversal of the policy that had led to Duncan's letter to the Dean. Wienckowski wrote:

The other issue that has arisen in connection with the handling of your [i.e., Horn's] application is the procedure of having the staff of Office for Protection from Research Risks write to the applicant's institutional review committee, when an initial review group calls attention to a problem in the treatment of subjects in application. The intent of these letters has always been as a means for providing feedback to the local review committees, and we are astounded and dismayed to learn that the letters have been used in some instances as negative evidence in faculty members' personnel files. We have previously had several discussions with Dr. Chalkley's office about these letters. . . . We have urged Dr. Chalkley to send a memo to the field decrying this practice and pointing out that ethical responsibilities are shared by the investigator and his university's committee.

Apparently Chalkley did not heed this last-mentioned urging, for in a letter to Mary Fillmore, Associate Director of the Federation of American Scientists Fund, Wienckowski wrote:

You also asked about our comment that we had urged Dr. Chalkley to send a memo to the field decrying the practice of using the letters from his office as unfavorable personnel actions against the applicant involved. Dr. Chalkley was . . . concerned that a general notice to the field might anger many persons, and he has decided to deal with such cases individually as they arise.

Thus it appears that the practice of sending letters from IRB to the administration of the applicant's university will continue.

The letter from DHFW also indicated that ethical questions pertaining to secondary analyses would be handled by review committees charged with calculating a risk-benefit ratio. In his letter to Fillmore and with specific reference to the Horn proposal, Wienckowski stated the matter thus:

. . . When proposals ask for support for secondary analyses, the consideration of subject protection includes an assessment of the risk/benefit ratio. As each application is evaluated, our reviewers assess whether the procedures of the study put the subjects at risk, and, if they do, whether the risks to the subjects are outweighed by the sum of the benefit to the subject and the importance of the knowledge to be gained so as to warrant a decision to allow the subject to accept these risks. In instances where risks are low and benefits are potentially high, review committees may well decide to waive the requirement that informed consent be obtained at the time the data were collected.

The implication is, too, that if informed consent had not been obtained in the gathering of the data originally, this could be a basis for denial of approval of a proposal to reuse that data. The conditions under which this could happen are presumably only those that would put the individual subjects at risk, as, for example, if the names of the subjects were a part of the data and an investigator could use this information to the detriment of a subject. There was no indication here, or in other communications from DHEW officials, that secondary analyses that might put a class of people at risk would be treated in any way different from proposals to gather new data that might put a social class at risk.

Communications from various DHEW officials covered a few points other than those mentioned above, but the comments here cited appear to well represent the major reactions that were both sent to the applicant and had some relevance to the issues raised by members of the scientific-academic community. In the main, the DHEW communications laid out the following basic positions:

1. Review committees charged with making both scientific and ethical judgments about proposals have done a good job, represent the best way to handle questions about the ethicality of research, and thus will be maintained in much the same form as they were in at the time the cases mentioned in this article came to the fore.

2. DHEW directives will continue to supply relatively little specific guidance to review committees about ethical matters, and thus the committees will be left on their own to decide whether or not a proposal is defective in respect to concerns about class risk, anticipation of social consequences, etc.

3. In the Small Grants Section, at least, and perhaps elsewhere in DHEW, increased care will be exercised and new procedures will be adopted to prevent future occurrences of cases such as those described here. As stated in the last written communication the writer received from SGS on these issues, this position was stated: "We plan to continue to be watchful. . . . The staff have developed new procedures for dealing with applications on which the review committee raises ethical questions. These applications now will be deferred until a response can be obtained from the investigator to the issues raised by the committee. In our opinion, this procedure will prevent other cases like yours from arising." (Louis A. Wienckowski & Stephanie B. Stolz, April 10, 1975)

To lay the case before the reader was the major purpose of this paper. But it is probably already evident that this presentation was not entirely objective. The writer has a position and this may have influenced the way he presented the facts, if not his choice of the facts as such. Partly in the interest of objectivity, therefore, what follows is a frank statement of the author's opinions about the major issues, as an aid to making implicit assumptions more nearly explicit.

There are other good reasons for having this statement. For one thing, more could be said than can be developed by trying to document statements made in written communications. On at least two occasions with Stephanie Stolz (there were probably more than two occasions) and at least one occasion with Louis Wienckowski, the author had rather extensive give-and-take discussions about various aspects of the specific case and matters pertaining to general policy. In being close to the issues as they were raised the author acquired viewpoints that may well represent "what went on," and thus indicate "what could go on" in the future, even though these viewpoints cannot be justified on grounds that so-and-so said such-and-such.

One impression that emerged clearly is that the ethical review process[5] of a DHEW bureau, even a bureau as small as SGS, is likely to have serious deficiencies and these are not likely to be corrected exclusively from within. As presently structured, at least, the bureaus and the ethical review process are not designed to be self-corrective.

The dominant response from the bureaus to criticism of the process, or even to simple questions about it, is a form of defense. It is implicitly maintained that the system is basically correct, or the best that can be devised in present circumstances, that the critic or questioner probably does not understand and thus needs to be "informed," that his objection or query might represent breakdown in communication, or that some simple, correctable mistake might have occurred in the operation of an otherwise exemplary set of procedures for doing a job that obviously is important and has to be done within DHEW in the manner in which it is being done. In considering the cases mentioned in previous pages there was virtually no mention by anyone within the DHEW system that perhaps, *just perhaps,* the ethical review procedures were *basically* wrong; there was no mention that perhaps, *just perhaps,* the entire assumptional foundation on which the review process was based was weak and that an entirely different system might be clearly superior. When the review procedures were found to produce what was acknowledged to be an "inappropriate decision," last ditch defensive stands were marshalled: the cause was attributed to ". . . the massive complexity of policy issues . . . (and) the rather bumbling processes of bureaucracy" (to quote from Schwartz) or the responsibility for the "inappropriate decision" was attributed to a diffuse other (as in Wienckowski's "explanation" that somehow the SGS review committee had gotten a wrong idea in using class risk as a basis for rejection of Horn's proposal).

There is virtually no evidence of initiative from within directed at defending what might be anticipated to be the applicant's position or at contesting a position stated elsewhere in the bureaucracy. For example, Stolz should have, and rather easily could have, questioned the initial decision rendered by the SGS review committee *before* sending the letter of rejection to the applicant. Similarly, Duncan should have, and easily could have, inquired herself or initiated inquiries by others into a few of the basics of the case before sending her letter to the Dean. The information of the MH-441 form that was reported to be absent in the review committee deliberations, and which absence was mentioned as a partial basis for the rejection decision, was acknowledged to be in the bureau at the times Stolz and Duncan wrote their letters. Yet apparently neither official read the brief statements of this form. There is no evidence that any of the DHEW officials who wrote the initial letters of "explanation" of the rejection decision (Brown & Plaut, as well as Stolz and Duncan) read any part of the proposal, as such. Each official restated the same incorrect statements that had appeared in communications issuing from another section of the Institute. Thus, there appear to be no checks, much less balances in the review system. In short, the system is not self-critical and, therefore, not self-corrective.

The vote to reject the Horn proposal on ethical grounds was reported (in the Wienckowski-Stolz letter of 10 April 1975) to be unanimous. This also illustrates the non-deliberate nature of the ethical review process. Apparently no one on the review board seriously questioned the ethical premises that later were found to be incorrect. Also, it seems that none of the DHEW officials who rubber stamped the review board's decision ever wondered how it was possible for a committee comprised of 15-20 thinking, conscientious individuals to all agree on the complex issues of this proposal. Unanimous votes are rare even when issues are simple and straightforward. They occur very seldom following truly democratic deliberations and when subtle issues are regarded seriously. Unanimous votes are recorded rather commonly in Fascist systems, in an emotional rush to judgment, or when the matters at stake are regarded quite casually.

The policies and procedures of an ethical review committee, and of the officials charged with sanctioning and communicating the decisions of such boards, are largely unspecified (notwithstanding directives such as Publication No. NIH-72-102, December, 1971, Institutional Guide, and that in the Federal Register, Vol. 39, 1974, 18914-18920). The review committees are accountable virtually to no one—not to officials in DHEW, as we have seen, not to the researcher, not to peers, and not to the courts. As was noted in previous sections, particularly in the communications of Chalkley, DHEW policy tends to favor the view that the review committees should be left free to develop their own definitions of ethicality and their own procedures for deciding on the ethicality of particular research proposals. This means that not only is it difficult to determine what the policies and procedures are for a particular review panel, but also that these may change from one panel to another and even from one case to another. There is thus no assurance that policies and procedures ever will become codified or that review committees ever will become accountable (e.g., to researcher peers, to the general public, etc.).

It is questionable whether in the peer review committees established under DHEW auspices there can ever be the concerted commitment in time and effort needed to work out proper procedures and do the very difficult and time-consuming analyses required to make really sound decisions about the ethicality of research. Moreover, it is questionable whether such review committees are, or can be, comprised of people who are capable in this respect. As Scriven (1966), for example, has pointed out, the ability to make sound ethical decisions is no less a skill and no more easily acquired than the ability to do sound mathematical reasoning. Many people, scientists as well as others, simply have not developed this ability to a very high level. The assumption that any otherwise competent person in a scientific field is also competent to provide judgment about the ethicality of research is not automatically warranted. It is not clear just how members of review panels are selected, but it seems evident that they are not selected specifically for competence in making ethical judgments. Indeed, a question directed at this point seemed to pass right by Wienckowski and Stolz. In their reply of 10 April 1975, they wrote:

You asked for a summary of the "ethical-judgment qualifications" of those who reviewed your application. We are not sure what sort of data would be appropriate to provide in response to this request. We can, if you want, give you biographical resumes of the committee members, although since they are all prominent in their fields, you can obtain much of this information from generally available directories.

The matter was not further clarified in oral communications. When it was suggested that members of the review panel should be selected specifically for their competence in ethical philosophy (Scriven types), Stolz and Wienckowski replied, in effect, that there are no experts in such matters, that persons chosen by their definitions of competence in the subject matter of psychology will also be competent enough in matters of ethics. When such Sunday-school naiveté about ethics is found at the level of directors and administrators in DHEW, it is no wonder that ethical decisions of the kind that were outlined in this paper can occur. Indeed, it seems that such decisions are likely to be the rule rather than the exception.

By way of summary, then, it is this writer's opinion that there are a number of very serious reasons for doubting that DHEW and the peer review panels created under the auspices of this bureau can do a consistently good job of ethical review of research. The structure of the bureau, the procedures that follow from it, the way in which review boards are created and the conditions under which the boards must work all discourage the kind of questioning and deliberative reflection that is required if the obdurate issues of research ethicality are to be cracked along clearly sensible lines. In particular all of these factors preclude adequate risk-benefit analyses (if such is even possible). Instead the conditions at DHEW are conducive to producing arbitrary and capricious ethical decisions; the record documented in this article shows that, indeed, the system already has produced such decisions.

But what are the alternatives? Surely we cannot return to a system in which investigators are left on their own to do what they choose to regard as ethical research? Probably not. For one thing, the public is not likely to stand for it right now. But there is a better way. The outlines of this were hammered out by the aforementioned UC-Berkeley Committee for Protection of Human Subjects (CPHS) under the direction of Herbert P. Phillips. Basically the idea is that instead of having two review committees, one at the university or research center or State level, and one at NIH or NIMH with the dual responsibility for ethical and scientific-technical review, there should be only the one committee at the local level. This has several advantages among which the following may be mentioned briefly:

1. Local review panels are not formed and dissolved each year, and called to Washington for a few weeks to decide on piles of applications. The membership of such panels can be reasonably stable. Experience can thus be built up within a committee in which members can understand how this came about. The members, and the committee, as such, can thus accumulate experience in handling the issues. This means that the procedures and policies in a board's decisions can become codified, justified, and thus known.

2. There can be extended and two-way negotiation and other interaction between the researcher and the review board. As Phillips argued, "When negotiation between researcher and local Human Subject Committees occurs at the campus level it typically results in permission to pursue the research, greater protection of human subjects, and considerable education for both the researcher and members of the committee." In contrast, ". . . a major disadvantage of having national review boards assume exclusive authority is that it would make the process of negotiating with researchers extremely difficult; and without negotiation a large number of very valuable high risk/high benefit projects may never be funded or done."

3. Local review boards are accountable to a number of agents. Again, as Phillips put it, "Members of local Human Subject Committees . . . have a juridical role, but . . . are subject to action in the public courts, to the direct criticism of . . . peers, and at all times have to provide full justification for . . . decisions."

4. To return to a system of local review would also eliminate conflict between local and national review boards. While this is not necessarily desirable, it surely is desirable if officials and review personnel at the national level cannot find time to gain and digest the materials of relevance for a decision. As long as the conflict between local and national boards is of the kind generated by the aforementioned letters from Duncan, the conflict is of very dubious value.

In sum, then, the experience of this investigator leads inexorably to a conclusion that ethical review of research at the level of DHEW is not desirable. It seems that the best way to accomplish this review is to vitalize, or revitalize, local review panels.

In the interim between the time this article was drafted and the time of final submission for publication, a proposal very similar to this one, involving the same subjects, and the same conditions of data-gathering, was approved and funded by the National Institute of Mental Health Advisory Council, Grant Number MH28455. This is a different agency of NIMH from the Small Grants Section that reviewed the original proposal. Although the reviewers provided several suggestions for improvement of the study, no objections pertaining to the ethics of the research were mentioned. It is impossible to know with confidence whether this means primarily that fundamental change regarding ethical review has occurred within DHEW, or that simply the membership of a particular review committee was not inclined to consider class risk, anticipation of undesirable consequences of the research, etc., as legitimate grounds for rejection of a proposal for ethical reasons.[6]

REFERENCES

a. Books and Articles

Cattell, R. B. A New Morality from Science: Beyondism. New York: Pergamon, 1972.

Horn, J. L. Experimental Tests of Fluid Intelligence in Children. Grant Proposal to Small Grants Section, National Institute of Mental Health, October 25, 1973.

Horn, J. L. The prima facia case for the heritability of intelligence and associates. A review of A. R. Jensen's Educability and Group Differences. American Journal of Psychology, 1974, 546-551.

Horn, J. L. Human abilities: A review of research and theory in the early 1970's. Annual Review of Psychology, 1976, 27, 437-485.

Horn, J., Bressler, M., Jensen, A. & Scriven, M. Ethical issues of behavioral science research. Journal Supplement Abstract Service, 1972, 2, 1-2.

Jensen, A. R. How much can we boost I.Q. and Scholastic Achievement? Harvard Educational Review, 1969, 39, 1-123.

Scriven, M. Primary Philosophy. New York: McGraw-Hill, 1966.

b. Letters cited

Brown, B. S., Director, National Institute of Mental Health. To Adlai Stevenson, U.S. Senate. January 2, 1975.

Cattell, R. B., Director and President, Institute for Research on Morality and Self Realization. To John L. Horn, Professor, University of Denver. August 22, 1974.

Cook, S. W., Visiting Fellow, Center for Creative Leadership. To John Horn. September 25, 1974.

Chalkley, D. T., Chief, Office of Protection from Research Risks, National Institutes of Health. To Benson Schaeffer, Chairman, Committee for the Protection of Human Subjects, University of Oregon. February 20, 1975.

Duncan, K. Institutional Relations Branch, Division of Research Grants, National Institutes of Health. To Nathanial H. Evers, Chairman, Committee on University Human Rights Review. August 9, 1974.

Horn, J. L., Professor, University of Denver. To Katherine Duncan. August 19, 1975.

Humphreys, L. G., Professor, University of Illinois. To Bertram S. Brown, Director, National Institute of Mental Health. February 4, 1975.

Humphreys, L. G. In APA Monitor, February, 1975.

Humphreys, L. G. In APA Monitor, March, 1975.

Plaut, T. F. A., Acting Director, National Institute of Mental Health. To Edward Madigan, U.S. House of Representatives. November 5, 1974.

Philips, H. P., Chairman, Committee for Protection of Human Subjects, University of California, Berkeley. To Dominick R. Vetri, Professor, School of Law, University of Oregon. June 10, 1974.

Purcell, K., Professor and Chairman, Department of Psychology, University of Denver. To Louis Wienckowski, Director Extramural Research, NIMH. August 20, 1974.

Schwartz, M., Dean, College of Social Science, Florida Atlantic University. In APA Monitor, March, 1975.

Stolz, S. B., Chief, Small Grants Section, National Institute of Mental Health. To John L. Horn. March 26, 1974.

Wienckowski, L. A., Director, Division of Extramural Research Programs, National Institute of Mental Health. To John Horn, December 9, 1974.

Wienckowski, L. A. To Mary Fillmore, Associate Director, Federation of American Scientists Fund. February 18, 1975.

Wienckowski, L. A. & Stolz, S. B. To John Horn. April 10, 1975.

NOTES

1. A form MH-441, "Protection of Human Subjects," did not accompany the proposal when it was sent, but was sent in time to be considered in the review. This indicated that consent for the testing was obtained from school officials, a practice accepted as ethical at the time the data were gathered. This form apparently was not assembled with the proposal at the time of the review, however, and thus the review committee simply lacked information on this point. Since individual parental consent for the testing was not obtained, and since it seems that the absence of such consent would have been a basis for rejection of the proposal, the fact that the information was lacking does not appear to be crucial. Thus it seems that the first basis for rejection specified in the SGS letter is either that parental consent for the original testing was not obtained or that parental consent for the analyses of the proposal was not obtained. It seems most likely that the former was intended.

2. In a widely publicized Harvard Education Review paper, Jensen (1968) had argued that much existing data was consistent with an hypothesis that individual differences in intelligence, and mean differences between racial groups, are largely due to genetic differences. It is ironic that the applicant whose proposal was turned down on grounds that his results might be interpreted as supporting the Jensen hypothesis is one of those who have been critical of Jensen's position (cf. Horn, 1975; 1976, as well as Horn, et al, 1972).

3. It turned out that she had suffered a severe illness about this time and no one had assumed her duties.

4. Among other statements in the proposal relating to these matters the following appeared on page 18:

A principal point to note about the two samples drawn for this study is that not only do they differ in respect to ethnicity, but also they differ, and in a very notable way, in respect to a larger number of other variables that are related to intellectual performances. Cobb County is made up largely from people associated with space travel and other technical industries which are located in the area, families in which the income and educational attainments of the father are frequently above the average for Georgia and for the Nation. By contrast, Hancock County is comprised mostly of Blacks whose educational attainments and incomes are well below the state and national averages. The persons of the two counties, and the two counties regarded as social-political entities, thus differ in respect to the many variables that are associated with income, education and ethnic differences. It is probably not abusing terms to say that the two samples of children of this study were drawn from different subcultures (some would say they were drawn from different cultures). Moreover, the variables other than ethnicity in respect to which the two samples differ are clearly related to the development of abilities to perform on intellectual tests, and there are no possibilities for controlling all of these variables. Hence by no stretch of the imagination or inference can the sampling of this study be construed as a basis for providing clear information about inherited racial differences in intelligence. The sampling was not designed to provide such information.

5. Maybe the scientific review process as well, but this possibility is not at issue here.

6. Preparation of this paper was supported in part by the University Centers for Rational Alternatives, Inc., and in part by research support funds supplied by the Army Research Institute, Grant Number DAHC19-74-G-0012, and National Science Foundation, Grant Number GB-41452.

The Fallout of the
Legal Mind in Research

L. G. Humphreys

University of Illinois

I will discuss two main issues in somewhat general terms and describe a second example similar to the one described by Dr. Horn. My theme is a quotation from Thomas Jefferson that is inscribed on the inner circumference of the Jefferson Memorial in Washington, D.C. "I have sworn eternal hostility to all forms of tyranny over the mind of man."

The two problems that I wish to discuss are these: first, the absurd decisions that are being made on the basis of legal reasoning, concerning the central role of free and informed consent of human subjects; and second, what I consider to be essentially the "fascistic" criteria being used to define sociological or social risk. I am not calling the people who use these criteria Fascists, but fascistic *actions* can be taken by people from the Left, the Right, or the center of the political spectrum.

First, with respect to free and informed consent, consider the following. Attorneys concerned with civil liberties have argued on the basis of seemingly impeccable logic that prisoners cannot possibly give free consent because of the constraints imposed by their imprisonment; therefore, one cannot do research on prisoners. And please bear in mind that by research I mean the full gamut of social science research, behavioral science research (I myself am a psychologist), and biological-biomedical research. Legal reasoning has led other attorneys to reach similar conclusions about research on children. Their logic runs like this. Children lack sufficient maturity to give informed consent. Therefore, one cannot do research on children. To my knowledge,

161

they have not considered a third group, but I introduce it for contrast. I could take a proposal involving great potential harm to a Congregation of Friends and get a fairly high rate of volunteering. I submit that psychologically they are no more free to give informed consent than are the prisoners. The constraints are different but are equally strong; they are ideological. They consist of the attitudes of the individuals concerned, their perceptions of the attitudes of their peers, and their perceptions of the expectations our society has for a Congregation of Friends. As a matter of fact, in the sense of Thomas Aquinas no one is free to choose.

It is necessary to look closely at this logic to determine the reasonable conclusions. The logic does point to the fact that the rights of prisoners and of children can be abused. As a matter of fact, the rights of any human subgroup can be abused and, therefore, the rights of the Congregation of Friends can be abused. What is evident to me is that the legal criterion of free and informed consent is not a sufficient safeguard. It is not an adequate control that leads to desirable results for the participants in research, or for society. Take a look at the situation of prisoners. A great deal of research is not nearly as dangerous to them as walking about the prison yard. They are in far greater danger from their fellow inmates and occasionally from guards than they are from any researcher. When they participate in a research project, they get a valued break in prison discipline. They are frequently given a little pocket money to spend on cigarettes or sundries. The legal mind leads to conclusions that are heavily punitive with respect to the daily lives of the individual prisoners directly involved. In the name of human rights, legal logic deprives prisoners of rights. Their prison experience is made more inhumane than it would be otherwise. It is also punitive with respect to the rights of prisoners in general, because research may help us do something about the problems of prevention and rehabilitation. Finally, research may be helpful to society generally without cost to the participants. It does not seem to me that attorneys can be proud of the existing prison systems. To deny opportunity to do research on prisoners is to reach an absurd conclusion.

One can also state with validity that children in many experiments learn as much or more than they would in a comparable time in a schoolroom. The children welcome a break in class discipline. There are individual rewards for the participants, and also potential gains for children in general. The most cursory examination of our current situation leads to the conclusion that children have problems, and that our society has problems with children. These problems cannot be solved by doing research only on adult human subjects. Neither will those problems be solved merely by embracing Jesus, to use a common metaphor, or by the adoption of some socioeconomic ideology.

Let us look at what I consider to be the Fascistic criteria that are being employed. These criteria are well illustrated by the second case to which I referred earlier. It occurred at the Dept. of Health, Education and Welfare (HEW). The study section predicted the outcome of the research directly opposite to the investigator's hypothesis. The investigator, however, was better qualified and more experienced in the area than the committee members. Secondly, the committee predicted that political action would probably ensue as a result of the study. In this case, the investigator was an American, but the research was to be done in Britain. The American committee was therefore predicting that there might be British political action. Furthermore, the committee decided that the presumptive political action by the Labor government would be undesirable for the ethnic group that was the focus of the research. In my opinion, this attitude is highly elitist and arrogant. The review panel assumed the functions of the British electorate and its elected representatives. However, the review panel may be less responsible for this decision than the confused directives they have been getting from the HEW bureaucracy. Dr. Horn reported that a HEW bureaucrat had in effect apologized for his committee's decision, but I have a subsequent letter from a different bureaucrat who reiterated the original principle. Thus, two different officers in HEW were stating opposite principles with respect to social risk.

I want to call your attention to something that happened at the University of California at Berkeley, that bears on the question of sociological or social risk. In the fall of 1972, a faculty committee recommended a policy concerning sociological risk that was accepted by the chancellor and circulated to deans, departmental chairmen, etc. This policy applied to all persons belonging to the groups sampled in the research. That is to say, risk to human subjects was defined to go far beyond the individual participants. Statements like the following gave the tone of the document. "Social risk places a reputation or status of a social group in jeopardy. Institutions such as churches, universities, or prisons must be guarded against derogation from information which would injure the reputations and self-esteem of those affiliated with those institutions. One must evaluate how the research findings will appear to persons belonging to any identifiable group affiliated with any institution reported upon."

If this policy had been followed explicitly, it would have prevented economic research on General Motors or on the National Association of Manufacturers. It would have prevented sociological research on the Ku Klux Klan. It would prevent research on the relationship of contraceptive practices to membership in the Catholic Church. It would also, of course, have prevented further research by Arthur Jensen on racial differences in intelligence. It is not surprising that the Senate Committee on Academic Freedom of the Berkeley campus pounced on this statement, and I am happy to report that a different statement has been substituted for the original. The new statement recognizes the possibility that research may cause a subject to suffer a loss of personal reputation in the eyes of other persons. Such risks can be minimized by confidentiality of files—i.e., concealing the identity of subjects in publications, refusing to release *individual* records, or deleting all information concerning *individual* identities from the research files.

The Scientific Versus the Adversary
Approach in Bio-Medical Research

Bernard Davis

The biomedical sciences seem to be as threatened as any by arguments over what is ethical or unethical in research. I would like to review briefly the ethical problems and the dangers of overreaction in two areas: fetal research, and experimentation on human subjects in general.

Vigorous objection to fetal research has arisen in recent years and has resulted in a national moratorium that is preventing most kinds of fetal research today, except those that involve tissues from an already dead fetus. In Massachusetts, recent legal actions are causing hospitals and doctors to be even more careful than the law actually requires, because nobody knows what interpretations are going to be attached to any action involving a fetus. The issue is highly charged because it is so closely linked to the problem of abortion and, hence, to very strong moral convictions on the part of many people who object to abortion, even though it is now legal. The issues are under extensive discussion and are gradually being sorted out.

There is widespread agreement that research on tissues from an already dead fetus are no different from research that may be permitted on adult cadavers. What will be permitted beyond this in Massachusetts is not clear. There has been extensive discussion between supporters of fetal research and some legislators, and the results seem to have been educational. I mention this because it offers hope for the possibility of getting people with diametrically opposed positions on such issues to see each other's point of view, and to adopt a better compromise. It looks as though the legislation will permit research on a fetus at *the time of* a legal abortion. For example, an investigator might want to test a diagnostic procedure that could lead to useful recognition of fetuses with serious hereditary disease. If the instrumentation involved is first tested on individuals about to be aborted it can be perfected without exposing wanted infants to the high risk of a novel procedure.

There is stronger objection to another kind of fetal research: one in which procedures are carried out, or drugs are given to a mother, a few hours or a few days ahead of a scheduled abortion. Even though it is recognized that somebody has to take the risk if you are going to test any new drug or any new procedure, and it seems logical to have the risk applied preferentially to fetuses that are scheduled for destruction, the groups opposing this want to preserve for the mother the right to change her mind up to the last moment. Any procedure that might irrevocably commit the mother to an already planned abortion is probably going to be legally blocked. There is an excellent article by Gaylin and Lappe in the *Atlantic Monthly* (May 1975), emphasizing that if we don't allow unwanted fetuses to undergo the risk we are going to condemn a great many wanted fetuses to undergo the risk.

The second, broader problem is that of human subjects in general in relation to medical research. Those of us in the medical profession have been astounded by the violence of the recent objection in large segments of society to many aspects of medical research. Indeed, biomedical ethics has become a major growth industry. This development is related to the consumer movement with its emphasis on individual rights and protection from institutions; it reflects loss of confidence in institutions in general, and reflects the fact that the tremendously increased scale of medical research over the last two decades, with the increasing funds appropriated by the government for this purpose, has involved many more people. Indeed, with this large scale there are inevitably incidents in which things are done that should not have been done. An atmosphere has arisen in which many investigators might be described as more enthusiastic than sensitive. It is, therefore, a good thing that we are being pressed to be more aware of this problem and to set up committees in hospitals and medical schools to review research projects for their adherence to ethical guidelines. Finally, a great deal of the reaction arises from a very small number of horror stories that have received a great deal of attention in the press. Among them are the Tuskegee study, in which treatment was withheld from some black patients with syphilis; injections of cancer cells in moribund patients; and a few other such studies.

It seems quite clear that we cannot solve the problem by saying that only those of us with a medical background can really understand the complexity of the problem. Now that we have been shaken up, we should be allowed to police ourselves again. It seems that there is too much concern on the part of too many other people. But I do think that the directions in which we are moving also present grave dangers. Initially some philosophers or theologians, with a serious and technical background in medical ethics, began a systematic inquiry into this field some years ago. Since they opened Pandora's box, everybody can be a professional on medical ethics and can write an article.

The best statement I have seen on this subject is one by Dr. Franz Ingelfinger, editor-in-chief of the *New England Journal of Medicine,* who has recently written a paper called "The Unethical in Medical Ethics" (*Annals of Internal Medicine 83,* 264, 1975). He points out that along with the value of having our attention called to the need for more awareness of the problem, there are also very serious dangers, which he describes under five headings. First is the righteousness with which people in the current climate of ethical opinion point the finger at horrors of the past. This action is no more justified than it would be to accuse a current Southern landowner of being responsible for previous Southern landowners thinking it ethical to have slaves. Ethical principles change and there is a great deal of righteousness in the horror stories that are getting so much attention about medical ethics and medical research. Second, this reaction is amplified by the desire of media for sensationalism. Third, a more basic problem is how to balance concern over individual rights with concern over society's needs. In the present climate of opinion, there are large groups who feel that there should be no more research on prison inmates because they cannot ever be considered to have given a truly voluntary consent. I believe this is an overreaction to a situation in which indeed there have been abuses. These could be better corrected by having committees of disinterested people, separate from the researchers, supervising the nature of the consent.

The fourth and fifth dangers that Dr. Ingelfinger mentions are those of bureaucratization and trivialization. If we have enormously detailed rules, and a dilution of real issues with innumerable trivial issues, the whole field becomes very unattractive. If we continue in this direction highly motivated people may be driven away from the field, since more energy, time, and money will go into filling out forms than into actions that are of benefit to the patient and to society.

There is a deep irony in all of this. For while researchers in teaching and research institutions have occasionally caused harm by actions that should be prevented, the general level of medical care in those institutions is undoubtedly far better than that in general practice in this country. The high visibility of these institutions could divert attention from the broad problem of the availability and quality of medical care in general.

One product of recent criticism of research practices has been insistence on informed and voluntary consent. While the principle is excellent, developing effective procedures is not easy. What is information to a doctor in a consent form may also mean a lot to a highly educated patient, but may mean little to another patient. Some people who are very concerned with this problem seem to me to be projecting onto the whole class of patients practices they would like for themselves, but that really do not fit most patients. Moreover, the problem of informed consent also gets pushed to an extreme when it is required for procedures that do not involve risk or serious invasion of privacy. Today it is necessary to have written informed consent in order to have waste products of a patient that are collected in the hospital used by investigators.

An example of silly interference has arisen in connection with some research on cell genetics in man that depends on cultivating human cells in test tubes. Cells from young individuals are required, and a convenient source is foreskins from newborns, a by-product of circumcisions. This material has been used now for a number of years. An investigator at MIT recently had his regular supply of foreskins from the Boston Women's Hospital cut off, if I may use the expression, because the doctor was afraid that he would have to have written informed consent from both the father and the mother. He didn't know what some Massachusetts prosecutor might do.

Perhaps the most general problem in medical research is that of risk-benefit analysis. In any new procedure there is, by definition, some risk involved. Who is going to take on that risk? One of the most valuable things that public interest lawyers can do in this area, I think, is to try to provide mechanisms for society to insure people for indemnity if they are harmed as a result of accepting this risk. But an added problem of social justice arises if one social class provides the guinea pigs for the benefit of another. That traditionally has been the way medical research was largely done, on the assumption that the risk of harm from research was traded for the much larger risk from less skilled medical care outside the teaching institutions. This is one area in which things clearly have to change. Unfortunately, at present the discussion seems unsatisfactory to me because much of it is contributed by a group of public interest lawyers, who act as prosecutors against a medical research community whom they place in the dock. At a forum on medical experimentation at the National Academy of Sciences recently, the lawyers and the medical investigators talked completely past each other. One reason for the lack of real communication was the adversary process, which is the natural approach of lawyers but is foreign to physicians and scientists. To many of us this approach seems to inject into the situation an atmosphere unconducive to the kinds of solution we are accustomed to seek. Unless we can agree on some less adversary kind of approach I predict a very unhappy course of events.

An Ethical Approach
To Bio-Medical Research

Seymour Seigal

Jewish Theological Seminary

"Utter helplessness demands utter protection" — Hans Jonas.

The application of moral principles to dilemmas raised by scientific research and experimentation requires knowledge of the scientific principles involved. Moralists who are ignorant of the details and procedures of scientific research can hardly be expected to make relevant judgments about such thorny issues as experimentations on humans; fetal research; genetic engineering, or any other types of research that arouse public controversy. This is equally true about other areas of public concern where moralists attempt to make relevant judgments, such as politics and international affairs.

There is a long tradition of ethical analysis embodied in the great religious and philosophical systems of our civilization. Methods of ethical reasoning have been developed over many centuries of experience and study. Just as one rightfully demands of those who render ethical judgments about science, to know something about science —one should also demand that they also know something about the *ethical* tradition.

Observation of discussions about the ethical dimension of scientific research often yields the melancholy conclusion that frequently ethicists are ignorant of science and that scientists are equally ignorant of ethical reasoning. Obviously, therefore, if one is to make sound judgments in this vital area, a creative partnership should exist between the disciplines of science and the traditions of ethics. This partnership should be genuine, not a situation where one party is respectfully silent. Morality is too serious a matter to be left merely to moralists—or to scientists.

Scientists frequently express some resentment when their activities are hampered by forces and interests that profess to be speaking for ethical traditions. This is especially true in the biomedical field. The feeling among those who work in such areas as fetal experimentation, experiments on human subjects, or genetic research, is that the groups speaking in the name of ethics propose unreasonable and even dogmatic restraints. Let the scientists monitor themselves, they say.

However, as Oscar Wilde once observed, morality is the attitude one adopts towards people whom one personally dislikes. This remark reflects a basic truth. Ethical restraints are especially necessary where one's self-interest, passions, commitments, and prejudices are involved. While it is sometimes difficult to fool others, it is simple to fool oneself.

Therefore, in questions relating to medical and scientific research where the researcher has much at stake—not only the pursuit of truth but also the furtherance of his career and reputation—the imposition of ethical restraints should be welcomed in order to overcome, as much as possible, the natural tendency to favor that which favors the researchers. This is especially important in questions involving biomedical research, where the subjects are human beings—and where it is possible to cause irreversible effects.

I am not implying that scientific researchers are somehow more self-centered and likely to cut corners to further their own self-interest than are other segments of society. My own observation is that these researchers are usually as good as, or even better than, professional ethicists. However, society must protect itself not only against the good people but mainly against the not-so-good people. Safeguards must be incorporated to make it possible to hinder those who need to be restrained. These restraints, although causing some hardship to those who do not need restriction, will enhance the community of science rather than needlessly hamper it. Some people are careful even if there are no rules. Since there are those who are careless without the enforcement of laws, everyone must follow the regulations set down by a community for its protection.

What are some of the ethical principles that should be applied to problems of research, especially in the field of human experimentation?

The most general principle that should influence our decisions is a *bias for life*. This bias is the foundation of civilization. The bias for life requires that all individuals—most especially those involved in the healing arts—should direct their efforts toward sustaining life where it exists. Means and procedures that tend to terminate life or to harm it are unethical; and when one doubts the benefits of certain kinds of research, that doubt should always be on the side of life. No experimental procedures should be carried out on a human being, if there is a risk involved that does not have as its aim the enhancement of the subject's health or well-being. Where an experiment involves no risk or minimal risk, this rule might be relaxed.

Another important principle that should guide researchers and those who carry out public policy is that no person should be called upon, without his consent, to sacrifice his well-being or to become the subject of experimentation or research for some "good" that might materialize. The progress of science, of knowledge, or the general good of society—however noble these concerns might be—does not oblige any individual to sacrifice his own well-being against his will. This, therefore, means that experiments on unborn fetuses or people in extremis who are by the nature of things unable or unwilling to give their consent, should not be carried on.

Professor Hans Jonas has profoundly discussed this subject in "Philosophical Reflection on Human Experimentation: Ethical Aspects of Experimentation on Human Subjects," Daedelus, Spring 1969, page 98 (reprinted in his Philosophical Essays: From Ancient Creed to Technological Man, Englewood Cliffs, N.J., 1974.) In no case, he argues, should the dying be told: "Since you are here in the hospital with its facilities—under our care and observation away from your job (or, perhaps doomed), we wish to profit from your being available for some other research of great interest we are presently engaged in." Nor, says Jonas, should one say to the fetus about to be aborted· "Since you are going to die anyway and are available and under observation, wouldn't it be more significant for you to die as our 'partner' in research of great interest and which might prove to be profitable to the uncondemned?" Only research that might help the patient before us is ethical. Jonas argues further, "Drafting him (the unconscious) for non-therapeutic experiments is simply and unqualifiedly not permissible; progress or not, he must be never used, on the inflexible principle that *utter helplessness demands utter protection.*" (italics mine.)

It is, of course, possible to ask people to submit to self-sacrifice for the good of scientific enterprise. Because there is generally a risk to the well-being of the subject, only those persons who can most genuinely identify with the end sought by nonthereapeutic experimentation should be accepted as experimental subjects. Genuine volunteers should be those who are committed to the experimental enterprise, who have—as Jonas describes it—"compassion with human suffering, zeal for humanity, reverence for the golden rule, enthusiasm for progress, zeal for the cause of knowledge and even longing for sacrificial justification." This description, incidentally, would most appropriately be applied to the researchers themselves.

This right of the individual to his own integrity over and above the interests of medical progress or scientific knowledge is not an absolute one. As Sidney Hook has perceptively pointed out, no right is absolute since—if carried to logical extreme—one right inevitably collides with another. For example, the right to free speech is not absolute because it is limited by the right to privacy or the right against defamation.

The same is true concerning the individual's rights to his well-being and to his not sacrificing himself for the general good. Societies do demand, on occasion, that individuals give up their rights in times of emergency. Thus, nations have laws making conscription and national service mandatory. An important distinction must be drawn between the right of countries to draft their members for the common defense and the right of researchers to use individuals unwillingly or unable to give consent to be part of medical experiments. Everybody is born into a society and becomes part of the social contract. Part of this social contract is the agreement to sacrifice for the common good whenever necessary—such as in the time of war or of a threat to the community's security. People are not, however, ordinarily born into a covenant that obligates them to participate in the furtherance of science or the enhancement of human knowledge to their detriment. Whatever the cogency of this distinction, the dilemma whether an individual should be part of an experiment where he has not given his consent, involves the clash of two or more values. One must then weigh the relative weight of each value. In my judgment, the individual's well-being and the integrity of his own body and personality would—in the majority of the cases—be greater than his possible contribution to the welfare of future generations or the growth of scientific knowledge.

What is needed is a revival of a refined casuistry. This concept, though ordinarily disdained, is part of all the great traditions of ethical reasoning. It involves applying general principles to concrete cases and recognizing there are factors inherent in individual cases that are unique, thereby requiring unusual decisions.

Even the issue of consent involves great problems. The problem of who can give consent for children or others who cannot make decisions for themselves has not been adequately solved. If prisoners are offered a shortening of their sentences if they submit to experimentation, and then they consent to be subjects—does this really involve consent or coercion? Even informed consent is problematical. A recent study at Yale University found that individuals who had given their consent to be part of an experiment, when quizzed later, were not sure to what they had really consented. Nor was it always true that the experimenters told the would-be subjects the details of the experiment in which they were to be involved.

Another important issue that requires much investigation and analysis is the question of the limits of scientific work. Does every problem or every possibility have to be explored? Should science and society surrender to the "Mount Everest syndrome," in which something is attempted merely because "it is there"? This question is of supreme importance in the area of genetic research. Do the social costs of such science fiction experiments as cloning, growth of fetuses *in vitrio*, outweigh whatever benefits might be realized by continuing research into these mysterious areas? It is encouraging that groups of genetic researchers recently have voluntarily put a limit on their own work for the greater good of the society.

As we proceed with the adventure of increasing human knowledge, we are bound to meet new problems fraught with ambiguities and difficulties that will present ethical problems. New solutions will most assuredly create new enigmas. However, a creative partnership between scientists, ethicists, and those who form public policy is not only desirable, it is indispensable. Perhaps the best way to concretize this partnership is to form committees on ethics and science. These committees should include scientists, ethicists, politicians, and representatives of the public at large. I do not wish to hold back scientific progress that has done so much to enhance human life. I do, however, wish to ensure that recognition of the ethical dimension will be considered in decision making that can affect mankind. Each person wishes to enhance our common life and to further that which is, after all, the main aim of science and of most human activity—to make one's sojourn on earth happier and more productive.

Ethical Principles and
National Security Research

Donald G. Brennan
Hudson Institute

The hardware that we have to deal with in the National Security business is certainly hard enough, but the issues are sometimes a good deal softer, and I am really going to talk about the issues related to the hardware.

Some people in the past have questioned, on ostensibly ethical grounds, the conduct by the American National Security establishment of research and development directed toward improving various kinds of weapon capabilities. I should like to claim that the research and development of weapons and weapon systems is on the whole entirely compatible with recognized ethical principles. I won't spend very much time on this because, I think, in some sense the National Security establishment, and in particular the military research and development community, is in fact not currently substantially threatened by the kind of fashion that is coming up in the biomedical sciences, for example. We have had a few tentative forays against the National Security establishment on allegedly ethical grounds but nothing like the kind of sustained attack that Dr. Davis was speaking of.

As to the ethical principles involved that would justify the usual kinds of weapon research and development, I should say first of all that it's not even questioned, even by the critics of some of this research, that sovereign states will defend themselves, can defend themselves, and should and ought to defend themselves against encroachments from the outside world. For example, it is stated very clearly in the

American Constitution that the government is charged with providing for the common defense. I have never heard anyone question that principle of the Constitution on ethical grounds. I think it is widely accepted.

I think it is also widely accepted that under a very wide range of circumstances it is ethically reasonable, proper and sometimes even mandatory to help protect others. Many of you will recall the Kitty Genovese case that took place here in New York City in 1964, in which some thirty-odd people apparently witnessed the murder of this girl without bothering to pick up a telephone and call the police, much less to intervene in any more forceful way. The behavior of these people was universally condemned on ethical grounds, and, I think, quite rightly. It is very easy to derive international parallels to the Kitty Genovese case in which governments may or may not choose to intervene in the aggression against some innocent state.

Well, if you accept these ethical principles as, in fact, everyone would, then you are inescapably in the weapon business; one can't avoid it. Ethically, one has no reason to avoid it at all.

If you wish to have ethical criteria for selecting some weapon systems as against others, one reasonable principle would be that the weapons you are going to develop should be reasonably controllable. You do not want weapons that are uncontrollable in a very substantial degree. To take what I believe is a thoroughly hypothetical case, I should think that one might resist on ethical grounds research that would be devoted or directed explicitly to finding a reaction that would ignite the entire atmosphere of the earth. I should be quite willing to resist it on ethical grounds, not to mention various pragmatic grounds as well. It is probable that some forms of biological warfare would not be sufficiently controllable to constitute a usable military weapon, and if they would not be, then I should think they would be subject to question on ethical grounds, among others.

It is conceivable that some kinds of weapons might be excessively repugnant in relation to their effectiveness, and I state that principle knowing very well that it might irritate some of you here that it has to be stated in relation to their effectiveness, but it is unfortunately necessary to state it that way. Otherwise, for example, one could not say that a flame thrower is more repugnant somehow than a nuclear weapon. Surely a large nuclear weapon is inherently more repugnant in the sense of what it might do, in the sense of large-scale damage, but there are some circumstances in the present world in which one should have nuclear weapons in the armories of some of the countries, not least in the United States. The ethical case against having flame throwers is much clearer than the case against nuclear weapons because they merely burn people in small numbers and may not have sufficient military effectiveness. This is a very tentative example and I don't necessarily wish to defend it ultimately, but this will give you an example of the kind of thinking that one should engage in in relation to the ethics of weapon development.

If you exclude only weapons that are insufficiently controllable or excessively repugnant in relation to their effectiveness, then choice among remaining weapon systems, those that are not excluded by these rather general principles, must be made on different grounds having to do with strategy, foreign policy, cost, and other issues of this kind that may be quite important but which are not inherently ethical.

In recent years, for example, ostensibly ethical arguments have come up about two military developments that are being pursued in part on university campuses and got into some trouble there. One was the development of MIRV—Multiple Independently Targetable Reentry Vehicles—I expect most of you are familiar with these; and another argument came up about the further development of accuracy in long-range strategic weapons. I picked these two examples because I happen to oppose one and support the other of those two particular developments. I was among those who felt unhappy about the advent of MIRV. I thought that there were various essentially strategic reasons why the world would have been better off if it had been possible to have avoided MIRV; it might have been very difficult to avoid then, but in any event, it was an unfortunate development. In the case of accuracy, however, I would be delighted to defend the development of further accuracy of strategic weapons because it does, in fact, permit more controllability of weapon effects and enables you better to avoid killing noncombatants when you don't want to, for instance. It takes a simple-minded theory to argue that accuracy is bad even on strategic grounds and nothing but an absolutely wild theory would support that assertion on ethical grounds.

I think that's probably enough for me to say about the subject of weapon development. If anyone has questions about it I shall be happy to respond to them.

An Engineer's Approach
to the Ethics of Research

A. R. Hibbs

California Institute of Technology

Although I will center my discussion on scientific research, I must approach this problem from the viewpoint of an engineer, and in particular from the viewpoint of one who administers engineering projects. Although my education was in theoretical physics, my closest contact with what is usually called "pure science" today is by virtue of teaching undergraduate physics at Caltech. It is important that you should know this, because I am discussing a subject—scientific research—which I am not personally involved with, always a slightly hazardous undertaking.

In the manner of my engineering colleagues, I will try to organize my approach into subsets and further subdivisions. Lacking a blackboard to diagram it, I will hope simply that you can follow it in the abstract, perhaps imagining the diagram here in the air above my head. It is not important that you agree with my organization, it is simply a convenient way to approach the problem and a help to me in explaining my thoughts to you.

We might identify the act of speculation as a scientific research undertaking. One can visualize a person simply sitting and thinking. I presume that for the most part this does not involve any major ethical problem, certainly not enough to demand our close attention.

I realize that there have been times and social situations in which thinking might be considered unethical, depending on the nature of the thoughts, but I trust that that does not apply to us here, and not to scientific speculation at least.

To proceed to Phase Two, we must presume that some interesting hypothesis has come from the speculative act, and perhaps the next idea is a visit to the library, first, to make sure no one else has already set forth the idea, and second to begin testing and analyzing the idea at least in the abstract (i.e., without laboratory experiments or field observations). It may be that the analysis accomplished in this step is sufficient to justify publication of an article.

I should note here that I am excluding mathematics from the scientific research. This is not done in any pejorative way, but simply because I think of mathematics as inherently different than physical science.

Now the question arises as to whether or not there are ethical questions involved with the publication of a speculation, analyzed perhaps but not yet experimented upon. I would guess that the ethical questions at this stage are still rather minor. It is interesting that quite often it is other scientists who tend to suppress the speculations of their colleagues. It is surprising how many scientists often feel threatened more by speculations than by experimental data. The case of Emmanuel Velikovsky and his speculation published as "Worlds in Collision" is a memorable example. There have been others. Perhaps closely fitting this pattern is a German geologist named Wegener, although it must be pointed out that his speculations were based to a large extent on observations. Many years ago he published a theory of continental drift. It was not translated into English for another ten years, but thereupon it was roundly denounced. Those who found his ideas interesting and sought to publish further articles along this line, at least in England and America, had a very difficult time of it.

It is rather interesting that now the pendulum seems to have swung the other way. I don't know if you are aware of this, but if you were a geologist today undertaking to publish a paper against continental drift, you would have a very difficult time getting it printed by any so-called reputable journal.

Phase Three would consist of data gathering. We've heard quite a bit about this already as it applies to a number of different types of research. I don't wish to duplicate the previous analyses. To avoid this I would like to subdivide the data gathering phase into two divisions. One, in which data gathering is done primarily by observation alone, such as astronomy, and the other, in which the data gathering results from laboratory experimentation, such as high energy physics.

In turn, both of these subdivisions have two general subclasses: data gathering on people and data gathering on non-people.

Within the box which we might title "Observation: People," we have such things as surveys, questionnaires, and other such data gathering with the implied subsequent phase of publication of the results. Such activities have already been discussed, and the potential and real problems which they encounter have been brought up. I will not go any further into it. The second box, "Observations: Non-People," might be considered reasonably safe and free from ethical difficulties. It would seem that looking at the stars does not present us with too many problems. But there are other types of observations, such as for example observing the behavior of the California condor.

There are very few of these birds left, perhaps one or two dozen. They are shy. They nest in remote cliffs. Observing them frightens them, disturbs their whole life pattern, and undoubtedly hinders their ability to rear their young. On the other hand, perhaps by learning more about them we will know better how to protect them and encourage their numbers to increase. There may be some ethical problems here, or perhaps it is simply a matter of technology: how to observe without being observed.

The other major subdivision is that of experimentation and again the first class is "Experimentation: People." Here again we've heard some discussion about this problem. Obviously there are a considerable number of ethical issues which are now being worked over. I would agree with the remarks of the others on this panel that there are unfortunately a number of cases in which the so-called ethical discussion does not seem very professional.

I would like to concentrate my attention on the other side of this experimentation division, namely, "Experimenting: Non-people." This is a very large area and it includes some cases in which there seems to be a clear danger such as, for example, experiments on the modification of bacterial genes.

This issue has already been discussed at some length by biologists involved with this type of research, both here and in other countries. They are well aware of the need to establish some ground rules for carrying out this type of experiment.

This is a danger which is upon us now. We are fortunate that the scientists involved recognize it and are attempting to deal with it. I know we all wish them success, for the stakes are high. On the one hand is the possibility of gaining a deep knowledge of the workings of the gene and the whole process of heredity. At the very least, such knowledge could be used to fight heredity diseases, but at the very most, such knowledge leads to a basic definition of the term "human being." On the other hand is a very real danger. If gene modifications of a harmless bacteria should make it harmful, then all of its descendents by the millions and billions and so on will carry the same change, and so become deadly instead of innocuous. What is to keep them in the laboratory? Truly this is a serious problem and one that deserves all the attention that it is currently getting.

But we must look forward to the future when other problems of this type will continue to spring upon us from the Pandora's Box which I and other technologists are opening for you. Consider, for example, modifications of the weather. At present, we have had a small amount of success in rainmaking. We have not introduced any major changes, but as this capability grows over the next few years, our power in this area may be quite impressive. Of course, in order to develop this capability we will have to carry out experiments—experiments which may themselves be on a vast scale, and affect not the presence or absence of a single local rain storm, but the weather pattern across half a continent. Surely we ought to have some thoughtful ground rules on this matter. The benefits of weather control are potentially enormous, but then so are the hazards. The problem is that we may be able to affect the weather before we really understand it—that is, before we can reliably predict the outcome of our experiments. It might be nice to say, "Well, don't do such experiments until you have enough understanding to predict the outcome." Unfortunately, the understanding may itself depend upon such experiments.

There are other examples of potential experimental activities in which there is enormous controversy on whether there is any danger at all. One such undertaking is the return to earth of a sample of soil taken from the surface of Mars. I will return to this question a little later, but now let me move on to Phase Four, that is, the publication of results.

My paper on this general subject which was mentioned earlier brought out the disturbing case of Dr. William Schockley and the question as to whether or not he should have the right to talk and to have his results published. There is also the interesting case of Dr. Linus Pauling, whether or not he should have the right to publish his opinions on the validity of megavitamin therapy. Wegener, the German geologist, did publish his theories about continental drift, but his intellectual descendents were in great difficulty for awhile. It seems clear that there are ethical difficulties in these areas, difficulties so far unresolved.

Phase Five takes us beyond this area of research and into the area of application, that is, the engineering activity of turning the scientific result into some sort of product. How can we approach the ethical issues of this operation? Is it possible to make any rules at all? Are we really intelligent enough to foresee the potential danger in the application of a new scientific principle? Perhaps one might attempt to apply the same principles of ethics that we have tried to develop for human behavior in general to scientific research and in particular to the applications of scientific results, but I confess I have serious reservations about the practicality and utility of that approach. I have the opinion that science and engineering, and particularly scientific research, is unique and demands a special approach to resolve the ethical problems that have arisen and will arise perhaps more often in the future.

In fact, I will go even further and say that each type of science is so unique in itself that we must have a separate ethical approach for each field—biology, physics, chemistry, etc. I do not see any way in which we can translate ethical systems developed as a guide for interpersonal relations into a guide for scientific activities. Of course, we can try, but I think the results would be no more than a rather interesting exercise in semantics. It is better to face the issue—science is unique. We are not going to find rules for its operation by deducing them from the Ten Commandments or any of the descendents thereof. But of course this is only my opinion, and perhaps a listener might claim—and with some justification—that it is an opinion based largely on the ignorance of the field of ethics.

But perhaps this is not the major issue—that is, the question of whether or not ethical principles for guiding scientific research can be derived from much more basic ethical concepts, or whether or not they must be created ad hoc for each new problem. The major issue is this: somehow these ethical questions must be resolved, and it might be reasonable to have those individuals who are deeply involved with the whole field of ethics to be involved also with the resolution of questions dealing with science. But then again, that might not be such a good idea. You see, this would require that philosophers and other humanists learn something about science, a task which they have so far steadfastly avoided. I realize this is a very arduous task, and I am sure that many of them will find it much more interesting and delightful to argue about how to make the ethical principles apply to science, without bothering to understand the science which they are attempting to apply the principles to. Every now and then I see books written by humanists about the philosophy of science, and so on. By and large they are a pile of rubbish. Often, for example, they attempt to define something called "The Scientific Method." Most of these definitions are offered by people who have never participated in scientific activities, and most successful scientists have never practiced any of the methods so defined as scientific.

I recall an opinion offered by Aage Bohr once in an informal conference at the Caltech Faculty Club. He suggested that there are two kinds of truths in the world. There are ordinary truths and then there are deep truths. Now an ordinary truth is something whose converse is obviously false. A deep truth, on the other hand, is a statement whose converse is also a deep truth. For example, ordinary truths would have it that "The sun rises in the east." Now a deep truth might be "To procreate is the only purpose of man," because it is also a deep truth that "To procreate is not the only purpose of man."

Perhaps you have gathered by now that I have a certain distrust of ethical principles and philosophy in general. I was in the audience yesterday afternoon and I was at a loss to understand an incident which took place, but I found myself quite intrigued by it. The discussion concerned the ethics of teaching. During the question and answer period, a gentleman near the back of the room stood up and made a reference of something I know nothing about. It concerned, I believe, five professors at the City College of New York who have recently been censured for something. He wondered what was the position of the American Association of University Professors on this issue. It so happened that the president of that Association was sitting on the stage approximately where I am now. The interrogator from the back of the auditorium pointed out that one of his colleagues in this group of five was also present. He went on to say they attempted to call the AAUP but never received any answer.

You can see how interesting the situation became. Here was a conference on ethics, and here is a specific ethical question raised. What happened next? First, the chairman, Mr. Hook, pointed out that we are here to examine principles not specific issues. He illustrated this by immediately bringing up two specific issues. Then when it came time for the president of the AAUP to respond, he pointed out that the Association really couldn't take a stand on this issue until the issue itself was a little more clarified. He went on to say that if there was any question about the ambiguity of the position of the Association he would be happy to clarify this and so on. I presume that this is the proper ethical response. In my business we would call it dodging the issue, but then of course I am an engineer, and not a philosopher. But I couldn't understand his failure to respond to the second question, which was, "Why can't we get you on the telephone?" It would seem to me to be quite possible for the person who is sitting down here on the stage to get up and say, "This meeting is going to be over at 3:30. At 3:35 I will meet you in the lobby and we'll have a talk." I mean, that would seem reasonable to me. I don't know what the right answer is, I don't even know what the issue is. I don't even know what the case is. But it seems to me that discussion doesn't commit you to anything, does it?

I am reminded of a quote by Mencken: "In politics it is often necessary to rise above principle." I am convinced that if you substituted the word "ethics" for "politics" the sentence would still be correct.

But now let me return to the question of how to make ethical decisions regarding the process of scientific research. Regardless of whether you agree with me that we must ad hoc our way through this morass or whether you believe we have a chance of deriving rules by deductions from deeper principles, nevertheless I think you must agree that anyone who attempts to face this issue must first do his homework and learn what is involved in scientific research. Leonardo da Vinci pointed out that the secrets of nature lie in her detail. We must learn these details. It is not enough to have some broad brush surface understanding of the nature of scientific research. If you are to speak upon it and how it is to be carried out, you must become familiar in detail with what it involves.

Let me give you a specific example. In about ten years or so we will have the technical capability to bring back to earth a sample of dirt from the surface of Mars. As yet, we don't know whether there is life on Mars or not. We will be sending a few instruments up to Mars to ask that question, a fascinating question, and one for which a single word is worth a thousand pictures: "yes," or "no."

Perhaps it is rather ironic that in analyzing the surface soil of Mars, one of the important steps is to burn it—an interesting first contact between life on earth and life on Mars.

Even if the answer is "no" from these instruments that really doesn't prove that there is no life. There are alternatives, one of the principle ones being that we lack sufficient knowledge to design instruments to ask the right questions. That is, we can't really understand the nature of Martian life, and so cannot devise the proper test.

Now it could be that not only is there life on Mars, but that life is particularly virulent to life on earth, which has never been in contact with it, has never had any opportunity to develop the hereditary disease-fighting mechanisms. Surely we recall the historical cases of aborigines in various parts of the world being nearly wiped out by diseases introduced by European explorers.

Why bother bringing back a sample of dirt from Mars? Many biologists believe that this is the only way we will ever be able to adequately analyze the soil of Mars and say definitely "yes" or "no" to the question of life. Furthermore, analyzing the nature of that life form, if it exists, enables us to understand the detailed differences between it and us, and so deepen our understanding of the nature of life itself. Surely these are enormous philosophical and scientific questions—the existence of life on another world, and of the detailed chemical nature of that life form. And yet, there is one eminent biologist at Stanford who says we should never undertake this particular approach, that is, returning a sample to earth. He is convinced that it would pose grave dangers, perhaps destroying much life on earth, including the human race.

There is another equally eminent biologist at Caltech, also involved with this problem, and in fact with the landing instruments we are sending there, who has said, "If you ever bring a sample back I will be happy to eat it." Of course, I think a sample would be a little too valuable to provide a salad for Professor Horowitz, but I point out to you the large difference of opinion between experts who are equally familiar with the issue. How might one do a risk-benefit analysis when we have no way of attaching any reasonable estimate to the top half of the ratio, the risk? The benefits perhaps we can appreciate, the new knowledge and the broadened human outlook which might result. But what about the risk? To some extent it depends upon how well we as technologists can isolate the sample and guarantee that none of it escapes. But perfect guarantees are impossible to come by, the best we can offer is a high degree of probability.

Would the community of ethical scholars care to enter this arena? If so, you have about ten years to do your homework, to learn about biology, Mars, and the technology of sealing up containers and laboratories.

Of course, I am a bit of a cynic and I suspect that most of you will not bother with such arduous undertakings but will reach your conclusions in the more traditional manner, in the manner of the ancients: on the basis of pure thought. But which ever way you go, you have about ten years to help us balance the risk of disaster against the benefit of discovery.

Rejoinder: Dr. Hibbs and the Ethics of Discussion

Sidney Hook

Even a sympathetic listener must be puzzled by Dr. Hibbs' discussion of the problem before us. For his position seems to be obviously incoherent. He starts out by recognizing that there are problems of moral decision both in the kind of research we undertake, for example in recombinant DNA, and in the application of the outcome of research, as in weather modification. Whatever decision we make, and often the refusal to make a decision, expresses a policy. A policy is a normative value judgment. It is an elementary truth of logic, which thankfully is the same for engineers and humanists, that no aggregation of facts by *themselves* uniquely determines any policy. When it appears to do so, it is only because of commonly accepted implicit values in the situation.

Despite the fact that Dr. Hibbs acknowledges the indispensability of these moral judgments, he seems to be skeptical about the existence of any moral principles. The source of his skepticism rests partly on the confusion between deducing moral rules "from deeper principles" and applying moral rules to different situations, and partly on the mistaken assumption that in applying moral rules to different situations we change those rules, something which is no more the case in ethics than it is in medicine. The rules of medicine or diet do not change when they are applied to different patients.

Dr. Hibbs then goes onto assert the even more extraordinary view that "each type of science is so unique in itself that we must have a separate ethical approach for each field—biology, physics, chemistry, etc." And since, he also makes the mind-boggling suggestion that "ethical concepts must be created ad hoc for each new problem," he must hold that there is a separate and unique ethical approach for each sub-field in every scientific discipline.

Unfortunately, Dr. Hibbs does not illustrate or give us the slightest hint of an ethical principle that is valid in one field but invalid in another. This is a great pity, for once more it suggests that all he really means is that applied to different *situations* the same ethical principles might give us different results. Offhand one can think of many ethical principles which are valid in all the sciences and even in other non-scientific areas. For examples, "It is morally wrong 'to cook' the results of one's experiment" or "If the same result can be achieved by an experiment that entails the least amount of suffering or pain on a sentient organism, it should be preferred to all other experiments (provided, of course, that there are no other moral objections to conducting the experiment)." I invite Dr. Hibbs to offer a case he believes invalidates these principles.

The contention that every science, and every problem in it, has its own unique ethical guiding principle, that "we must ad hoc our way through the morass" of ethical decisions entails the view that there really are no ethical principles, that anyone may take any policy position whatsoever with respect to any problem, that anything goes. The kindest assumption would be that Dr. Hibbs is blissfully unconscious of this but his rewording of Mencken's *bon mot* to read that it is neccessary to rise above principle in ethics, suggests that he can have no objection to unprincipled ethical behavior. On what grounds then could he morally condemn the experiments of the Nazi physicians at Buchenwald?

There are further assumptions in Dr. Hibbs' position that invite examination. One of them is that only those "who do their homework and learn what is involved in scientific research" have a right to make ethical decisions in scientific matters. I agree but wonder on what moral grounds Dr. Hibbs would defend this statement against those who denied it. He could only do so by invoking an ethical principle which is *not* unique to any one field. Knowledge of the relevant facts should be a *sine qua non* of judgments of policy in any field.

Unfortunately, Dr. Hibbs goes beyond this. It is not enough for him that one must have a "broad understanding" of the problem of scientific research; one must be "familiar in detail with what it involves." In other words, one must have more than knowledge of the gross relevant facts, one must have knowledge of the intricacies and details of the problem. What Dr. Hibbs is in effect saying is that one must be expert in the field in which the ethical decision is to be made in order to make a justifiable and wise decision about the moral issues that arise therein.

I should like to challenge this on many grounds. One does not have to be an expert to assess or evaluate properly the recommendations of experts. If a decision is to be made about an operation, the surgeon can inform me what is involved, the risks, the costs, etc., but I am in the best position to make the decision. Whether to go to war or not, is a question that cannot be intelligently decided without acquainting oneself with the expert knowledge of the generals. But the final decision should not be left to the generals. Indeed, the whole logic and ethics of democracy presupposses that it is possible for citizens or their representatives to judge and decide intelligently on the recommendation of experts without being experts themselves.

Further, in any controversial situation the recommendations of experts always disagree—sometimes vehemently. Indeed, the controversial situation is characterized by such disagreement. Dr. Hibbs' own illustration about the wisdom of bringing back a sample of dirt from Mars is a case in point. One eminent biologist at Stanford warns against returning the sample to earth. Another eminent biologist at Caltech is enthusiastically in favor. Since neither one can be denounced as full of philosophical hot air and nonsense, what does Dr. Hibbs recommend we do? Dr. Hibbs is unjustifiably harsh with philosophers whom he taxes with inability and unwillingness to acquaint themselves with the scientific material. But on his own showing, since the experts from Stanford and Caltech fundamentally disagree, why should philosophers become experts?

As a matter of fact philosophers in the field are much more familiar with the developments of modern science than Dr. Hibbs is with the elementary distinctions of logic and philosophical analysis. He does not seem to be able to distinguish between logical contraries and contradictions, and he is ignorant of what a converse proposition is. He asserts that "an ordinary truth is something whose converse is obviously false." But the converse of "Some engineers are boors" is "Some boors are engineers" and the converse of "No man is infallible" is "No one infallible is a man," and neither converse is false. On the other hand, the converse of "The sun rises in the East" is not false, as he asserts, but meaningless. Dr. Hibbs must have got Bohr's illustration of a "deep truth" all wrong. "To procreate is the only purpose of man," far from being a deep truth, is obviously false. And if it is modified to read "To procreate is the only purpose of X" is true, then the statement, "To procreate is not the only purpose of X" is necessarily false, and not a truth at all—deep or ordinary.

Dr. Hibbs has provided us with a paradigm case of the arrogant and dogmatic scientist who illustrates to a rather comical degree the faults and failings he attributes to others. Happily he is not representative of the general run of scientists concerned with ethical issues or of the engineers with whom he identifies. A singular lack of consistency indeed of awareness, characterizes his easy judgments. Contemptuous of those who make pronouncements on matters with which they are unfamiliar, he himself brashly passes judgment about something of which he says: "I don't know what the right answer is. I don't even know what the issue is. I don't even know what the case is." It is precisely what he doesn't know that prevents him from understanding the impertinence and irrelevance of an attempted disruption of a session devoted to a discussion of the academic rights and responsibilities of scholars and teachers. Anyone who reads Professor Van Alstyne's judicious remarks will appreciate that the occasion and time of its delivery was the last place in the world to raise a specific question about a matter that required prolonged inquiry by a Faculty Senate whose action ultimately might fall under the purview of Committee A of the AAUP. Had the President of the AAUP expressed a judgment about something that was at the time *sub judice* at the institution in question, he would have violated the guidelines of his own organization. There was no more reason for his discussing or replying to the disruptive question than for a speaker at an academic colloquium who had presented a paper on the principles of accountancy replying to a bill collector in the audience who wanted to know why the wife of the speaker's colleague didn't pay her bills.

Dr. Hibbs' intellectual manners and tone speak for themselves. But I cannot permit his denigrating references to those of my colleagues who have written about the philosophy of science and the nature of scientific method to pass unchallenged. It would have been more instructive if he had offered evidence to substantiate his assertion that what philosophers who concern themselves with the philosophy of science turn out, is "by and large . . a pile of rubbish," and that most definitions of scientific method are incompatible with the scientific methods practiced by the most successful scientists. Actually most philosophers of sciences take their point of departure from the scientific methods that have been employed by the most successful scientists. The literature of the field shows that when successful scientists write about the philosophy of science they often write in the same vein and about the same issues as their colleagues in philosophy. Dr. Hibbs does not conceal his disapproving, cynical view that most of us will eschew learning about scientific developments and in the manner of the ancients revert to "pure thought." He seems unaware that philosophical speculations—or "pure thought"—about the nature of space, time, numbers, infinity, causality, evolution, mind, to mention only a few themes—have profoundly influenced the history of science. But whether thought is pure, impure, or practical is not so important in what we say and do as is the presence of sound thought. What is distressing in Dr. Hibbs' contribution to the discussion is not only the deficiencies in his thought but the absence on his part of thoughtfulness in the several senses of that term.

Wanted: A Rational Decision Procedure for Value Conflicts in Science

Miro Todorovich
CUNY

A few years ago, speaking to a dinner audience at the Stony Brook campus, physicist Max Dresden explained the reasons for his move to the East. He was attracted by its intellectual vigor, he said. *The New York Times* reaching the West Coast was full of excellent articles on science. Occasionally some of the descriptions of physics were really not up to par, but reports about developments in the field of chemistry or biology or medicine were in his opinion truly excellent. So he decided to move to Long Island in order to be closer to New York. Subsequently he has become somewhat perplexed — Dresden continued — after talking to some biologists. They indicated that they found the *Times* articles on *physics* and chemistry excellent though reports dealing with *their* subject, biology, could stand some improvement.

This brief anecdote came vividly to my mind while listening to members from various disciplines discuss questions of professional ethics. Views expressed seem to be a function of distance from one's own field. There was often sweeping agreement about the shortcomings of others, their egocentric approaches, and their disregard of broader implications of their professional action. Conversely, with the exception of Judge Frankel, there was an equally sweeping consensus that one's own specialty is in fine shape but is usually poorly understood.

"Were the critics only willing to learn more about the field they criticize, they would probably have a quite different attitude." This local tug-of-war, which was felt during the two days of meetings, is quite typical of what happens elsewhere in our society. Medical researchers are accused of unethical use of biological objects, psychiatrists are said to trample over the privacy and civil rights of inmates, lawyers are allegedly concealing the truth in the course of the adversary process, while weapons designers operate in a Frankenstein creature's spacetime which excludes any ethical dimension. Therefore, all professional schools should, we are told, adopt courses in ethics as part of their curricula.

Conversely, all these professionals, physicians, attorneys, scientists and strategists contend quite vehemently that their basic and predominant commitment is to the good of humanity. They insist that the fruits of their endeavors, when available, far outweigh any undesirable side effects, and claim that their devotion to ethical principles is second to none. If only the critics would make the effort—so the reasoning goes—to acquaint themselves with the facts, professional procedures would be promptly and fully vindicated. Thus philosophers should learn about science, bureaucrats take mandatory courses in medicine, journalists study penal rehabilitation, etc.

This tension between the various segments of our society (and individuals within it) should not come as a surprise. As Sidney Hook pointed out at numerous occasions, difficulties on the ethical front rarely occur as a clash of good and bad: in a sense such a clash would not be an ethical *problem*. Difficulties mostly appear when one is asked to choose between good and good, adopt one of the two desirable but irreconcilable alternatives. Public right to know may conflict with a defendant's right to a fair trial. One man's search for truth may invade another person's right to privacy. By maximizing merit, one may move away from some aspects of equality. What *is* surprising is the intensity with which the conflict has come to the fore at this time. It may be worthwhile inquiring into the causes of this conflict which has erupted all over the sociological landscape. This may help us understand the need for, and the implications of, the selection of one among the ethical alternatives. Finally, one may wish to search for the vehicles required to establish a new consensus or, as some have preferred to call it, a new "social contract."

For many centuries Western culture coasted more or less consistently along a path which was laid out for it by its Judeo-Christian heritage. It was, broadly speaking, characterized by the centrality of human existence, the quest for the betterment of the human condition (through trade and the development of productive forces), and the acceptance of the sanctity of human life. The centrality of human existence led to the creation of various instruments like *Magna Carta,* national constitutions, and various human rights statutes. The quest for betterment (which included learning) resulted in the unique technological world of today. The sanctity of human life was developed to its farthest conclusions in the dogmas and teachings of the Catholic Church. Let us note, for didactic purposes, that an extension of sanctity of life to *all* life would result in a vegetarian civilization which would encounter, among other things, considerable difficulties when attempting to develop any significant and efficient medical research. While the tradition developed, the actors of this Greatest Social Play on Earth were kept busy trying to materialize their own dreams. Much had to be done with very meager resources. People lived generally under conditions comparable to the current situation in many underdeveloped countries. The break-through point occurred some time during the period of the industrial revolution when an accelerated movement towards general economic wealth and personal fulfillment appeared possible. Still, it took a couple of centuries before the post-industrial, consumer-oriented society began to emerge. Until recently, the main task of any leadership group was to secure for its constituency a reasonable chance for decent survival. During the trying times of primitive struggle, human beings were, by and large, apt to accept the dicta of given principles without question. The work ethics remained uncriticized. The value of a structured family life was accepted as self-evident. Deviants were simply "crazy children of the good society." Justice, derived from natural law, punished the guilty and protected the victim. And if the vicissitudes of life in this world turned out to be too tough or too unjust to some individual, there was always a reward waiting in some other world.

The more primitive world lacked mechanisms by which to transform numerous theoretical concerns into day by-day practical action. Legal services were rudimentary and medical help available only to those who could afford the cost. Consumers were at the mercy of merchants distributing limited amounts of scarce goods. The security forces existed more often for the protection of the rulers than to protect the rights of the common man. Furthermore, even if lofty ethical ideals had been general, the sheer poverty of the milieu under such circumstances made the implementation improbable. Persons of good will usually do what they consider feasible. To act otherwise and spend one's energies in an attempt to achieve unrealizable ideals of artistic and liberal education for all, of equality in athletic competitions, or universal access to incorruptible justice would seem to them both impractical and foolish in a world of material scarcity.

At the same time, such restrictive material circumstances often went hand in hand with considerable social stability. History is full of examples of people who were proud and at peace with themselves while struggling for daily survival. Today such stoicism is encountered in numerous underdeveloped countries—a circumstance which often baffles Western visitors who try, erroneously, to associate such an attractive phenomenon with the ruling political system.

Presently, the Western World is far beyond this state of materially constricted morality. We have reached an abundance of means and an abundance of individuals capable not only of articulating the aspirations of the many as well as of the few but of organizing for their realization. Name any cause or formulate any purpose and there will materialize somewhere in the United States a council or committee supportive of such a goal.

The West has also in many respects succeeded in implementing its working agenda. We are able now to maintain human life even beyond the time some people think worthwhile. We have the capacity to educate almost anyone. We have the resources to feed the population with more calories than is medically advisable. We can travel faster over a landscape than we can enjoy its features. We can and should, of course, do many more things for many people—for those who are not yet there and would like to get where others already are—and this will require among other things a further expansion of our productive capacities.

Still, in the eyes of those devoted to creative intellectualism—writers and journalists, college and university professors—all such endeavors represent only more of the same. It induces in them a feeling of boredom associated with a *deja vu*. For many a contemporary activist to amplify the known is to belabor the obvious and they have little patience with such pedestrian tasks. It is the search for alternative approaches which intrigues their imagination and energizes their creative ego. Thus one observes frantic searches for alternative life styles, efforts towards counter-cultures, the rise of the antihero and the promotion of nonmother's day. What in the past were sporadic ethical skirmishes for the improvement of existing rules or for the development of original ways to further a common goal have now become a fullfledged war. Whether one likes it or not, the United States is in the midst of a cultural revolution—American style. The thoughtways and practices of the past have been challenged. Traditional authorities have lost their legitimacy. Flux, if not chaos, is king. The best we can do is to contribute to a process that will facilitate the emergence of a viable synthesis for the future.

From the practitioner's point of view the establishment of a workable consensus should be a reasonably straightforward process. Barring obvious research excesses associated with the Nazi era, the normal operating framework for professional activities seems to justify claims by just about everyone in the field that in one way or another their actions are in the best interest of humanity. It is at the same time recognized that any goal-oriented endeavor has some side effects which may be viewed as undesirable. Thus from such a vantage point the consensus building seems a simple one-two proposition: society need only agree that (1) a goal is worthwhile and (2) the associated side effects can be viewed as negligible or subordinate compared with the benefits resulting from the achievement of that goal, and presto! —disputes will be resolved.

While this simplified scenario seems quite accurate to some simple souls the ingredients needed for its implementation are neither simple nor close at hand. Let us see why in the context of some of the examples cited at our conference.

The medical profession, we were told, wishes to help human beings live longer and fuller lives free of anxieties engendered by potential or actual illness. For that purpose, in addition to trained cadres, the health services necessarily rely on a comprehensive body of medical data derived from actual cases, on tests performed on a series of specimens, and on experiments that involve predominantly animal organisms but also some humans. These goals and practices are questioned for diverse reasons by various groups.

Critics of current medical practices include, e.g. those who object to any use of animals for experimentation, those who demand "informed consent" for the gathering and use of even the most trivial human specimens material (sweat, sputum), those who question the validity of "informed consent" elicited from children and inmates, those who object to case studies as an invasion of privacy and those who on religious grounds object to certain medical practices altogether. Their criticism is strident and forceful. It is constantly updated for better persuasiveness and wider appeal. Research on fetuses, for example, has become embroiled in the broad public controversy over the meaning of life and what constitutes murder.

In addition to this kind of questioning addressed to specifics, the value of the very goals that define the objective of medical activity has been increasingly subjected to uncertain resolution and critical doubts. "Isn't modern medicine contributing to the world population explosion with potentially catastrophic consequences?" "Should we save lives that will not be worth living if we succeed?" "Is the continuous extension of human life a blessing or a curse?" Of course, rarely does one encounter a direct rejection of the need for and the usefulness of the basic medical services. Nevertheless, the questions cited above convey if not, a negative judgment, a corrosive skepticism that may dislocate the self-assurance of doctors in the value of their mission. The image of professionals in the public eye has gradually been tarnished. Those questioning the validity of some medical practices have at their disposal easy access to the courts in their quest for a temporary or permanent halt of the procedures they find objectionable. The establishment of consensual guidelines has therefore become very important precisely at a time when because of the absense of a common core of understanding their actual formulation seems more elusive than ever.

This impasse is further exacerbated by the continuous and often shrill verbal sparring between uncompromising adversaries. The ethics of medical research is thus in need of some rational decision procedures to keep the peace.

Similar problems are encountered in debates about our system of legal defense. The protagonists of the adversary trial approach assert that with all its limitation it is still the best possible mode of discovering truth and doing justice in a world of incomplete facts and approximate verities. They point out that a wrong decision may entail disastrous consequences to the one who suffers it. In turn, critics cite the increasing body of evidence that raises doubt in the belief in the utility of the adversary system. They refer to instances where lawyers for the defense concealed their knowledge of the location of the murdered victims, deeming this information damaging to the case of their clients. Was such a behavior ethical? Is a lawyer's obligation to the defendant so presumptive as to override the rights of the parents of a victim, not to mention the court, to knowledge of the victim's whereabouts? And what about the arrogant claim by some attorneys that the art of scientific jury selection and publicity management has attained such a state of predictability that given a sufficient amount of money and talent a preselected verdict can be guaranteed in advance?

These criticisms are given added weight by reports describing the recourse to technicalities during the pretrial hearings or post-trial challenges. The result is numerous acquittals even in cases where the relevant evidence, which has been ruled inadmissible, would incontestably be sufficient to convict the accused. The question is then naturally raised whether the concern for the protection of the presumably legally innocent defendants has not been stretched to a point where the rights of the actual victim, and of other potential victims, have been denied.

As these examples accumulate, it becomes increasingly difficult to formulate a convincing argument in defense of the adversary proceedings. Clearly, at no point in the past could philosophical arguments in favor of the legal adversary approach and its practical consequences have been persuasive enough to sway society in favor of such a system. Only historical causes rather than rational moral grounds can account for its past acceptance. However, current experience which has made so acute the conflict between the right of a defendant to a fair trial and the right of the public (really the press) to know, poses questions that cannot be dismissed without eroding public confidence in the capacity of the courts to deliver justice. We encounter once more the elements of an impasse that cannot be overcome and resolved by a new consensus without a rational decision procedure.

Similar conflicts come to light in other areas wherever we turn. Industrial research is asked to make a choice between product effectiveness and consumer protection; journalists to choose between objective reporting and advocacy journalism; economic planners between growth and retrenchment; labor unions between concerns for the economic welfare of their members and the public interest. All of these opposing views are formulated in ethical terms and carry an emotional impact far beyond the simple weighing of rational alternatives. In view of the complexity of the matter it seems advisable to preface the search for solutions by a survey of the necessary ingredients for a successful action.

1. Investigations and resolutions of conflicts must necessarily involve experts from the field under scrutiny. Attempts by critics to impose unilateral solutions in areas which are outside their primary competence result in cures which are usually worse than the disease they are supposed to medicate. Recent regulatory efforts by certain bureaucratic governmental agencies are a clear case in point. Conversely, search for new modalities must be a cooperative effort involving the critics as well as those they criticize. Specialized professionals all too often develop a technically biased view in relation to which vigorous criticism is both salutary and invigorating. An understanding born of a frank and open discussion also has a better chance to be accepted by a broad enough majority — a sufficient condition for the durability of any societal views.

2. The understanding of the nature of ethical conflicts is an important ingredient of the process of resolution. As long as each contending party sees itself as right and others as wrong, choice of other "good" alternatives is precluded and a solution without one side oppressing the other is impossible.

3. The framers of ethical social contracts must be aware that the choice of any possible ethical alternative is associated with definite unintended consequences of a far reaching character. We mentioned earlier that the adoption of the sanctity of all life would necessarily result in an obligatory vegetarian society with immense economic, medical, and legal consequences. It would take the imagination of a science fiction writer to project all the ramifications of such a compact! Another perspective would be the unequivocal adoption of the principle "an eye for an eye and a tooth for a tooth." Such an ethical principle may lead to a stable and durable society but its legal system, educational upbringing, and other social institutions would profoundly differ from our own. In particular, it is questionable whether in such a society labor unionism of the American variety could exist. The process of collective bargaining encompasses various degrees of forgiveness (refraining from reprisals, propensity toward compromises, etc.) which a strict application of an eye for an eye justice would make totally impossible.

Incidentally, we are witnessing the final phases of the worldwide abolition of political and economic slavery. This is a logical consequence of the universal adoption of the ethical principle that "all men are created equal." We naturally should welcome the abolition of any kind of slavery. But do we understand and are we prepared to accept *all* the ramifications of a guiding ethical principle that goes beyond equality of opportunity for all to equality of results for all? Can we have excellence without some kind of inequality?

4. Ethical principles cannot be viewed as absolutely valid in the sense that strict adherence to them would result in universal satisfaction. We have seen already that even if we disregard human frailty, unavoidable contradictions may preclude absolute bliss: the fair trial ideal demands controls over what is said and how things are publicized which is in direct conflict with the ideal of absolutely uninhibited free speech. Things become even more complicated when human weakness becomes a factor. Take the case of euthanasia. In principle, a consistent application of such an ethical proscription would make various avenues of life much more dignified and esthetically pleasing. But what about its potential for abuse, what about the moral of Maupassant's story of a man who consoled his aged relative by offering her his company during sustained sessions of wine sipping until the old lady died of cirrhosis and he inherited her fortune? What assurances have we that today's ultimate decision is not a statistical attitudinal fluctuation which, alas, can be reversed tomorrow? These are some of the unavoidable questions that make the path of the ethical decision-maker difficult. We can only hope that persons entrusted by society with making decisions on moral codes for professional practice will have the experience, talent and wisdom to present their conclusions aware of the imperfections and contradictions which are an integral part of life.

We operate in a world whose basic ethical norms in the West were first laid down in Biblical terms, subsequently refined in ecclesiastical councils, challenged by reformers and conterreformers and finally translated by secular writers into the language of today. With the growth of society into a complex organism composed of many interdependent specialized subgroups, the overall ethical concept was transformed and differentiated in its applications. Today, for example, we have the famous Hippocratic oath and its lesser known derivative recited by the graduates of the City University of New York; we talk of the ethics of lawyers and of teachers, and scrutinize the ethical code of our congressmen. Businessmen seem to operate under one code at home and another abroad. Incidentally, the extension of our ethics overseas, e.g., to countries like Japan, may result in unexpected consequences in their social and political life.

Existing professional codes grew with the professions and were authorized by the very professionals whose comportment they were supposed to regulate. They formalized views held within an occupation and were usually adopted by professional societies at some of their meetings. The outside polity may have occasionally expressed concern about the lack of ethical norms or unethical behavior of professionals, but the actual writing of rules within the generally acceptable framework of the prevailing social ethics was left to the specialists.

Is such an internal procedure still open to us today? Can, for example, the society of geneticists, within their professional walls, develop a set of rules guiding genetic manipulation research without a prompt challenge from the Friends of the Earth, HEW, Ralph Nader, National Institutes of Health, and the Boston Municipal Council? Can the association of textbook writers develop their professional code without an active input from the National Organization of Women, the Editorial Board of McGraw Hill Corporation and other pressure groups? Clearly, the openness of our society has been extended from previously privileged domains and has acquired new meanings. Consequently, an adequate understanding of what is possible and necessary for a new ethical consensus within the given social climate of today is of paramount importance for anyone who wishes to participate in such a creative and constructive process.

There are several reasons why nowadays the codification of desirable professional attitudes cannot be accomplished within closed professional circles. Foremost among them is a lingering suspicion of the general public vis-à-vis the professions in the wake of numerous scandals involving professional groups or associations. Existing codes appear to have failed either because they have been outmoded by professional or social developments or because the long periods of mid century tranquility have invited complacency and a creeping rascality.

This general lack of confidence in professionals has been reinforced by a spreading feeling of malaise towards rationality. Scientific achievements which in the past were hailed as a boon for humanity have lately, in the minds of the public, become associated with negative headlines about chemical pollution, atomic danger, and other scary themes. In addition, the social sciences have failed to achieve the predictive accuracy of the natural sciences and this has generated a feedback casting clouds of doubt on all the scientific disciplines. With suspicion often comes the desire for control.

Public reaction would still not necessarily lead to public rule-making were it not for the belief of the average citizen that he or she is competent to design meaningful and effective controls. This naive belief is partly a consequence of mass public education in which everyone has been exposed, at least in theory, to the many elements of our contemporary civilization and thus deemed capable of evaluating even the most complex subjects.

The willingness of the public to judge and to issue verdicts on the most recondite matters has found further encouragement in the pages of the daily press and magazines and in the easy-to-digest presentations of other media. The simplifications which are unavoidable, given the limitations of available journalistic space-time, actually conceal the intrinsic complexity of the problems reported on. The very glibness of the presentations make the issues seem easily intelligible. Laymen are therefore emboldened to exercise their political prerogative dogmatically and opt for solutions that even experts would advance with great tentativeness.

This, then, is the era of the consumer tribunes, public interest outfits, and people's lobbies who have achieved standing in matters of rule-making, legislative as well as ethical. The self-assurance and political skill of these individuals and groups as demonstrated in hearings and media appearances should be contrasted with the prevailing mood of insecurity and doubt within the professions and a considerable degree of ineptitude among existing professional associations when acting on matters of interest to their membership.

As a result of the interplay of these factors, American society feels itself imperiled and tries to protect itself against real or imaginary dangers by all available means including the services of legitimate or self-appointed public guardians. Whether one finds merit in these developments or not, this involvement of the public-at-large in the drafting and implementation of ethical codes and professional activities will be with us for the forseeable future. This means that more probably than not codes and rules produced only within closed professional circuits will not enjoy public support and acceptance. Efforts to develop codes along these lines will generate only greater frustrations on the part of well intentioned professionals if any crisis situation develops.

What, then, is a possible line of approach?

Firstly, members of any profession must restate in contemporary terms their professional goals and the ways to achieve them. Unless a profession can point to a set of rules and practices that the overwhelming consensus of its members supports, it will experience great difficulties defending its *raison d'etre* against outside criticisms, if and when they come.

Second, every profession through the active participation of its members must be willing to enter the public arena and in concert with other segments of society work towards the establishment of viable guidelines to direct its functioning. This will include participation in official or unofficial commissions, symposia, meetings, publishing ventures, debates and the like. However, such participation will be counterproductive unless those acting as representatives of their profession convey their deep, personal conviction in the value of the work they are doing and a sense of dedication to the basic ideals of their calling.

Third, one should not expect that the resolution of conflicts will mean a return to the innocent optimism of the past. Each historical period has its own insights and its own tastes and postulates. Hopefully current debates conducted on a high intellectual level will provide transition from one state of metastable equilibrium to another one better suited to the realities of the day.

Any particular transition to a new social equilibrium is not definitive since there is a number of possible final states of such a transition. The appeal of any one of such possible goal-states depends on one's vantage point. For a scientist, a society in which astrology is subsidized and given pride of place and rational analysis is discouraged by superstition and fear would be highly undesirable. Within a democratic context, the search for a new societal consensus is then equivalent to a search for equilibrium states with the greatest appeal to the largest number of societal subgroups. It is in a certain sense a bargaining process where bargainers who are best prepared and have the greatest visible support from their constituencies are the probable winners. It is something members of professions and their representatives should keep in mind when preparing themselves for the next round in which they will have to defend their views, their values, and their integrity. Their greatest strength and most convincing argument, when it can be honestly made and persuasively presented, is that the rational pursuit of the professional interest is a pursuit of the public interest, too.

The Ethics of Free Inquiry

Paul Kurtz
State University of New York at Buffalo

History records the continuing efforts to censor free inquiry. We are all too familiar with the attempts by theologians to prohibit free thought. Obstacles were placed in the way of each new development in science—usually in the name of God and in opposition to "blasphemy" and "heresy." Galileo was condemned for contesting the orthodox theistic view of the universe; Darwin, for his dangerous theory of evolution; and Freud, for his novel interpretations of human nature. In the long struggle between religion and science, higher religious "truths" were called on to restrict the range of scientific investigation.

Similar calls for censorship have been made in the name of politics, economics, and ideology. Vested interests have often opposed new ideas that are considered seditious to the established order. Since the time of Socrates, we have been familiar with the repression of inquiry for political ends. In our time, Nazi racist theories prohibited non-Aryan physics and social science, Stalinism banned those scientific theories that ignored dialectical materialism, and Lysenkoism exorcised genetic theories that contradicted its environmentalist dogma.

Today there are similar efforts to limit scientific research, but now they are made primarily on ethical grounds.

In the conflict between free inquiry and censorship, science presupposes conditions of freedom that may themselves be justified on ethical grounds. The arguments are basically utilitarian in character: We ought to be committed to free inquiry because of long-range consequences for the common good. No one can predict what scientists may discover, nor the therapeutic uses that these findings may have for humankind. Once the door to inquiry is closed, we are never certain what criteria will prevail or when the door will be slammed shut again. A society that does not allow freedom for its intellectuals, writers, artists, and scientists, will eventually stagnate and die. Creativity is the source of vitality and life. Thus, both science and an open society presuppose the right to knowledge and the free use thereof.

Recently, however, these assumptions have come under heavy attack. Indeed, there has been a frontal assault on the whole scientific enterprise itself. Many people have become profoundly disillusioned with the promise of science. Science is held responsible for many serious problems in the contemporary world. Atomic physics gave us nuclear power and thermonuclear weapons. Biology and chemistry provided the means to wage biochemical warfare. Although scientific research has had immense positive results, it has also resulted in pollution, ecological destruction, and resource depletion. Thus the first indictment raised against science concerns haphazard technological growth. The fear of technology—fed by the popular media—often considers the scientist to be an amoral Frankenstein, fanatically dedicated to a research that may be dangerous to society's basic welfare. The only way to guard society from these destructive tendencies, it is said, is to tame the scientist and police his research and the consequences of it.

This disenchantment with science has assumed other forms. The scientific world view has been criticized as too narrow. The counterculture has rejected the logico-empirical method, and sought to expand the range of consciousness by means of psychedelic drugs. The counterculture has questioned the rationale for pure research and academic freedom, and sought to politicize the academy and judge it by aesthetic or moral criteria. Attendant to the counterculture, a whole series of cults of unreason has proliferated—from the importation of Asian sects to the revival of astrology, the occult, exorcism, belief in reincarnation, magic, and spiritualism. In the quest for meaning, rigorous standards of evidence are considered too limiting to the imagination; even where scientific authority is sought, science fiction and speculative audacity reign. There is widespread belief in unidentified flying objects, extraterrestrial visitations, and doomsday prophecies. The realm of the paranormal, from telekinesis to faith healing and psychic surgery, has expanded.

In this broader context of the growth of irrationalism and obscurantism, the attack on scientific research must be appraised. For it is one thing to raise serious doubt about the abuses of scientific technology in contemporary society—this is a meaningful and important concern. It is another thing to extend this indictment to the possibility of free scientific research.

Regarding technology, the results of scientific research obviously are used by industry and fulfill ancillary economic, political, and military purposes. In a democratic society, it is not the scientist alone who should judge the efficacy of a technological application. The entire society should decide, through debate, the costs and hazards of the applications of scientific knowledge. Hence, a society may decide to curtail certain products if they are considered noxious to the public health. It is industry that is being restricted here, not science. If cyclamates or artificial coloring are found to be carcinogenic or if fluorocarbon sprays do destroy the stratospheric ozone layer, their production can be prohibited. So far as technological applications have social consequences, society itself should evaluate and determine the uses of these applications by open discussion and the legislative process.

That is not at issue. What is at issue is the ensuing indictment, not of technology *but of scientific research itself.* This has taken many forms in recent years. We are told that there are certain things that should not be researched (for example, nuclear energy or the genetic basis of IQ and race) because of possible misuses, or should be made illegal (such as behavior modification, fetal research, or genetic engineering).

Again, this indictment of science is made basically on ethical grounds. In some circles this has reached a kind of moral hysteria. It involves a sweeping denunciation of the "high priests" of medicine and psychiatry, a suspicion of psychologists, geneticists, biologists, and other scientists This ethical critique is not much different from earlier calls for censorship, and religious and political criteria are usually accompanied by a moral bias. Science was "wicked" because it contradicted religious pieties, or because it opposed the prevailing political shibboleths. Whatever the grounds, all such calls for censorship involve the intrusion of extrinsic criteria on scientific research.

We cannot, then, object to ethical evaluation by society of the effects of technology—for the goal here is no longer truth per se but practice. What is at stake is whether ethical objections should be taken as decisive in the area of pure research. Matters are complicated, for there is no absolute dualism between theory and practice; and all theoretical constructs have a practical impact, since thoughts are related to human conduct, interests, and purposes. Although there is no sharp distinction in kind, there is one of degree—for some theories do not seek directly to change the world. And in the area of knowledge and truth, *scientists ought, on utilitarian grounds, to be allowed to inquire as they see fit and to publish their results without the imposition of external standards of judgment as to the ethical worth of their investigations.*

Some scientific theories, however, can only be tested by experimental practice. Here is the rub. For in the act of inquiry, there may be a direct modification of the subject matter; this may be negative and harmful. I can best illustrate this by reference to the field of genetic research. Recent discoveries in recombinant E. coli DNA research in molecular biology are significant, but there is also some danger that a new and virulent strain of virus may be formed that will be resistant to medical treatment. If unleashed, even accidentally, such artificially created strains can be greatly hazardous to human life. Should such research be allowed to continue? The pure quest for truth is one thing; but if in testing one's hypothesis a highly noxious fallout can occur, should we permit it? The fears expressed by people in the greater Cambridge-Boston area about the possible dangers inherent in such research proposed at Harvard, may be justifiable. Some people think that such research need not be dangerous and that objections are based on a fear of the unknown. In any case, the issue is at least arguable.

Clearly a commitment to free scientific inquiry cannot be taken as an absolute. No right is absolute, not even the right to free inquiry. There may be some situations in which one would want to limit the actual experiments performed to test theories, because they may be too dangerous

If that is the case, one should not therefore move to the other extreme and question each and every claim to free inquiry or judge it on extrinsic ethical grounds—as many people increasingly seem ready to do today. Scientists should not be kept continually on the defensive to justify their inquiries.

I would suggest that the right to free inquiry should be taken as a prima facie general principle, which we ought to respect save in exceptional cases. If we are to make an exception to the principle, this would depend on the possibilities of extraordinary dangers to life and limb. The general principle is justified on ethical grounds because of the proven value of knowledge to humanity.

Since some forms of moral opposition can become as tyrannical or fanatical as religious or ideological objections in destroying free inquiry, I would suggest that *the burden of proof always be placed on those who would limit inquiry.* It is the exception to the principle that needs justification, not the principle itself.

Should a question about the efficacy of a research project arise, the first step should be a peer review by those competent within a field. In a democratic society, the public at large may have a justifiable stake in the outcome—and the public's input in the decision is relevant. In pursuing their craft, scientists no more than lawyers, businessmen, or teachers can ask for the right to harm others without their consent. Scientists are not gods. In some kinds of research they may abuse their calling—as did Nazi doctors in experimenting with helpless concentration camp inmates. The fact that they were scientists did not give them legal immunity.

The best safeguard against the undermining of scientific research is an informed, intelligent public. The larger task facing scientists is to help educate the public about the nature of the scientific method and the roles of science and research in human progress. We have recently failed to accomplish this task, and the rising tide of subjectivism is due in part to a failure of people to appreciate the character of scientific intelligence in understanding nature. The assault on scientific research likewise is symptomatic of a failure by the broader public to appreciate how society has benefited from the untrammelled search for knowledge.

The freedom of scientific inquiry ultimately depends upon a public enlightenment that must be nurtured not only in the schools but through every media of communication in society. The task is heavy and unremitting and sometimes like the labors of Sisyphus. But it must be shouldered by all who have faith in human freedom furthered by the arts of intelligence.

Contributors

Fred Baumann   UCRA

Dr. Baumann is the Assistant Executive Secretary of the University Centers for Rational Alternatives.

Donald G. Brennan   Hudson Institute

Dr. Brennan heads National Security Studies at the Hudson Institute.

Francis Canavan, S. J.   Fordham University

Father Canavan is Professor of Political Science at Fordham University.

Bernard Davis   Harvard University

Since 1968 Dr. Davis has been Adele Lehman Professor of Bacterial Physiology and Director of the Bacterial Physiology Unit, Harvard Medical School, and formerly Chairman of the Bacteriology Department there.

Martin Diamond   Northern Illinois University

Professor of Political Science at Northern Illinois University, Professor Diamond has been a member of the National Advisory Council, American Revolution Bicentennial Administration. He is the co-author of several historical works including *The Democratic Republic; Essays in Federalism;* and *The Thirties: A Reconsideration.*

Gray Dorsey   Washington University

Dr. Dorsey is Nagel Professor of Jurisprudence and International Law in the School of Law, Washington University, St. Louis. He is the author of *American Freedoms* and Editor of *Constitutional Freedom and the Law* and *Validation of New Forms of Social Organization*.

Charles Frankel   Columbia University

Dr. Frankel, Old Dominion Professor of Philosophy and Public Affairs, Columbia, was chairman of the U.S. delegation to the UNESCO General Conference in 1966 and was Assistant U.S. Secretary of State for Educational and Cultural Affairs, 1965-67. He is the author of *The Case for Modern Man* and *Pleasures of Philosophy*.

Marvin E. Frankel   Judge, United States District Court

U.S. District Judge Frankel was formerly Professor of Law at Columbia University and the College of the City of New York, and Editor-in-chief of the *Columbia Law Review*.

Robert A. Goldwin   The White House

Dr. Goldwin is Special Consultant on Education to the President of the United States.

A. R. Hibbs   California Institute of Technology

Dr. Hibbs is Senior Staff Specialist at the California Institute of Technology.

Sidney Hook   New York University

Emeritus Professor of Philosophy at New York University, Dr. Hook is currently a Senior Research Fellow at the Hoover Institution on War, Revolution and Peace, Stanford, California.

John L. Horn   University of Denver

Dr. Horn is Professor of Psychology at the University of Denver.

L. G. Humphreys   University of Illinois

Dr. Humphreys is Professor of Psychology at the University of Illinois.

Paul Kurtz   State University of New York

Dr. Kurtz, Professor of Philosophy at the State University of New York at Buffalo and Editor of *The Humanist,* is the author of *The Fullness of Life* and *Decision and the Condition of Man.*

Abraham H. Miller   University of Cincinnati

Dr. Miller is Professor of Political Science at the University of Cincinnati.

Lee Nisbet   *The Humanist*

Formerly Assistant Professor of Philosophy at Alfred University, Dr. Nisbet is currently Executive Editor of *The Humanist* magazine.

Henry R. Novotny   California State College

Dr. Novotny is Associate Professor of Psychology at California State at Bakersfield and a psychological consultant to the California Correctional Institution at Tehachapi. He also holds degrees in Chemical Engineering and Physics.

Norman Redlich   New York University

Currently the Dean of New York University Law School, Professor Redlich has served as a counsel for the President's Commission on the Assassination of President Kennedy, and the New York Committee to Abolish Capital Punishment.

Robert M. Rosenzweig   Stanford University

Dr. Rosenzweig is Vice-President for Public Affairs, Stanford University.

Seymour Seigal   Jewish Theological Seminary

Rabbi Seigal is Ralph Simon Professor of Theology and Ethics, Jewish Theological Seminary.

Miro M. Todorovich   City University of New York

Dr. Todorovich, Associate Professor of Physics at Bronx Community College, City University, is Executive Secretary of the University Centers for Rational Alternatives.

William Van Alstyne   Duke University

Currently the President of the American Association of University Professors, William Van Alstyne is a frequent contributor of articles to professional journals. He has held various teaching posts and served as an attorney in the Civil Rights Division, U.S. Department of Justice.

Eugene Wigner   Rockefeller University

Born in Budapest, Hungary, Professor Wigner has had a lifetime of teaching posts and distinguished awards, including a Nobel Prize for Physics in 1963.

Marvin Zimmerman   State University of New York

Dr. Zimmerman is Professor of Philosophy at the State University of New York at Buffalo.